ROBERT LOUIS STEVENSON

ROBERT LOUIS STEVENSON

edited by
Andrew Noble

VISION
and
BARNES & NOBLE

Vision Press Limited
Fulham Wharf
Townsmead Road
London SW6 2SB

and

Barnes & Noble Books
81 Adams Drive
Totowa, NJ 07512

ISBN (UK) 0 85478 424 1
ISBN (US) 0 389 20369 6

Printed and bound in Great Britain by
Unwin Brothers Ltd.,
Old Woking, Surrey.
Phototypeset by Galleon Photosetting,
Ipswich, Suffolk.
MCMLXXXIII

Contents

Introduction

by ANDREW NOBLE

Contemporary literary criticism is singularly challenged, indeed, given not a few of its predilections, singularly tempted by the work of Robert Louis Stevenson. One stresses Stevenson's work because almost all his biographers have provided us with material which is not only thin and repetitive but distracts from the fiction. Such biographies often insinuate either that the art has the undoubted power and charm of that extraordinary life or that the life, somehow, compensates for inadequacies in the art. Fortunately Stevenson has been the subject of one truly great biography: J. C. Furnas's *Voyage to Windward* is a true labour of love and masterpiece.[1] It and Stevenson's letters, rightly praised by Henry James, do truly illuminate the art. As in his underestimated travel books, the letters in their direct response to contingent reality drew the best out of Stevenson.

The fundamental challenge still presented to critics of Stevenson is provided by that extraordinary change which took place in his reputation almost immediately after the First World War. While there is no question of our returning to the inflated fame of the late-Victorian period, we are faced with the complex problem of assessing the degree to which the dismissive Modernist critiques of Stevenson's language and form are definitive, or were rather the products of the prejudiced literary values of these troubled post-war years. This extreme oscillation in Stevenson's standing is particularly remarkable and, hence, revealing in Scottish criticism. In the eyes of the Scottish pre-war sentimentalists of Kailyard persuasion, Stevenson assumed near-deified proportions. Thus Ian MacLaren:

> There are certain who compel words to serve them and never travel without an imperial body-guard; but words waited on

7

Stevenson like 'nimble servitors' and he went where he pleased in his simplicity because everyone flew to anticipate his wishes. His style had the thread of gold, and he was the perfect type of the man of letters—a humanist whose Greek joy in the beautiful was annealed to a fine purity by his Scottish faith; whose kinship was not with Boccaccio and Rabelais, but with Dante and Spenser. His was the Magical touch that no man can explain or acquire; it belongs to those only who have drunk at the Pierian spring. There is a place at the marriage feast for every honest writer, but we judge that our master will go to the high table and sit down with Virgil and Shakespeare and Goethe and Scott.[2]

It is perhaps better to pass over such Scottish self-esteem in pensive silence. Obviously these notions could not be justified, far less sustained. A fall in Stevenson's stock was inevitable but was undoubtedly deepened by the nature and consequences of the First World War. The great Modernist writers considered that civilization had been borne to a bloody shambles on a tide of false eloquence. Rightly or wrongly, Stevenson was felt to have been an active participant both in his language and form in this self-destructive impulse. Such a luxuriant style, with its arguable disrelation of word from concrete, specific thing, was associated with the sinister eloquence of political rhetoric. The form of the 'romantic' adventure story, with its stress on naïve, masculine courage, was also viewed as deeply suspect in a world which had seen the enactment of such 'heroism' in the context of the mass production of weaponry. In some respects, therefore, we can see Hemingway as Stevenson's polar opposite.

If Scottish sentimentalists had reason to place Stevenson absurdly high, the post-war realists, partly in reaction, placed him correspondingly low. This was particularly true of the two great Scottish members of European Modernism, Hugh MacDiarmid and Edwin Muir. In a world corrupted by mendacious eloquence, MacDiarmid saw anglicized Scotland as particularly debased. Believing the Rabelaisian spirit and precise factuality to be congruent with the true Scottish literary tradition, MacDiarmid saw Stevenson as anaemically genteel and linguistically florid. He had betrayed his linguistic birthright.[3] MacDiarmid believed that Stevenson's ornate rather than simple English was, like the Kailyarders, part of his mercenary talent for fabricating an exportable image of Scotland. Further, he considered that, like Barrie's, Stevenson's boyhood tales were not the stuff of true imagination but fanciful work which kept bourgeois Scotland in a state of willed immaturity. Such literary immaturity both expressed and created Scotland's dependence on England by denying its adult nationhood and making it the middle-management, if not servant class, of English imperialism.[4]

Though he somewhat qualified his initial, if less political, opinions, Edwin Muir was equally acerbic.

> Stevenson—and it was the sign of his inferiority, his lack of fundamental merit—never had this struggle, nor realized that it was necessary that he should have it. He was from the first a mere literary man, a man to whom language was a literary medium and nothing more, and with no realization of the unconditional mystery and strength of utterance. He sweated over words, but the more laboriously he studied them the more superficial he became, and to the end his conception of an English style remained that of a graceful and coloured surface for his thoughts and sensations. Below this were concealed, as pieces of unresolved matter, almost an irrelevancy, the plots of his novels, his knobbly or too smooth characters, and his thoughts which he never had the courage to face.[5]

In *The Structure of the Novel*, written five years later, Muir returned to the question of the Stevenson plot in terms of the genre it represented. Defining, as, indeed, Stevenson himself did, the adventure novel or novel of action as the simplest, weakest form of fiction because of its obsequies to our desire for fantasy rather than imaginative truth, Muir wrote:

> But the action is the main thing, the response of the characters to it incidental, and always such as to help the plot. The actors have generally such characters, and so much character, as the action demands. In *Treasure Island* Trelawney must be unable to keep a secret, otherwise the pirates would never know he was sailing to find the treasure. Silver, in the same way, must be diplomatist, otherwise the crew would not reach the island without being suspected; and the pirates must conveniently quarrel, or the few faithful hands would never win in the end. Had Silver and his followers killed all the loyal ship's company,

9

secured the treasure, sailed away, been captured, taken to England and executed, *Treasure Island* would not have been a novel of action, but something else, probably of far greater value.[6]

Muir thought what he described as 'the vulgarity of the happy ending' was a product of our questionable desires, and that there was a consequent mercenary temptation for the artist to pander to this element of pervasive fantasy both in himself and his audience. Muir considered Stevenson's work as almost always seriously impaired by this sycophantic genre:

> In its course the novel of action will generally deal out death to certain of the subsidiary characters; the wicked will be slaughtered, and some even of the good may safely be sacrificed, so long as the hero returns to peace and prosperity after his tumultuous vacation. The plot, in short, is in accordance with our wishes, not with our knowledge. It externalises with greater power than we ourselves possess our natural desire to live dangerously and yet be safe; to turn things upside down, transgress as many laws as possible, and yet escape the consequences. It is a fantasy of desire rather than a picture of life. It is never of much literary consequence except when, as in Scott and Stevenson, it is also in some measure a novel of character.[7]

Muir's concluding qualification of the adventure novel as also capable of, in part, bearing the mature burden of character is a specific important example of the problems of form and genre which provide the substance of the following essays. Indeed, the essential theme of this collection is the nature of the novel of action in Stevenson's hands. It would be pleasant and, certainly, much easier to report that in such manifestly crafty hands what we have generally discerned is a subtle evolution of the adventure story: that, covertly, Stevenson freights it with a depth of psychological complexity and truth different in principle from that characteristically found in that genre. Sadly this is not the case in the majority of our analyses. MacLaren described Stevenson as a Magician. Stevenson was more specific as to his power: 'The magician after he has prepared his sleight of hand will sometimes afford a second, and a fresh, pleasure by explaining the method of his dexterity.'[8] With unhappy frequency our essays show our explanations of the formal, aesthetic sleight of hand at work behind the highly finished surface of the work. Stevenson's stories consequently open themselves to a near-mechanistic analysis of a sort quite impotent to deal with the organic nature of genuine art. Extraordinarily in a writer so stylistically self-conscious and one who could write that 'any story can be made *true* in its own key; any story can be made *false* by the choice of a wrong key of detail or style',[9] Stevenson frequently indulges within his stories in the most astonishing 'key-changes'. One of the most infamous of such transpositions is that reported to James concerning the conclusion of *The Master of Ballantrae*:

> For the third supposed death and the manner of the third reappearance is steep; steep, sir. It is even very steep, and I fear it shames the honest stuff so far; but then it is highly pictorial, and it leads up to the death of the elder brother at the hands of the younger in a perfectly cold-blooded murder, of which I wish (and mean) the reader to approve.[10]

But this is alarmingly characteristic of the manner in which, arbitrarily and often *consciously*, Stevenson aborts a serious enterprise into escapist, picturesque adventure. 'The Merry Men', 'The Beach of Falesá' and *The Ebb-Tide* are outstanding examples of other stories which share this auto-destructive capacity. *Weir of Hermiston* would arguably have suffered a similar fate. What *Weir* shows is ambiguous. Stevenson longed to write not fantasies of action or realistic violence but to recreate a genuine epic spirit. Edwin Muir believed that, at the very end of his career, *Weir* demonstrates such a capacity:

> Had it been finished *Weir of Hermiston* would have been something unique in fiction, a modern saga, a novel combining two elements which are almost always disjoined: a modern sensibility and a heroic spirit. It is a fragmentary monument not only to Stevenson's own unfulfilled powers, but to an un-fulfilled possibility in modern literature.[11]

Yet this is doubtful on the basis of earlier failures of nerve. As well as the notes which suggest the avoidance of the tragic ending the book undoubtedly called for, there is also present throughout the story a reductive, ironic authorial voice which demonstrates Stevenson's chronic disease with an authentic epic form. Indeed, both in tone and form, so much of Stevenson's aesthetic theory and practice seems to be designed to provide him with defences against depth of feeling. Thus, though he was influenced by an extraordinary range of truly major nineteenth-century novelists, he never seems capable of *creatively* learning from them. In these essays, we have consequently sought to perceive Stevenson, as he saw himself, in a comparative context. It is a context in which he almost always fares badly. Consciously modelling himself on Poe, Hawthorne, Dostoevsky ('Markheim' and *Crime and Punishment*), Twain (*Kidnapped* and *Huckleberry Finn*), Scott, Charlotte Brontë and, in his Pacific stories, Herman Melville, he usually emerges from such encounters discredited. While Edwin M. Eigner's *Robert Louis Stevenson and Romantic Tradition* is an often interesting and informative study, one simply cannot assent to his thesis regarding Stevenson's relationship to the great nineteenth-century novel. Eigner commented that:

> Stevenson's official biographer, his cousin Graham Balfour, wrote that while the author took the best wherever he found it, 'he rendered it to the world again with interest.' Such a statement may appear immodest, especially if we consider that the best from which Stevenson took included such masterpieces as *Wuthering Heights, The Marble Faun, Huckleberry Finn,* and *Crime and Punishment.* The partiality is understandable, though, for in 1901, when Balfour's book was published, Stevenson was almost as much over-rated as he is neglected today. And while it is perhaps improper to regard Stevenson as having improved on these books, it is just as wrong to dismiss him as a mere copier of the ideas he took from the great masters of his tradition. Always, as we shall see, he modified their themes with his own insights and concerns, and he made their ideas fitter to be transmitted into our own century.[12]

Is a middle-man inevitably a middle-brow? An earlier and more perceptive American, John Jay Chapman, thought that Stevenson's ability so to *dilute* major fiction was the true cause of his enormous, commercial success. Such success was created by a perverse talent and paid for at heavy personal and creative cost.

> Writing was to him an art, and almost everything that he has written has a little the air of being a *tour de force*. Stevenson's books

and essays were generally brilliant imitations of established things, done somewhat in the spirit of an expert in billiards. In short, Stevenson is the most extraordinary mimic that has ever appeared in literature.

. . . When Stevenson, writing from Samoa in the agony of his 'South Seas' (a book he could not write because he had no paradigm and original to copy from), says that he longs for a 'moment of style', he means that he wishes there would come floating through his head a memory of some other man's way of writing to which he could modulate his sentences.[13]

Chapman related this quality of Stevenson's to arrested development. Stevenson seemed partly aware himself that he had never progressed beyond the puerile apprentice stage to be his own master. He himself would perhaps not have finally disagreed with Chapman's remark that:

The instinct at the bottom of all mimicry is self-concealment. Hence the illusive and questionable personality of Stevenson. Hence our blind struggle to bind this Proteus who turns into bright fire and then into running water under our hands. The truth is that as a literary force, there was no such man as Stevenson; and after we have racked our brains to find out the mechanism which has been vanquishing the chess players of Europe, there emerges out of the Box of Maelzel a pale boy.[14]

Indeed, in a last letter, depressed by his again fragile health, Stevenson wrote an even bleaker self-portrait. A final, truthful stocktaking on the brink of death or mere low spirits?

I know I am at a climacteric for all men who live by their wits, so I do not despair. But the truth is I am pretty nearly useless at literature, and I will ask you to spare *St. Ives* when it goes to you; it is a sort of Count Robert of Paris. But I hope rather a *Dombey and Son*, to be succeeded by *Our Mutual Friend* and *Great Expectations* and *A Tale of Two Cities*. No toil has been spared over the ungrateful canvas and it *will not* come together, and I must live, and my family. Were it not for my health, which made it impossible, I could not find it in my heart to forgive myself that I did not stick to an honest, commonplace trade when I was young, which might have now supported me during these ill years. But do not suppose me to be down in anything else; only, for the nonce, my skill deserts me, such as it is, or was. It was a very little dose of inspiration, and a pretty little trick of style, long lost, improved by the most heroic industry. So far, I have managed to please the journalists. But I am a fictitious article and have long known it. I am read by journalists, by my fellow-novelists, and by boys; with these, *incipet et explicit* my vogue. Good thing anyway! for it seems to have sold the Edition.[15]

As well as immaturity, Chapman thought that Stevenson's fate as a deracinated Scotsman on the loose if not the make at the end of a great period of English literature contributed to this chameleon-like behaviour. 'He is', he wrote, 'the mistletoe of English literature whose roots are not in the soil but in the tree.' Of course, it could be argued, and indeed has been so argued, by writers of the enormous talent and ingenuity of Borges and Nabokov that what we should see in Stevenson is not decadence but sportive innovation. Nabokov, another ethnically displaced person, who could write that 'style and structure are the essence of a book; great ideas are hogwash' and '*Mansfield Park* is a fairy tale, but then all novels are, in a sense, fairy tales . . . There is no such thing as real life for the author of genius' is manifestly one who would hold Stevenson dear.[16] Thus in our essays we have also tried to show Stevenson in a post-Modernist perspective. Further, we have attempted to show him in at least one of his books, *The Amateur Emigrant*, as finding his own, authentic voice in dealing with the hardships of his age. He was capable of the highest order of social realism. With regard to his relationship to Henry James we have suggested that he did not by any means adhere entirely to the restricting, petrified, geometric notions of 'ideal' form which his debate with James would suggest. In practice, as opposed to theory, they came into *living* proximity.

On the whole, however, this volume of essays, based as they are on close, formally attentive analyses of Stevenson's most important work, does *not* suggest it is time for a radical revaluation in his reputation. In the last twenty years or so there have been, for various reasons, certain attempts to so revalue Stevenson. The aesthetic values of post-Modernism hold some degree of promise in such a task. Given its theory as adequate to the nature of the relationship of literature to life, it is a cogent and consistent system. At the moment, however, in academic literary criticism, while *systems* breed apace, the capacity to read imaginatively declines. We seem intent on manufacturing states of spurious cerebration—abusing literature in so doing. Such critical ideologies, of course, are by no means wholly new phenomena. Writing of Henry James in 1918, T. S. Eliot remarked on the bitter contrast between intelligence in literature as opposed to ideation. These comments are highly salutary for much of the current critical promotion of Stevenson.

> James's critical genius comes out most tellingly in his mastery over his baffling escape from Ideas; a mastery and escape which are perhaps the last test of a superior intelligence. He had a mind so fine that no idea could violate it. . . . In England ideas run wild and pasture on the emotions; instead of thinking with our feelings (a very different thing) we corrupt our feelings with ideas; we produce the political, the emotional idea, evading sensation and thought.[17]

The forms of such corruption and evasion are now legion. We seem increasingly unable to read literature in that Jamesian state of grace which perceived it as a form of knowledge, of revelation even, which is not subject to reduction to inferior 'closed' forms of cerebration. Behind this lurks not only critical inadequacy and bad faith but also a desire for power over the imagination inspired by ambition, fear and perhaps even hatred. With Stevenson this has led to some particularly tortuous commentary. Given his own predilection for the unconscious, he is, of course, an obvious target for the psychoanalytic systematizer. Hence Mark Kanzer:

> The recurrent themes of finding treasure, as employed by Stevenson, are couched in typical symbols of castration anxiety. The searchers are evil men—pirates—and the lust for gold terminates in disaster and death. The end of the quest in *Treasure Island* is characteristic; the deluded men stand in horror before an empty pit (the female genital) and into it tumbles Merry (significantly named), shot as the result of his wickedness and obviously condemned, beyond the moment, to the eternal damnation of a deeper Pit. Unmistakably representative of the sexual aspects of the treasure hunt is the description of the place of concealment in another Stevenson story, 'The Treasure of Franchard', where loot is found in the cleft of a rock that is covered over with moss. Again and again, however, the alluring

spot is turned into a grave, the chests of buried gold into coffins, the surrounding earth into a repository for men's bones—viz., Long John (phallic pseudonym and successor to Mr. Hyde!), experienced in the ways of wickedness, has lost a leg.[18]

Alas for our lost innocence; without knowing it we were all the time in the domain of the Lord of the Flies.

Like psychoanalysis, contemporary hermeneutic criticism aspires to the revelation of hidden, latent inner meanings. Also, like psychoanalysis, it frequently feels freer in dealing with literature not of the first order. Perhaps because it is easier to impose meaning on such work. Perhaps, too, because since it insinuates that we applaud its cleverness rather than the visionary power of genius, such cleverness is more startling in the context of finding depth and complexity where we had assumed relative simplicity. Henry James thought that *Treasure Island* was 'delightful, because it appears to me to have succeeded wonderfully in what it attempts'.[19] While James considered that Stevenson's mature work required a more sophisticated critical response, he at no time considered it required an allegorical reading. Indeed, even in an allegorical master such as Hawthorne, James, as Poe, was far from convinced that it was a literary mode of the first order.

> Hawthorne, in his metaphysical moods, is nothing if not allegorical, and allegory, to my sense, is quite one of the lighter exercises of the imagination. . . . Allegory is apt to spoil two good things—a story and a moral, a meaning and a form; and the taste for it is responsible for a large part of the forcible feeble writing that has been inflicted upon the world. The only cases in which it is endurable is when it is extremely spontaneous, when the analogy presents itself with eager promptitude. When it shows signs of having been groped and fumbled for, the needful illusion is of course absent and the failure complete. The machinery alone is visible, and the end to which it operates becomes a matter of indifference.[20]

While Stevenson did unsuccessfully experiment with allegory, Professor Alastair Fowler tends to look for depth not only in a story like *The Ebb-Tide* but, improbably, in *Treasure Island* and *St. Ives*. His belief that 'Stevenson's better stories have the

16

implication of an inner, secondary narrative' is certainly put to the test by his choice of texts. Thus *Treasure Island*:

> So far, the story leads to individualism as much as individuation. But at last the achieved self is restored to society, and the individual to the fold. Outwardly, this comes about through reconciliation with Dr. Livesey and partial reconciliation with Captain Smollett. Indirectly, there are several statements of a similar idea. Perhaps the clearest is Ben Gunn's return to the human race. Another may be concealed in the treasure's final lodgement. We are told that Jim was 'kept busy all day . . . packing the minted money into breadbags'. The symbol of the achieved self is thus enclosed and fused with another symbol: containers of bread, the element of community.
>
> The quest occasioned many deaths—fifteen, in fact, in the tradition of the island called The Dead Man's Chest. But the conclusion demands still more subtractions from the microcosmic community. Three mutineers were marooned to continue the harsh process of individuation. And Silver, helped by the anarchic Ben Gunn, subtracted himself, with a little Treasure-manna. His escape is variously interpreted. It may be merely to save him from the legal embarrassments of repatriation. Or it may imply doubt about civilised society's ability to arrest Silver's tendencies. Or perhaps Robson is right to see a connection with the abandonment of the bar silver. Stevenson may hint at deferred judgement and the silver of Jeremiah 6.30—'Reprobate silver shall men call them, because the Lord hath rejected them.' If so, Ben Gunn was right to warn that the lives of the company 'would certainly have been forfeit' had Silver remained aboard. It is sobering that Captain Smollett can think of a comparable exclusion of Jim, and proves to be right in his prediction: 'I don't think you and me'll go to sea again. You're too much of the born favourite for me.' But to press the point farther might be 'not to enrich but to stultify the tale': to break a butterfly on the wheel, or make it walk the plank.[21]

Would that Edwin Muir had such erudition at his disposal to prevent his generic misinterpretation of *Treasure Island*. Happy, too, that Professor Fowler should stop short of plunging into really deep water. Do students feel that they are being made to walk the plank at the cutlass point of such esotericism? Can the academic teaching of literature, in general, or

Stevenson, in particular, withstand such a perverse compulsion for meaning? As Saul Bellow has remarked, 'deep reading has gone very far. It has become dangerous to literature.'[22] Like Eliot, Bellow sees this kind of cerebration, this allegorical compulsion maintained in the absence of faith in imagination, as evidence of a repression and corruption of emotion.

> 'Why, sir,' the student asks, 'does Achilles drag the body of Hector around the walls of Troy?' 'That sounds like a stimulating question. Most interesting, I'll bite,' says the Professor. 'Well, you see, sir, the *Iliad* is full of circles—shields, chariot wheels and other round figures. And you know what Plato said about circles. The Greeks were all mad for geometry.' 'Bless your crew cut head,' says the Professor, for such a beautiful thought. You have exquisite sensibility. Your approach is both deep and serious. Still I always believed that Achilles did it because he was so angry.'
>
> It would take an unusual Professor to realize that Achilles *was* angry. To many readers he would represent much, but he would not *be* anything. To be is too obvious. Our Professor is a 'square', and the bright student is annoyed with him. Anger! What good is anger? Great literature is subtle, dignified, profound. Homer is as good as Plato anytime; and if Plato thought, Homer must surely have done so, too, thought just as beautifully circle for circle.
>
> . . . Perhaps the deepest readers are those who are least sure of themselves. An even more disturbing suspicion is that they prefer meaning to feeling. What again about the feelings? Yes, it's too bad. I'm sorry to have to bring in this tiresome subject, but there's no help for it. The reason why the schoolboy takes refuge in circles is that the wrath of Achilles and the death of Hector are too much for him. He is doing no more than most civilized people do when confronted with passion and death. They contrive somehow to avoid them.[23]

We hardly need to hide from the emotions of *Treasure Island*. As James remarked of his early work 'everything he has written is a direct apology for boyhood; or rather (for it must be confessed that Mr. Stevenson's tone is seldom apologetic) a direct rhapsody on the age of little jackets.'[24] Undoubtedly Stevenson continues to play a continuing role in the literature of childhood. Exegesis such as Professor Fowler's would lay this waste. Stevenson was not, though on occasion he aspired to be, Nathaniel Hawthorne. His actual efforts at allegory either waxed incoherent or were surrendered up to the pressure of violent events in the story. Often he wrote manifest, self-confessed pot-boilers. Of *St. Ives*, that late, bad entertainment, he remarked 'it is merely a story of adventure, rambling along; but that is perhaps the guard that "sets my genius best", as Alan might have said.'[25] Despite such avowals this work, too, is replete for Fowler with hidden depths. To quote Bellow again:

> Are we to attach meaning to whatever is grazed by the writer? Is modern literature Scripture? Is criticism Talmud, theology? Deep readers of the world, beware! You had better be sure that your seriousness is indeed high seriousness and not, God forbid, low seriousness.[26]

Modern literary criticism is seriously endangered by a false, high priesthood prepared to sacrifice art and artists on their ritual altars of alleged esoteric meaning. Stevenson's worth is not to be increased by such tactics. Nor is he to be revalued by superficially opposite tactics. Rather than the excluding, sacerdotal mantle, Professor Leslie Fiedler assumes the blue-jeaned garments of the people. The avowed advocate of not only bridging the gap between High Art and Pop, but, indeed, of asserting the new dominance of the latter over the former, Fiedler considers Stevenson as an alleged manifestation of this process. Fiedler's lust for aristocrat-beheading revolution leads him in a direction so opposed to Fowler's as to be comical:

> Before the Bible of the Christians and Jews ceased to be central to the concerns of men in Western society, it had become merely a 'book' among others; and this, indeed, may have misled the Arnoldians who could not believe that a time might come when not merely *the* Book ceased to move men, but even books in general. Such, however, is the case—certainly as far as all books which consider themselves 'art', i.e. scripture once removed, are concerned; and for this reason the reborn novel, the truly New Novel must be anti-art as well as anti-serious. But this means, after all, that it must become more like what it was in the beginning, more what it seemed when Samuel Richardson could not be taken quite seriously, and what it remained in England (as opposed to France, for instance) until Henry James had justified himself as an artist against such

self-declared 'entertainers' as Charles Dickens and Robert Louis Stevenson: popular, not quite reputable, a little dangerous—the one his loved and rejected cultural father, the other his sibling rival in art. The critical interchange on the nature of the novel to which James contributed 'The Art of Fiction' and Stevenson 'A Humble Remonstrance' memorializes their debate—which in the thirties had been won hands down by James's defense of the novel as art; but which in the dawning seventies we are not sure about at all—having reached a time when *Treasure Island* seems somehow more to the point and the heart's delight than say, *The Princess Casamassima*.[27]

Given that *The Princess Casamassima* is about the covert nihilism of apparent espousers of the people's cause, Professor Fiedler does well to feel some reservations about it. What such Pavlovian responses to popular whim always entail is, among much else, a lamentable ignorance of history. Stevenson did delight the heart of an earlier generation of Americans than that of Professor Fiedler. Sadly for his thesis they were delighted because he was bringing them 'High Art'. As John Jay Chapman wrote:

> The American market rules the supply of light literature in Great Britain. While Lang culls us tales and legends and lyrics from the Norse or Provençal, Stevenson will engage to supply us with tale and legends of his own—something just as good. The two men serve the same public.
>
> Stevenson's reputation in England was that of a comparatively light weight, but his success here was immediate. We hailed him as a classic—or something just as good. Everything he did had the very stamp and trademark of Letters, and he was as strong in one department as another. We loved this man; and thenceforward he purveyed 'literature' to us at a rate to feed sixty millions of people and keep them clamoring for more.
>
> . . . The state of mind it shows is a definite and typical state of mind which each individual passes through, and which precedes the discovery that real things are better than sham. When the latest Palace Hotel orders a hundred thousand dollars' worth of Louis XV. furniture to be made—and most well made—in Buffalo, and when the American public gives Stevenson an order for Pulvis et Umbra—the same forces are at work in each case. It is Chicago making culture hum.[28]

Introduction

A full study of Stevenson with regard to the complex sociology of literary taste in the late nineteenth century is beyond the scope of a collection of essays such as this. What we have tried to suggest is Stevenson's ambivalent relationship to his audience and to money. No one is, in fact, more revealing about the ambivalence and anguish of this relationship than, in his letters, Stevenson himself. Attention to them might have cured Fiedler of his assumption that Stevenson was, like himself, an untroubled medium of the popular will. As so many of his heroes, Stevenson felt trapped by superior, if corrupt, forces which he had neither the will or strength to break free from. His audience was not the least of these masters.

> What the public likes is work (of any kind) a little loosely executed; so long as it is a little wordy, a little slack, a little dim and knotless, the dear public likes it; it should (if possible) be a little dull into the bargain. I know that good work sometimes hits; but, with my hand on my heart, I think it is by an accident. And I know also that good work must succeed at last; but that is not the doing of the public; they are only shamed into silence or affectation. I do not write for the public; I do write for money, a nobler deity; and most of all for myself, not perhaps any more noble, but both more intelligent and nearer home.
>
> Let us tell each other sad stories of the bestiality of the beast whom we feed. What he likes is the newspaper; and to me the press is the mouth of a sewer, where lying is professed as from an university chair, and everything prurient, and ignoble, and essentially dull, finds its abode and pulpit. I do not like mankind; but men, and not all of these—and fewer women. As for respecting the race, and, above all, that fatuous rabble of burgesses called 'the public', God save me from such irreligion!—that way lies disgrace and dishonour. There must be something wrong in me, or I would not be popular.[29]

NOTES

1. *Voyage to Windward: The Life of Robert Louis Stevenson* (London, 1952).
2. 'In Memoriam', *Robert Louis Stevenson: His Work and His Personality* (London, 1924), pp. 113–14.
3. As part of his anxious awareness of his 'Scottishness', Stevenson had an acute sense of the distinctive nature of the Scottish language. *R.L.S.:*

Stevenson's Letters to Charles Baxter (Yale, 1956), is replete with his often happy if playful use of his native tongue.

4. 'Sir J. M. Barrie', *Contemporary Scottish Studies* (Edinburgh, 1976), pp. 3–4. References to Stevenson are scattered through these studies. For the immaturity in Scottish fiction represented by Stevenson and Scott see John Speirs, *The Scots Literary Tradition* (London, 1962).
5. 'A Note on the Scottish Ballads', *Edwin Muir: Uncollected Scottish Criticism*, ed. Noble (London & New York, 1982), p. 156.
6. *The Structure of the Novel* (London, 1960), pp. 20–1.
7. Ibid., pp. 22–3.
8. 'A Note to *The Master of Ballantrae*', Valima Edition, Vol. XXIV (London, 1924), p. 479.
9. *The Letters of Robert Louis Stevenson*, ed. Colvin, 4 vols. (New York, 1969), Vol. II, p. 321.
10. *Henry James and Robert Louis Stevenson*, ed. Janet Adam Smith (London, 1948), p. 171. Henceforth *James and Stevenson*.
11. 'Robert Louis Stevenson', *Edwin Muir: Uncollected Scottish Criticism*, p. 235.
12. *Robert Louis Stevenson and the Romantic Tradition* (Princeton, 1966), p. viii.
13. 'John Jay Chapman on Stevenson's Sham Art', *Robert Louis Stevenson: The Critical Heritage*, ed. Maixner (London, 1981), pp. 489–90.
14. Ibid., p. 494.
15. *Letters*, Vol. IV, p. 362.
16. *Lectures on Literature, Volume One: British, French and German Writers*, ed. Bowers, introduced John Updike (London, 1981).
17. 'On Henry James', *The Question of Henry James*, ed. Dupee (New York, 1973), pp. 110–11.
18. 'The Self-Analytic Literature of Robert Louis Stevenson', *Psychoanalysis and Culture*, ed. Wilbur and Muensterberger (New York, 1951), p. 433.
19. *James and Stevenson*, p. 80.
20. *Hawthorne* (London, 1967), pp. 70–1.
21. 'Parables of Adventure. The Debatable Novels of Robert Louis Stevenson', *Nineteenth-Century Scottish Fiction*, ed. Campbell (Manchester, 1979), pp. 114–15.
22. 'Deep Readers of the World, Beware', *Opinions and Perspectives from The New York Times Book Review*, ed. Brown (Boston, 1966), p. 25.
23. Ibid., pp. 25, 27.
24. *James and Stevenson*, p. 131.
25. *Letters*, Vol. IV, pp. 172–73.
26. 'Deep Readers of the World, Beware', p. 26.
27. *Cross the Border—Close the Gap* (New York, 1972), p. 67.
28. 'Stevenson's Sham Art', p. 493.
29. *Letters*, Vol. II, pp. 312–13.

1

Stevenson and Henry James: A Crossing

by KENNETH GRAHAM

1

It was natural that their two lives should cross. And it was their art, and their views of art, that helped to make it natural. James's unusually firm emphasis on mimetic representation in 'The Art of Fiction'—'the air of reality (solidity of specification) seems to me to be the supreme virtue of a novel'—evoked Stevenson's counter-emphasis in 'A Humble Remonstrance'— 'A proposition of geometry does not compete with life; and a proposition of geometry is a fair and luminous parallel for a work of art.'[1] Out of such discursive opposition, and within a few months, grew their very real, warm friendship. A formal debate on art produced a relationship in life, and in that relationship the issues of the debate were repeated, and fleshed out. If the interplay of art and life, mind and nature, is one of the longest-running dramas of our intellectual history, it produced one small but perfectly paradigmatic scene in this encounter between James and Stevenson. Their ideas took issue in a relationship; the ideas were *about* relationship; and the art they respectively created was a naturalization and therefore a rich qualification of these ideas. The facts of their friendship are quite well known, as are their views on art and on one another. But there is an aptness, a sense of recognition and significance about their conjunction, both historical and personal, that enforces some further consideration, even meditation. James himself, brooding on the significances, would have called it a 'case'. At any rate, it is a crossing-place for more than just the lives of two friendly Victorian writers.

James's 'The Art of Fiction', which began it all, is a famous but quite inadequate document of his thinking on art. When Stevenson very distinctly took issue with him, mainly over his statement that the novel 'competes with life', James made little attempt to stick to his guns: 'we agree, I think, much more than we disagree', he wrote to Stevenson on 5 December 1884. '. . . Excellent are your closing words, and no one can assent more than I to your proposition that all art is a simplification.'[2] James's movement here towards friendly compromise is more than just a social grace. It exemplifies the quite unfixed nature of his basic concept of artistic form; for even in his critical, theoretical thinking James is always the artist, distrusting categories and dramatizing in the shifting emphases of what he writes the necessary openness and the kinetic quality of the concept he is considering—Form itself. Form is never a fixity or a clearly-willed outline simply because of the perpetual pressures against it of the real; and in this fact alone we can detect the very pattern of response, both critical and creative, so characteristic of James's 'opponent' in the little debate of 1884—Stevenson, the purported champion of the geometrical proposition.

Let me look in a little more detail at this doubleness or openness of thinking on James's part. It is likely to be more subtle, and certainly articulated over a wider area, than Stevenson's critical utterances; but it may lead us towards some things fundamental to Stevenson's own art, and perhaps fundamental to all artistic expression. And if that is to widen the 'case' too extravagantly, we can then narrow it quite drastically by finding the elements of so universal an issue at work in one very limited and little-regarded story by Stevenson, which lay germinating in his mind that very summer of 1885 when James was becoming a fireside *habitué* at Skerryvore, amid the Bournemouth pine-trees.

In 'The Art of Fiction' James writes with his eye quite closely on Walter Besant's published lecture, to which his own essay is a studied reply, and this no doubt occasioned the one particular emphasis, not fully typical of his criticism, that aroused Stevenson's friendly disgruntlement. For example, this:

> Many people speak of [the novel] as a factitious, artificial form, a product of ingenuity, the business of which is to alter and arrange the things that surround us, to translate them into conventional, traditional moulds. This, however, is a view of the matter which carries us but a very short way. . . . In proportion as in what [fiction] offers us we see life *without* rearrangement do we feel that we are touching the truth; in proportion as we see it *with* rearrangement do we feel that we are being put off with a substitute, a compromise and convention.[3]

This offers a perfect peg on which Stevenson can hang his eloquent and modern-sounding argument that art pursues not 'correspondence with life' but 'a certain figmentary abstraction . . . neat, finite, self-contained, rational, flowing, and emasculate'.[4] But there is one brief moment in James's essay where we can detect the other direction he *could* have taken, the qualifications he *could* have elaborated, had the immediate purposes of his rhetoric allowed him. He writes, in passing: 'All life solicits [the novelist], and to "render" the simplest surface, to produce the most momentary illusion, is a very complicated business.'[5]

'Life' as a 'solicitation', and art's 'rendering' as a perpetual complexity and struggle: here we have the very key-note of James's whole theory—or experience, rather, since it is far more rich and complex than a theory—of aesthetic form. It is too easy to cite by themselves such famous instances of James slighting the claims of 'life' in favour of 'form' as these: the critique of the Tolstoian novel as 'large loose baggy monsters, with their queer elements of the accidental and the arbitrary'; his impatience at 'the fatal futility of Fact'; and the attack on 'saturation' and the 'slice of life' in his exchanges with H. G. Wells—'It is art that *makes* life, makes interest, makes importance.'[6] No less characteristic, however, are those instances where James describes the 'life versus art' issue in terms of something that is moving and incomplete: a perpetual struggle and drama, rather than an equation or a choice to be made. The drama is most clearly, and most appropriately, expressed by

James's elaborate images or metaphors describing the very act of creating, the act of struggle between solicitous, sensuous, multitudinous life and the 'sublime economy' demanded by the shaping mind and the 'cold passion of art'.[7] For example, his reminiscences of battling to write *Portrait of a Lady* in Venice, or *The Tragic Muse* in Paris:

> The Venetian footfall and the Venetian cry . . . come in once more at the window, renewing one's old impression of the delighted senses and the divided, frustrated mind. How can places that speak *in general* so to the imagination not give it, at the moment, the particular thing it wants? . . . Such, and so rueful, are these reminiscences; though on the whole, no doubt, one's book, and one's 'literary effort' at large, were to be the better for them.[8]

And again:

> Re-reading the last chapters of 'The Tragic Muse' I catch again the very odour of Paris, which comes up in the rich rumble of the Rue de la Paix—with which my room itself, for that matter, seems impregnated . . . to an effect strangely composed at once of the auspicious and the fatal. The 'plot' of Paris thickened at such hours beyond any other plot in the world, I think; but there one sat meanwhile with another, on one's hands, absolutely requiring precedence . . . there being so much of the confounded irreducible quantity still to treat.[9]

These same two 'plots' represent the stress and the dynamic in James's concept of form: the dangerous stream of experience within which the artist's mind must seek to live, and the contending 'plot' of fictional device, compression, 'discrimination', and 'value'. There can be no adjudication between the two. Between them they make for stress and difficulty—'the deep difficulty braved'—and between them they make art what it is.

One last example, from one of James's most revealing and subtle works of criticism, his 1905 lecture, 'The Lesson of Balzac', shows James, as so often, trying to take us, through impression and metaphor, through the evoked senses and through little fictions, into the creative personality of the writer concerned. Even as a work of criticism the whole lecture enacts the two-way drama of *relationship*—between the over-

26

bearing, alluring object and the impression-receiving inter-preter—which in itself adumbrates a theory of art. And in this one extract we have the attempt to hold together the two currents of life and form, in the metaphor of the creative mind as a window overlooking the world in flux while seeking to control and to 'frame' the images that still draw their life from that external world:

> It takes attention not only to thread the labyrinth of the *Comédie Humaine*, but to keep our author himself in view, in the relations in which we thus image him. But if we can muster it, as I say, in sufficient quantity, we thus walk with him in the great glazed gallery of his thought; the long, lighted and pictured ambulatory where the endless series of windows, on one side, hangs over his revolutionized, ravaged, yet partly restored and reinstated garden of France, and where, on the other, the figures and the portraits we fancy stepping down to meet him climb back into their frames, larger and smaller, and take up position and expression as he desired they shall look out and compose.[10]

2

This may seem to have taken us some distance from Steven-son. And indeed James's attempt to grasp, through luxuriant metaphor, so complex an affair of interrelationships is a far cry from Stevenson's much brisker decisiveness: 'the great creative writer shows us the realization and the apotheosis of the day-dreams of common men'; or, 'the motive and end of any art whatever, is to make a pattern.'[11] James would have agreed, with a genuine interest and friendly admiration—then pro-ceeded to qualify Stevenson's position at great, perhaps at interminable, length. No doubt the visiting metaphors bur-geoned by the fireside each evening, below those Bournemouth pine-trees. But on the fructifying presence of *struggle*, at least, the two men would have been united; and each succeeds in conveying quite tangibly the central kinetic relationship and pressure which I am suggesting is the key to James's conscious aesthetic and a source of both men's most significant, most personal creativity. Here is Stevenson on the artist in the very act of engagement:

It is, then, first of all, at this initial and decisive moment when execution is begun, and thenceforth only in a less degree, that the ideal and the real do indeed, like good and evil angels, contend for the direction of the work. Marble, paint, and language, the pen, the needle, and the brush, all have their grossnesses, their ineffable impotences, their hours, if I may so express myself, of insubordination. It is the work and it is a great part of the delight of any artist to contend with these unruly tools, and now by brute energy, now by witty expedient, to drive and coax them to effect his will.[12]

Stevenson goes on, characteristically, to emphasize the controlling force of selection, omission, design, and rigorous relevance—'the greater outlines' and 'the one excuse and breath of art—charm'—though acknowledging that the 'idealist' in achieving these high virtues runs the risk of losing 'all grip of fact, particularity, or passion', the latter being always Stevenson's firmest and most unswerving concession to the demands of 'the real'.[13] In the Preface to *Daisy Miller* James similarly describes what I have called the act of engagement, but with a more sustained and intricate attempt to celebrate the redeeming, if disruptive, force of the artist's material. For James it is the continuing but formally resisted pressure of the real—of the view *against* the frame, as it were—that creates intensity and 'the *rich* effect':

the simplest truth about a human entity, a situation, a relation, an aspect of life, however small, on behalf of which the claim to charmed attention is made, strains ever, under one's hand, more intensely, *most* intensely, to justify that claim; strains ever, as it were, toward the uttermost end or aim of one's meaning or of its own numerous connexions; struggles at each step, and in defiance of one's raised admonitory finger, fully and completely to express itself. Any real art of representation is, I make out, a controlled and guarded acceptance, in fact a perfect economic mastery, of that conflict: the general sense of the expansive, the explosive principle in one's material thoroughly noted, adroitly allowed to flush and colour and animate the disputed value, but with its other appetites and treacheries, its characteristic space-hunger and space-cunning, kept down. The fair flower of the artful compromise is to my sense the secret of 'foreshortening'— the particular economic device for which one must have a name and which has in its single blessedness and its determined

28

pitch, I think, a higher price than twenty other clustered loose-
nesses; and just because full-fed statement, just because the
picture of as many of the conditions as possible made and kept
proportionate, just because the surface iridescent, even in the
short piece, by what is beneath it and what throbs and gleams
through, are things all conducive to the only compactness that
has a charm, to the only spareness that has a force, to the only
simplicity that has a grace—those, in each order, that produce
the *rich* effect.[14]

This dialectic between form and life, which Stevenson and
James as critics each recorded and revealed in their differing
ways, was the central dialectic of their age—or, at least, of the
age's thinking about art and literature. Behind and around the
public Stevenson–James exchange of 1884, and the same dialectic as it fluctuated within the fiction of each of them, should be
detected the pulse of that post-Romantic debate which has
never quite subsided even in our own time. The 'striving'
between form and matter that characterized art for Pater is
described, for example, in his great essay, 'The School of
Giorgione', first published in 1877. The highly contentious
reception given to Zola's novels throughout the '80s and '90s—
and to the novels of James and Howells—focused the same
issues explicitly on the novel-form, as did the so-called revival of
the Romance, centring on the writing of Stevenson, Haggard,
and Hall Caine.[15] In 1885 Vernon Lee's 'The Value of the
Ideal' and, most famous of all, Wilde's 'The Decay of Lying' in
1889 struck the top-note of the Idealist register; while looming
behind them all, in this crucial decade of the '80s, was the figure
of Nietzsche, whose belief in the demonically joyful and transformative powers of art, and in the illusive but vital subjugation
of the natural world to the force of the artist's creative will,
carried these terms of the James-Stevenson debate on to an
altogether higher, more vertiginous, stage, and ushered in the
age of extremism that still overshadows us.

More whole-heartedly than James—and much more clearly
than James the cautious realist of 'The Art of Fiction'—
Stevenson would seem to belong, and to belong quite ostenta-
tiously, to the Idealist camp.

All bad art comes from returning to Life and Nature, and
elevating them into ideals. Life and Nature may sometimes be

used as part of Art's rough material, but before they are of any real service to Art they must be translated into artistic conventions. The moment Art surrenders its imaginative medium it surrenders everything.

No, that is not Stevenson—it is Wilde, in 'The Decay of Lying'.[16] But it could well have been Stevenson: it has something of the same bravura, the Alan Breck swagger. And the insistence on convention is a consistent trait—as when Stevenson, quite uncharacteristic of his time, describes characters in fiction as 'only strings of words and parts of books; they dwell in, they belong to, literature; convention, technical artifice, technical gusto, the mechanical necessities of the art, these are the flesh and blood with which they are invested.'[17] And this is the nub of his disagreement with James in 'A Humble Remonstrance': that James has emphasized the novel's capacity to *represent* at the expense of the novel's conventionality, its formal devices, its pursuit of singleness and relevance, its need to *omit* for the sake of harmony and coherence:

> Our art is occupied, and bound to be occupied, not so much in making stories true as in making them typical; not so much in capturing the lineaments of each fact, as in marshaling all of them towards a common end. For the welter of impressions, all forcible but all discrete, which life presents, it substitutes a certain artificial series of impressions, all indeed most feebly represented, but all aiming at the same effect, all eloquent of the same idea, all chiming together like consonant notes in music or like the graduated tints in a good picture . . . The novel which is a work of art exists, not by its resemblances to life, which are forced and material, as a shoe must still consist of leather, but by its immeasurable difference from life, which is designed and significant, and is both the method and the meaning of the work.[18]

But for all Stevenson's eloquent firmness there is a saving contradictoriness in much of what he says. That is, just as James's position in 'The Art of Fiction' that the novelist competes directly with life was qualified and subtilized a thousand times by his own contrary tendency in the direction of artifice and 'consonant notes', so Stevenson's aestheticism frequently came up against his inalienable sense of experience—his respect for the basic 'leather' from which his fine shoes must be cut. His very description of the 'life' with which 'emasculate' art must never compete is a paean to experience. And—this is the heart of the contradiction, as it was that of James's—the more his imagination contemplates the multitudinousness of life the more his language seems to draw energy from the spectacle and to extend and intensify the tropes of art in order to express the distance of experience from art. So *un*self-contained is his art— despite his very words to the contrary—that its most florid and highly-formed rhetoric is directly occasioned by the perception and the pressure of life's shapeless variety:

> Life goes before us, infinite in complication; attended by the most various and surprising meteors; appealing at once to the eye, to the ear, to the mind—the seat of wonder, to the touch—so thrillingly delicate, and to the belly—so imperious when starved. It combines and employs in its manifestation the method and material, not of one art only, but of all the arts. Music is but an arbitrary trifling with a few of life's majestic chords; painting is but a shadow of its gorgeous pageantry of light and colour; literature does but drily indicate that wealth of incident, of moral obligation, of virtue, vice, action, rapture, and agony, with which it teems. To 'compete with life', whose sun we cannot look upon, whose passions and diseases waste and slay us—to compete with the flavour of wine, the beauty of the dawn, the scorching of fire, the bitterness of death and separation—here is, indeed, a projected escalade of heaven; here are, indeed, labours for a Hercules in a dress coat, armed with a pen and a dictionary to depict the passions, armed with a tube of superior flake-white to paint the portrait of the insufferable sun.[19]

Similarly, when Stevenson finds fault with the writing of his friend the 'remonstrances' in his letters are rather different from the 'Remonstrance' of the formal debate. Far from remonstrating with James for continuing to compete with life, he urges on him the virtue of what sounds remarkably like realism and representation. For example, he writes about the first two numbers of *The Princess Casamassima*, in October 1885:

> yes, sir, you can do low life, I believe. The prison was excellent; it was of that nature of touch that I sometimes achingly miss from your former work: with some of the grime, that is, and some of the emphasis of skeleton there is in nature. I pray you

31

to take grime in a good sense; it need not be ignoble; dirt may have dignity; in nature it usually has; and your prison was imposing.[20]

And while it is in a way understandable that Stevenson should have preferred James's *Roderick Hudson* to *Portrait of a Lady*, he accounts for his preference not in terms that point to the former novel's more brightly coloured 'conventions' or sharper 'geometry' but apparently to its greater realism:

> I must break out with the news that I can't bear *The Portrait of a Lady*. . . . I thought *Roderick* was going to be another such at the beginning; and I cannot describe my pleasure as I found it taking bones and blood, and looking out at me with a moved and human countenance, whose lineaments are written in my memory until my last of days.[21]

Stevenson, that is, like James, knew the 'solicitations' of the real world, and showed this in the cross-currents of his criticism—though not as clearly as in his art. It was one of the things that James most admired in him. From the first he saw in Stevenson a prime 'case': an image, to haunt his own imagination, of the interplay of art and life; a living crossing-place of the contraries that, for James, comprised the very stress and tension of the mind in its finest creativity. For all that James is drawn naturally and strongly to Stevenson as a conscious cultivator of style and a rare believer in the novelist's high calling he is also very concerned, in his 1888 essay on Stevenson, to defend him from William Archer's suggestion that he is a mere technician, a gamesman of the *mot juste*:

> Much as he cares for his phrase he cares more for life, and for a certain transcendently lovable part of it. . . . youth, and the direct expression of the love of youth is the beginning and the end of his message.[22]

A certain affectionate half-disparagement is detectable in parts of the essay, I think, as James spins out his account of Stevenson's jaunty love of heroics and of 'the romance of boyhood', and there is rather a tell-tale reliance on words like 'delightful' and 'delectable' and 'this little masterpiece'. But his happiest touch is reserved for *Kidnapped*, in which he singles out Stevenson's great strength as 'the imagination of physical states', and admires the scene of the quarrel between David and Alan for having 'the very logic and rhythm of life—a quarrel which we feel to be inevitable, though it is about nothing, or almost nothing, and which springs from exasperated nerves and the simple shock of temperaments'.[23]

James had a very particular sense of Stevenson's life: an imaginative grasp of it as ruminative and as extravagant as the impressionistic method by which, in his own account of Balzac, the critic slowly circles, broods over, and mentally takes possession of the considered subject.[24] He sees in Stevenson something of a hero of a Jamesian fiction: a Ralph Touchett, stricken by disease but living vividly, and tragically, through the vicarious imagination; even a Hyacinth Robinson, aspiring to altruistic heroism, but under the burden of a quivering, lonely sensibility and an ineradicable guilt: 'His appreciation of the active side of life has such a note of its own that we are surprised to find that it proceeds in a considerable measure from an intimate acquaintance with the passive.'[25] And clearly, as Stevenson, against all expectation, moved out of invalidism to his brief consummation in the life of apparently exotic act and freedom as Tusitala (like a somewhat less haunted Lord Jim on Patusan), James's prose, swelling its plumage in half-conscious envy, begins to take an almost unhealthy mental possession of his friend's image, as though the very fact of distance served to release the benevolently prehensile and vicarious quality of James's imagination. At this stage, in the letters to Samoa and above all in the letter of condolence to the widowed Fanny, Stevenson has become something of a figment—though a true and illuminating figment—of James's own creative urge. It is a matter of inter-penetration—a relationship—a value found, and a dense fact responded to. James's mind and art—often quite wittily—convert Stevenson's newly active and achieved life into a nugget to be hovered over by the contemplative, sedentary, and *shaping* beholder. It is our crossing-place again: a paradigm for the act (and not just the art) of fiction.

With gentle comicality, James is genuinely intent on the problem of recapturing, through imagination and words, the forfeited reality of an absent person:

33

Hang it all—sink it all and come back. A little more and I shall cease to believe in you: I don't mean (in the usual implied phrase) in your veracity, but literally and more fatally in your relevancy—your objective reality. You have become a beautiful myth—a kind of unnatural uncomfortable unburied *mort*. You put forth a beautiful monthly voice, with such happy notes in it—but it comes from too far away, from the other side of the globe, while I vaguely know that you are crawling like a fly on the nether surface of my chair. . . . A little more and I shan't believe in you enough to bless you. Take this, therefore, as your last chance. I follow all with an aching wing, an inadequate geography and an ineradicable hope.[26]

Or again, the quaint half-salacity of this:

until a few days ago I hugged the soft illusion that by the time anything else would reach you, you would already have started for England. This fondest of hopes of all of us has been shattered in a manner to which history furnishes a parallel only in the behaviour of its most famous coquettes and courtesans. You are indeed the male Cleopatra or buccaneering Pompadour of the Deep—the wandering Wanton of the Pacific. You swim into our ken with every provocation and prospect—and we have only time to open our arms to receive you when your immortal back is turned to us in the act of still more provoking flight.[27]

This is all quite light, of course; and perhaps—but only perhaps—it is a mistake to see such self-indulgent whimsicalities as much more than a variation on James's friendly and rather more straightforward wish that 'I could send a man from Fortnum and Mason's out to you with a chunk of *mortadella*.'[28] But much more unmistakable is the impassioned letter to Fanny, of December 1894, with its refrain (extraordinarily near the bone, considering the occasion and the recipient) that Stevenson's death was aesthetically *right*, the perfect consummation of the life as work of art. The letter, one of James's characteristic *tours de force*, brilliantly succeeds (but only just succeeds) in fusing such intellectual appreciation with an accompanying wholehearted feeling of personal grief and discerning sympathy: the love of shape with the 'throb' of the real, once again:

To have lived in the light of that splendid life, that beautiful, bountiful thing—only to see it, from one moment to the other, converted into a fable as strange and romantic as one of his own, a thing that has been and has ended, is an anguish into which no one can enter fully and of which no one can drain the cup for you. . . . He lighted up one whole side of the globe, and was in himself a whole province of one's imagination. . . . with all the sad allowances in his rich full life, he had the best of it—the thick of the fray, the loudest of the music, the freshest and finest of himself. It isn't as if there had been no full achievement and no supreme thing. It was all intense, all gallant, all exquisite from the first, and the experience, the fruition, had something dramatically complete in them. He has gone in time not to be old, early enough to be so generously young and late enough to have drunk deep of the cup. There have been—I think—for men of letters few deaths more romantically right. Forgive me, I beg you, what may sound cold blooded in such words—or as if I imagined there could be anything for you 'right' in the rupture of such an affection and the loss of such a presence. I have in my mind in that view only the rounded career and the consecrated work.[29]

Commentators before now have detected a morbid trait in James's imagination, by which his desire to 'possess' or 'grasp' the imaged reality of a person is apparently fulfilled by the person's death: as though the predatory and transformative powers of the contemplative mind are sometimes heightened by the physical *wasting* of what it contemplates.[30] Be that as it may—and James, it should never be forgotten, was like Stevenson an inheritor of some of the more opulent burdens and styles of Romanticism—James's most committed and intense piece of writing on Stevenson is something of an *oraison funèbre*: the review-article on the Colvin edition of *Letters to his Family and Friends*, published in 1899.[31] 'In short, we grew to possess him entire' is the key-note, struck in the very first paragraph; and though James is aware of the great dangers of the cultist approach to Stevenson, and of turning him into 'a Figure', his own approach is to blend the life and the works into one richly-constituted and eminently appreciable 'case'. And the 'case', as before, is that of the man who wrote but who also *did*: 'he belongs to the class who have both matter and manner, whom life carries swiftly before it, and who communicate and signal as they go. He lived to the topmost pulse. . . .' James recognizes in Stevenson, with a perceptible *frisson* of admiration, the stylist who was also 'the recusant engineer', the 'shameless Bohemian haunted with duty', and the life of luxurious freedom that nevertheless hung by a 'beautiful, golden thread'. All the opposites—strength with extreme vulnerability, passion with restraint, dandyism with oppressive guilt, the love of form with the rejection of artifice and the adoration of experience ('There was only one thing on earth that he loved as much as literature—which was the total absence of it')—all these things comprised the supremely rich but supremely *open* 'case' of Stevenson. These are the unreconciled opposites that spoke so intimately to James, and spoke to him not just of his friend but of himself and his own 'case'. These are the very opposites out of which he created his own imaginative world, in his fiction. And when he writes this about Stevenson, in 1899—'Almost the last word about him . . . would be that he had, at any rate, supremely written, were it not that he seems still better characterized by his having at any rate supremely lived'—we are reminded by the very phrases that only a few months later James was to begin *The Ambassadors*, of which the very germ and radiating centre was the scene of the elderly Strether, in the alluring garden of the supremely successful Gloriani, urging little Bilham to 'live'. Gloriani's garden was James's Samoa of the mind; and in the Stevenson whom he loved in life and evoked in his writing he recognized the scruples of his Strether, the worldly and artistic panache of Gloriani, and the youthfulness— always the youthfulness and *potential*—of his Bilham, his Chad: his young men leaning, appreciatively, imaginatively, on their balcony, taking in the spectacle of a dire but alluring world.

3

The rich, dire world, and the balcony of the imagination: life and art, experience and the mind, passion and withdrawal, possession and loss. They are Jamesian images, Jamesian themes; but they cross directly into the Stevenson *oeuvre*, and help to define the lineaments of his creative imagination. The ecstatic but doubting view of experience Stevenson took from his particular balcony—as he watched the miserable image of Hyde trampling over the child in the darkened street or heard the ranting victory-song of Alan Breck rise above the tumult and blood of the round-house on the brig *Covenant*—this responsiveness to the two-facedness of life is perfectly caught in a letter he wrote three months before his death. Significantly, James quotes the letter with emphasis in his article on the letters:

> But as I go on in life, day by day, I become more of a bewildered child; I cannot get used to this world, to procreation, to heredity, to sight, to hearing; the commonest things are a burthen. The prim obliterated polite face of life, and the broad, bawdy, and orgiastic—or maenadic—foundations, form a spectacle to which no habit reconciles me; and 'I could wish my days to be bound each to each' by the same open-mouthed wonder. They *are* anyway, and whether I wish it or not.[32]

Against the 'burthen' of the material and sensual foundations of life Stevenson sets his own perpetual capacity for 'wonder'. It is a matter of interplay—at times, of tragedy. The burthen is never to be ignored, for between them the stress of the real and the free play of the shaping, wondering mind comprise the very drama of art. And this was precisely James's own concept of form, at its most profound: not an imposition of conventions or devices but a struggle and multiplication of relationships: an event, not an achieved stillness; and closely akin to the nature of perception itself—'the state of private poetic intercourse with things, the kind of current that in a given personal experience flows to and fro between the imagination and the world.'[33]

James passed no comment on *Olalla*, that extraordinary Christmas story which Stevenson was writing at Bournemouth in 1885 and which even so sympathetic a reader as J. C. Furnas dismisses as 'misbegotten'.[34] Stevenson himself seems not to have known what to make of it:

> *Markheim* is true [he writes to Lady Taylor in 1887]; *Olalla* false; and I don't know why, nor did I feel it while I worked at them;

indeed I had more inspiration with *Olalla*, as the style shows. . . . I admire the style of it myself, more than is perhaps good for me; it is so solidly written. And that again brings back (almost with the voice of despair) my unanswerable: why is it false?[35]

Olalla has its demerits and its strict limitations, most of them obvious. But I want simply to offer it, quite briefly and partially, as a dramatic working out, in fictional terms, of some of those stresses and currents that run through the James–Stevenson 'encounter'. As well as being an effective half-Gothic tale in its own right—considerably more striking, in my opinion, than the slightly mechanical and moralistic *Markheim*—its resonances are fundamental to the 'case' we have been exploring: a typical Stevenson crossing-place of 'burthen' and 'wonder', inchoate 'world' and perfecting 'imagination'.

The narrator, at the outset, is to move, for convalescence, from a world of war, sickness, and the 'poisonous city' into an upper realm of mountain quietness and purity, where the keen air will 'renew your blood'; but the account of the family with whom he will lodge suggests a counter-movement of degeneracy and gracelessness, weighted by a burden of family pride and a sense of the past. *Damnosa hereditas*, of blood and body, hangs over the whole plot. The doctor (as though unconvinced by 'A Gossip on Romance'!) ironically articulates what will be the narrator's predicament:

> 'I would not romance, if I were you', replied the doctor; 'you will find, I fear, a very grovelling and commonplace reality.'

The journey into the mountains is suitably ominous: a vivid, and distinctly Hawthornean, induction into the half-world of unredeemed Nature, attractive but alien. The loutish Felipe, who convoys the narrator, is a child of Nature, 'of a dusky hue, and inclined to hairiness', who perceives all things freshly but disjointedly; sings, birdlike, without art or order—'it seemed to breathe a wonderful contentment with what is, such as we love to fancy in the attitude of trees or the quiescence of a pool.' The volatile animalism of the boy—one of those people who live 'by the senses, taken and possessed by the visual object of the moment and unable to discharge their minds of that impression'—is blurred into the impression on the narrator of the landscape, as the road begins to descend into a dark ravine loud with wind and the roar of a torrent. The voice of the river suggests the Scottish water-kelpie; and the Spanish boy, the child of nature, is haunted by a terror of the sound, though it is the voice of the elemental world he belongs to. The paradoxes—the ascents and descents, idyll and nightmare— are beginning to declare themselves.

The arrival at the castle-like *residencia* by darkness, the guest's room 'carpeted with the skins of many savage animals' and fitfully illuminated by the flames of a fire, and the striking discovery of a mysterious and haunting portrait of a woman on the wall—these are Gothic clichés, no doubt. But Stevenson brazens them out with fine confidence, aided by his usual mastery of cinematic clarity, by his sharp sense of place, his fresh-minted phrases, and by an imaginative commitment to the details and the intensity of each scene as total as the instinctive, almost obsessive impressionism of the 'innocent' Felipe. And not least, the ideas and suggestions in the story are becoming fully orchestrated, far beyond the scope of mere melodrama; never quite to the allegorical degree of a Haw-thorne, but insistently and feelingly, nonetheless. There is the pleasure of the senses in wine and the softness of sheets— Felipe caresses them with a 'grossness of content' that disturbs the narrator. The woman's portrait is an evocation simul-taneously of the past, of cruel sensuality, and of the uncon-trollable pressures of inheritance and degeneracy. The very appeal of the senses and of the 'natural' seems necessarily to evoke the idea of threat and degeneration in the mind of the narrator; as though attraction must be accompanied by revul-sion and (though only implicitly) by guilt. And the image of the sullen, feline woman, long dead, becomes an oppressive image in his mind, a Lamia-figure from some primal world whose reincarnation might yet enthrall him.

The contrasts and contradictions thicken. The narrator is puzzled at the degree to which the primitive Felipe can allow his sense of duty to overcome his instincts in his domestic labours; but is appalled when he finds the child of nature extravagantly torturing a squirrel. But we then see the

narrator himself torture the boy as a punishment, purportedly
in order to make a moral point but in effect to establish a
bodily mastery over him. 'Degeneration', we can see, is always
at hand; and the qualities of mind and order are perpetually
interwoven with their opposites, often each wearing the other
as a mask—just as the narrative, so stylized, dream-like, and
'romantic', is obsessed with physicality and the senses. So too,
in the quickening interest and pace of the narration, weather
and place now perform a dance of contrasts. The large, free
movement of the wind and sky, all vigour and change, clashes
against the shuttered introversion of the ancient house,
gathered around its dust-laden courtyard 'like the sleeping
palace of the legend'. And in the centre of that centre—as
though to illustrate something of the 'proposition of geometry'
that Stevenson took as his theoretic analogy for the work of
art—exactly repeating the motif of the narrator's own bed-
room, with its blazing wood fire and skins of animals, is the
strange 'pillared recess' where his hostess sits. The mother of
Olalla is an avatar of the woman in the portrait, and bears the
same burden of degenerate physicality. Richly dressed—like
the suggestive pomegranate that grows in the courtyard—and
noble of attitude, she is also mindless in her 'idol-like impass-
ivity', and sits in a swoon of regressive sloth and languor. She
belongs to the same 'nature' as her son, Felipe, half-noble,
half-primitive, responding to the moment-by-moment excite-
ments of passing impressions—the movements of doves and
swallows—but with her eyes distended in an appalling, haunting vacancy—'devoid of either good or bad—a moral blank
expressing literally naught'. This 'naught' lurks like a shadow
at the heart of natural, sexual plenitude, and expresses the
latent fear and distrust that bulks so large in the story. It is a
High-Romantic nightmare, of course, with hints of Keats and
of Poe; but it seems to be particularly Stevensonian, too. And
in such a context of highly controlled Gothicism, it is more
than faintly reminiscent of the occasionally-revealed nightmare world of Henry James, as in, say, *The Aspern Papers* (with
its similar emphasis on alluring but menacing eyes, on
imprisonment and repression; on a vital but ravening secret
hidden in the heart of a house or behind a screen; on the power
of the past, on degeneration, on sensual promise of weather or

garden offset by the vulpine threat of the woman or by personal fear in the predatory narrator). At any rate, there seems to be a half-articulate but rich quality of feeling beneath the rendering of *Olalla* that strongly qualifies and fills out the 'geometric' nature of its orchestration (including its frequent use of formal parallels, ironic prefiguring, echo, and premonition).[36]

Clearly, some ritual of induction or initiation is being enacted by the narration; and the critical change of weather—the dust-laden 'black wind' that wails off the mountains, like the animal screams that fill the house at night and fill the narrator 'with a deadly sickness and a blackness of horror'—is part of a physical, as well as neurotic, process of partial disintegration and descent. This middle section of the story produces two integrally linked revelations, two 'secrets' which the narrator uncovers, in the house and by analogy in himself, as he prowls, maddened by the desire to penetrate the central mystery, from chamber to chamber (again, but for the absence of Jamesian wit, one is reminded of *The Aspern Papers*). The first revelation is the encounter with Olalla herself, who is found at the end of a journey into the oppressive weight of human inheritance and decay—as though the liberating appeal of her beauty must be accompanied by the counter-impulse of guilt and the sense of being trapped and determined within time. Her home is a house of decay:

> The spider swung there; the bloated tarantula scampered on the cornices; ants had their crowded highways on the floor of halls of audience; the big and foul fly, that lives on carrion and is often the messenger of death, had set up his nest in the rotten wood-work, and buzzed heavily about the rooms.

And the family portraits everywhere, while expressing, in contrastedly positive terms, 'the miracle of the continued race, the creation and recreation, the weaving and changing and handing down of fleshly elements', can also delimit the self:

> an ancient mirror falling opportunely in my way, I stood and read my own features a long while, tracing out on either hand the filaments of descent and the bonds that knit me with my family.

The inmost chamber, where Olalla lives, is a place of asceticism, where the spirit endeavours to atone for, and even to

41

redeem, the animalism of the flesh. And the beauty and awakened passion of the girl—which the narrator evokes in uncomfortably ecstatic apostrophes: this is the weakest area of the story—now seem to offer possibilities beyond those of atonement: above all, the possibility, no less, of reconciling the natural animalism of passion—'the most exuberant energies of life'—with mentality and grace—'the torches of the soul'. 'She lived in her body; and her consciousness was all sunk into and disseminated through her members, where it luxuriously dwelt.' It is an artistic dream, as well as a sexual one—a very recognizable and age-old dream in which *mimesis* and *armonia* achieve their consummation—and the powerful appeal of it distinctly survives even the garish prose to which the over-committed Stevenson has succumbed.

But the second revelation is contradictory—the story pulses continually, in opposition to itself. Even as lover, the narrator knows retraction and disgust. James-like, he recoils from the possible 'mere brute attraction' that the girl might feel for him, from 'nature' as a determining and degrading power:

> she was drawn to me as stones fall to earth; the laws that rule the earth conducted her, unconsenting, to my arms; and I drew back at the thought of such a bridal, and began to be jealous for myself.

He reacts strongly against this impulse; and when Olalla in her turn begs him to leave, seemingly about to take herself back into the world of spiritual atonement instead of advancing into a world of soul-and-body fulfilment, he pleads blasphemously for the laws of earth: ' "Nature," I told her, "was the voice of God" '. What she represents for him is:

> the link that bound me in with dead things on the one hand, and with our pure and pitying God upon the other; a thing brutal and divine, and akin at once to the innocence and to the unbridled forces of the earth.

And at the thought of losing such primal reintegration he awakens to 'a weariness and horror of life':

> The vacancy thus suddenly opened in my life unmanned me like a physical void. It was not my heart, it was not my happiness, it was life itself that was involved.

Here is a crisis of dread, a crisis sealed in the extraordinary moment—a perfectly successful *coup de théâtre* in Stevenson's handling of it—where the narrator, blood spurting from a cut in his wrist, finds that Olalla's mother is something of a vampire after all. The 'monstrous horror of the act'—she sinks her teeth in his bleeding wrist 'to the bone'—evokes the fullest and most inhibiting revulsion from 'the laws that rule the earth', and signalizes the return of the-world-as-burden: the closing-in of the paralysing dead-weight of history and inheritance, and the crisis of the disillusioned sexual idealist. The narrator is left staring into the fatal gap that has re-opened in his love; and Olalla, too, is forced to look at her own body, with its desires, as a thing apart from her soul. Her body is not even her own, but has been handed down by her forbears: this is the horror of *her* recognition and of her final self-alienation— 'I that dwell apart in the house of the dead, my body, loathing its ways.' The insistence throughout on the monstrousness of physical inheritance is strange, and a little obsessive: as though the concepts of philosophic determinism *and* Calvinist pre-destination (the latter, at least, well known to Stevenson as a very personal and very national devil) have in this way taken physical form and limitation. It provokes some of the strongest rhetoric in the whole story:

> The hands of the dead are in my bosom; they move me, they pluck me, they guide me; I am a puppet at their command; and I but re-inform features and attributes that have long been laid aside from evil in the quiet of the grave. Is it me you love, friend? or the race that made me?

The idea of impersonality appals Olalla: she feels extinguished in it. The narrator vainly argues on behalf of impersonality:

> the clay of the earth remembers its independent life and yearns to join us; we are drawn together as the stars are turned about in space, or as the tides ebb and flow, by things older and greater than we ourselves.

It is a very clear, very dramatic, indeed very stagey debate: is the *otherness* of the body, its time-bound flesh, its genetic fixity, a curse and an obliteration of the self; or is such otherness, in the impersonality and universality of passion, a release and a fulfilment? In its deterministic aspects, the debate is a little reminiscent of some of the tones of Ibsen—it is very late-century. In its sexual aspect (though the rhetoric is different) it is almost pure Lawrence. And if these issues, in their overt-ness, seem outside the world of Henry James, the romantic-elegiac tone and—what now follows ineluctably—the con-cluding acts and gestures of abnegation, sacrifice, and parting could have come straight from the inner world of, say, *Roderick Hudson* or *The Spoils of Poynton*.

The story ends—and ends rather finely—on the image of the crucifix. And it ends, being true to its own inner alterna-tions, in doubleness. Olalla forswears happiness in emulation of the Man of Sorrows, bowed beneath the weight of inherited sin; and the narrator, though he is persuaded by her eloquence and accepts the lesson of Christian stoicism—'suffer all things and do well'—also notes the grimacing crudity of the carved crucifix and the 'painful and deadly contraction' of the face on the cross. The story has generated too much energy—energy of a frenetic kind at times, it is true—to find a complete resolution in ascetic resignation. Like any successful work of art it is founded upon, and it expresses, perpetual desire, as well as disillusionment. Exactly as for Henry James—for all their many differences—Stevenson's sombre distrust of life is vitally dependent on his love of life, each encircling and defining the other. And in the end we have to reverse the dictum that Stevenson addressed to James in 'A Humble Remonstrance' and suggest that for both writers the 'prop-osition of geometry' *does* 'compete with life'. The clear symme-tries and studied gestures of *Olalla* express a world of private feeling and general idea that flows straight back into the world of experience, and, indeed, challenges quite explicitly the finality of any containing, restraining form. Stevenson's own unconscious life pushes too insistently, too revealingly, too enrichingly, against the elegances of fairy-tale, and turns a part of geometry into voice, metaphor, and drama. And neither the concluding clarity of the Cross nor the impassioned and idealistic desire of the narrator to fuse the opposites that rend him can alter the fact that life remains all intersection and paradox, convergence *and* dispossession, and that art, being a life-bound compromise at the last, performs rather than resolves that same struggle. Perhaps it was some dim sense that they shared this recognition, at a level and at a point of crossing far deeper than their public dissension, that made James concede, 'we agree, I think, much more than we disagree'; and made Stevenson, paradoxical Stevenson, keep his remonstrance humble.

NOTES

1. *Henry James and Robert Louis Stevenson. A Record of Friendship and Criticism*, ed. Janet Adam Smith (1948), pp. 67, 92. Hereafter referred to as J. A. Smith. James's relevant essays and letters are available in various other editions, but it seems convenient to refer throughout to the Janet Adam Smith collection.
2. J. A. Smith, p. 101.
3. J. A. Smith, p. 75.
4. J. A. Smith, pp. 91–2.
5. J. A. Smith, p. 68.
6. Preface to *The Tragic Muse*, reprinted in *The Art of the Novel*, ed. R. P. Blackmur (New York, 1934), p. 84; Preface to *The Spoils of Poynton*, ibid., p. 122; letter to Wells, 10 July 1915, reprinted in *Henry James and H. G. Wells*, ed. L. Edel and G. N. Ray (London, 1958), p. 267.
7. The latter phrase occurs in Chapter 19 of *The Tragic Muse*.
8. *The Art of the Novel*, p. 41.
9. Ibid., p. 87.
10. Reprinted in *The Future of the Novel*, ed. L. Edel (New York, 1956), pp. 112–13.
11. 'A Gossip on Romance', *Memories and Portraits*, Tusitala Edn. (1924), xxix, p. 123; 'On Some Technical Elements of Style in Literature', *Essays in the Art of Writing*, ed. cit., xxviii, p. 35.
12. 'A Note on Realism', *Essays in the Art of Writing*, ed. cit., xxviii, p. 72.
13. Op. cit., p. 74. In 'A Humble Remonstrance' Stevenson singles out James's avoidance of passion and scenes of passion in his own work (J. A. Smith, p. 96).
14. *The Art of the Novel*, ed. R. P. Blackmur, p. 278.
15. For a fuller account of this debate see my own *English Criticism of the Novel, 1865–1900* (1965), pp. 19–70.
16. *The Works of Oscar Wilde*, ed. G. F. Maine (1948), p. 930.
17. 'Some Gentlemen in Fiction', *Lay Morals and Other Ethical Papers*, Tusitala Edn., xxvi, p. 110.
18. J. A. Smith, pp. 91–2.
19. J. A. Smith, pp. 89–90.
20. J. A. Smith, p. 106.
21. Letter of November 1887. J. A. Smith, p. 166.

22. J. A. Smith, p. 130.
23. J. A. Smith, p. 159.
24. See 'The Lesson of Balzac', in *The Future of the Novel*, ed. L. Edel (New York, 1956), pp. 97–124.
25. 'Robert Louis Stevenson', in J. A. Smith, p. 144.
26. Letter of 31 July 1888. J. A. Smith, pp. 173–76.
27. Letter of 28 April 1890. J. A. Smith, p. 187.
28. Letter of 12 January 1891. J. A. Smith, p. 202.
29. Letter of December 1894. J. A. Smith, pp. 248–49.
30. One of the most extreme of such commentators is Maxwell Geismar, in his 'debunking' *Henry James and his Cult* (London, 1964).
31. 'The Letters of Robert Louis Stevenson', in J. A. Smith, pp. 250–78.
32. Letter of September 1894. J. A. Smith, pp. 271–72.
33. 'Gabriele D'Annunzio', *Notes on Novelists* (New York, 1969), p. 281.
34. *Voyage to Windward* (1952), p. 217. *Olalla* was published in the Christmas number of *The Court and Society Review* (1885); and can generally be found in *The Merry Men and Other Stories* in the various Stevenson collected editions. I have not felt it necessary to give page references in the account that follows.
35. *Letters*, ed. S. Colvin (1911), ii, p. 306.
36. It is worth noting, for its suggestive value, that *Olalla* was one of the stories 'given' to Stevenson in a dream. See 'A Chapter on Dreams', *Random Memories*, Tusitala Edn., xxx, p. 52.

2

Dr. Jekyll and Professor Nabokov: Reading a Reading

by ANDREW JEFFORD

Between 1950 and 1958, Vladimir Nabokov taught Literature 311–12, 'Masters of European Fiction' at Cornell University. Despite the course title, the lectures given focused on individual works, and Nabokov chose four that were written in English.[1] *Ulysses* and *Bleak House* perhaps elected themselves, and can have raised few eyebrows. The third choice, *Mansfield Park*, was suggested to Nabokov by Edmund Wilson, a suggestion Nabokov at first received indifferently, preferring to use 'The Strange Case of Dr. Jekyll and Mr. Hyde'. 'I shall take Stevenson instead of Jane A.', he wrote to Wilson. (Cited by John Updike, 'Introduction', in Nabokov, 1980, p. xxi; henceforth N, p. xxi, etc.) Eventually, however, both were accommodated.

In this essay, I propose to consider the main points of Nabokov's reading of 'Jekyll and Hyde', extending his useful but sometimes unthoroughly explored lines of approach. I shall pay particular attention to Nabokov's predilection for apparently eccentric aspects of the story, his structural analysis, and his pronounced anti-thematics. This will then be briefly linked with his silence on the more usually remarked facets of

47

the story (the complex narrative, the use of the double motif), an eloquent silence in the light of Nabokov's own short stories and novels, in which the double motif and its elaboration in complex narrative discourse receives lengthy treatment.

A brief summary of Nabokov's lecture is given at the end of this essay. Page references to Stevenson's story refer to its reprinting in *Dr. Jekyll and Mr. Hyde and Other Stories*, ed. Jenni Calder (London: Penguin, 1979)—henceforth S, page number. Other references are either in full, or refer to the select bibliography at the end of the essay.

1

' "Dr.Jekyll and Mr. Hyde" was written in bed, at Bourne-mouth on the English Channel, in 1885 in between hemor-rhages from the lungs' (N, p. 179). Thus begins Nabokov, deliberately echoing the opening of his book on Gogol, which offers an elaborate reconstruction of Gogol's miserable end, complete with details of the half-dozen 'plump leeches affixed to his nose', and the fact that 'you could feel the spine through the stomach' (Vladimir Nabokov, *Nikolay Gogol* (London: Weidenfeld and Nicolson, 1973), p. 2). This opening sentence is a useful abstract of Nabokov's entire approach—to Steven-son, to literature in general, to his own work. 'In high art and pure science,' he declared in an interview, 'detail is every-thing' (Nabokov, 1973, p. 168).[2] It seems likely that Stevenson would have substantially agreed with Nabokov here, though he would probably have conceptualized the point rather differently. For Stevenson, it was not detail that was important,[3] but *incident*. 'Eloquence and thought, character and conversa-tion, are but obstacles to brush aside as we dig blithely after a certain sort of incident, like a pig for truffles' (Stevenson, 1882, reprinted 1920, p. 151). That 'certain sort of incident' was what typified the romantic ideal for Stevenson (the quotation is from 'A Gossip On Romance'), just as the detail of taxonomic precision (the *sine qua non* of lepidopterological research) typified the scientific ideal to which Nabokov aspired. (Both, we might note *en passant*, practised their cynosure: Stevenson working away at *Ballantrae* on the 'Casco', threading her way through the Dangerous Archipelago en route to Fakarava

(Calder, 1980, pp. 252–53); Nabokov working away at *Ada* and the other late novels in hotel rooms, writing with his scalpel-like pencil on slide-like index cards. He also spent 'seven or eight years' as Research Fellow in Entomology at the Harvard Museum of Comparative Zoology.)

Furthermore, both talked of the ideal to which they aspired in terms of poetry: for Stevenson, romance was 'the poetry of circumstance' (Stevenson 1882, reprinted 1920, p. 153) and Nabokov wrote of his scientific activity as possessing 'the precision of poetry' (1973, p. 79).[4] This link through poetry— used in the generalized sense of 'poetry, of course, includes all creative writing' (Nabokov, ibid., p. 44)—is but one junction in a substantial hierarchy of creative values that Nabokov shares with Stevenson. These seem to be fleshed out very differently— the writer as scientist appears at first a far cry from the writer as brinkman—but this is perhaps largely a question of signifiers in history, for scientists have been without doubt among the most significant brinkmen of our century.

More important than this, however, is the background and tradition in which both Stevenson and Nabokov saw them-selves as writing subjects: a specifically European tradition, rather than a narrowly national or monocultural tradition. In both cases, too, linguistic facility and enforced exile added to the uncertainty and rootlessness of their creative subjectivity,[5] with the result that both placed enormous emphasis on the craft and business of writing. There was nothing else to fall back on: no 'natural' language, no 'natural' themes, no 'natural' history. It is perhaps significant, too, in this respect, that both writers possessed fluent French, for as *writers* the lessons that both practised endlessly were those of the French post-Flaubertian tradition that later flowered in European Modernism. Steven-son had as little time for Scott's 'practice of writing' as Nabokov did for Dostoevsky's.[6]

Thus when Nabokov focuses on 'artistic problems' in 'Jekyll and Hyde', and draws attention to the story as 'a phenomenon of style', he is, after all, reading Stevenson much as Stevenson asks to be read. Only two years before writing 'Jekyll and Hyde', Stevenson had opened his essay 'A Note On Realism' (1884) with a resounding paragraph beginning 'Style is the invariable mark of any master . . .' (Stevenson, 1884, reprinted

1907, p. 262). This was no isolated broadside: in addition to this essay, Stevenson expanded his ideas further in another essay written the following year, 'On Some Technical Elements Of Style In Literature' (1885), and these essays, which Nabokov knew from the 1905 collection *Essays In The Art Of Writing* (N, p. 180), show that Stevenson had devoted considerable thought to this issue. It is enough for present purposes to note that 'style' for Stevenson meant the 'engagement of the whole forces of the mind' (Stevenson, 1884, 1907, p. 265)—the mind of both writer and reader. Style was the whole part of writing, sensual and supersensual: 'From the arrangement of according letters, which is altogether arabesque and sensual, up to the architecture of the elegant and pregnant sentence, which is a vigorous act of the pure intellect, there is scarce a faculty in man but has been exercised' (Stevenson, 1885, 1907, p. 288).[7]

What, though, comprises Nabokov's reading of 'Jekyll and Hyde' as 'a phenomenon of style'? At first sight this might seem a perverse approach to what is, in popular terms, perhaps the most celebrated fictional realization of the double motif in English and American literature.[8] Or if one wishes to consider Stevenson as (shifting objects) a phenomenal stylist, surely *Weir of Hermiston* or *Island Nights' Entertainments* would provide more rewarding study?

The key to these minor mysteries is twofold. First, the nature of Literature 311–12 and its addressees meant Nabokov was under some obligation to re-present well-known works, accessible texts. Secondly, and more importantly, Nabokov's tastes in literature, and statements on literature, were always 'perverse', and avowedly so. The importance and value of this cannot be underestimated, particularly in approaching a text like 'Jekyll and Hyde', in which the original all-important suspense device has been, paradoxically, utterly annihilated by the very fact of the narrative's own success. The mythology of 'Jekyll and Hyde' has, for many, rendered any reading superfluous. Even where this is not the case, a conventional, *fabula*-bound[9] reading is still difficult to achieve for exactly the same reason. Nabokov's seemingly 'oblique' approach has the virtue of *initiating* possibilities for a number of new readings (image-linked, spatial, discursive: see sections 2–4), all of which are essential if the complexities of this richly shortened text are to be (and are to continue to be) activated and reactivated.

Hence Nabokov's 'main injunction': 'Please completely forget, disremember, obliterate, unlearn, consign to oblivion any notion you may have had that "Jekyll and Hyde" is some kind of a mystery story, a detective story, or a movie' (N, p. 179). Although this is partly a historical point—the genres mentioned by Nabokov were developed to the forms we know by Stevenson's readers (Conan Doyle among them[10]) rather than by those whom Stevenson had read—it is also a plea for as a-generic a reading as possible.[11] Or, to follow Nabokov a little further, to situate the text within the genres Stevenson himself mentioned: the 'fine bogy tale' that he was dreaming when woken by his wife (Calder, 1980, p. 220), which provided the catalysing impetus for a piece he had been long considering; or the 'Gothic gnome' that Stevenson wrote of on 2 January 1886 to Will H. Low (Stevenson, ed. Colvin, 1899, Vol. 2, p. 11) after the work was complete. A 'bogy tale' is perhaps best described as a personal genre: a dream-work genre peculiar to each individual; whereas a 'Gothic gnome' suggests dwarf-Gothic, enigmatic Gothic.[12] With either description, in sum, we are left with free play, room to read: they situate the text in areas imaginatively fecund, rather than leaving it high and dry on the shores of a fiction of frozen codes.

2

The first of the other readings that Nabokov can be said to initiate is that based on the text's image repertoire. Nabokov focuses primarily on the role of wine in the narrative, developing this from a parenthetical suggestion of Stephen Gwynn's.[13] Wine is seen by Nabokov as all-pervasive ('There is a delightfully winey taste about this book . . .'), suffusing even the narrative discourse itself ('Everything is very appetizingly put. . . . there is an appetizing tang about the chill morning in London . . .' and so on (N, p. 180)). Nabokov then contrasts this 'sparkling and comforting draft' with the 'icy pangs' of the 'chameleon liquor' that Jekyll uses to 'hydizate' (N, ibid.)—and thus we are provided with the two elementary poles in the image repertoire. Considerably more could be made of this line of approach, however.

If we examine the points at which wine is mentioned in the text (S, pp. 29, 36, 43, 49, 53, 62) we find that in each case (p. 49 excepted) it marks a major point of reference within the text. Initially (S, p. 29) it is used to establish ambience and characterize the best part of Utterson, the essential Utterson; on p. 36 it marks the first, genial encounter between a chuckling Dr. Lanyon and Utterson; on p. 43 this ambience of civilized and discerning bibulousness is reinforced and Jekyll simultaneously inserted within its hearth. On pp. 53–4 it marks the first 'close' of the Carew murder case, and the wine now takes on a decidedly ameliorative function, 'setting free' and 'dispersing' the fogs of London outside, 'melting' the lawyer and his Guest inside. Then finally on pp. 62–3, the last night, on the verge of 'calamity', the situation is now such that wine can no longer be consumed: it is mentioned twice that Poole leaves his glass of wine untasted—Utterson's wine, the man with a taste for vintages (S, p. 29), whose house is built on *foundations* of unsunned particular old wines (S, p. 53). Utterson's wonder at this is marked.

Wine, therefore, is the litmus of the text. When it is possible or present, or even drinkable, we are among the positive image clusters; but the absence or impossibility of wine situates the reader in a limbo of negative images. Under normal conditions, in its natural state, wine is the marker of well-being in this narrative world, linked with fire, talk, and interiors. Indeed the impossibility of speech, and the invariably hostile (cold) exterior, are two of the chief negative forces at play in the text, and wine stands opposed to both of these.

To take the former first, at the dinner party of section three ('Dr. Jekyll was Quite at Ease'), Jekyll, when probed, describes the business of Hyde as ' "one of those affairs that cannot be mended by talking" ' (S, p. 44)—though by then the wine is within, and Utterson does learn somewhat more. Lanyon, a fortnight before his own death, can only countenance talk ' "of other things . . . if you cannot keep clear of this accursed topic, then, in God's name, go, for I cannot bear it" ' (S, p. 57). Utterson asks Jekyll about this quarrel: Jekyll replies ' "you can but do one thing, Utterson, . . . and that is to respect my silence" ' (S, p. 58). At the penultimate 'Incident at the Window', even though Jekyll cannot allow his two friends into his interior, Utterson offers speech 'goodnaturedly': ' "the best thing we can do is to stay down here, and speak with you from where we are" ' (S, p. 61). The doctor consents with a smile—but 'hydization' commences, and speech has to cease abruptly. Finally, on the last night, the situation is so dire that class form is thrown to the winds outside, and Utterson proposes to Poole ' "that we should be frank. We both think more than we have said" '—thus the difficulties of speech are acknowledged. (*En route* to Jekyll's house, we note, the wind 'had made talking difficult' (S, p. 63).) And when Utterson finally proposes to break down the door, Poole responds with an enthusiastic ' "Ah, Mr. Utterson, that's talking!" ' (S, p. 67). Furthermore in a text of such carefully chosen names,[14] it can be no accident that the threat to speech is met primarily by a character whose very name speaks, even through his own natural reticence: Gabriel John Utterson. The forces that underlie the threat to speech are Jekyll's excesses and Hyde's evil: the *unutterable* (see section 4). It is perhaps fitting, too, that the truth is finally brought to light, not by a lengthy speech or discussion over wine by the fireside, revealing all; but by sealed testaments, read by Utterson at home 'in quiet' between ten and midnight.

As for the image group of the exterior, the first point to be noted is that a reconstructed chronology shows all the events of the text to take place in the autumn or winter months: sections 1–3 in November/December, followed by a gap of 'nearly a year'. Sections 4 and 5 take place in the following October, section 6 in January, section 7 in February, and section 8 on a 'wild, cold, seasonable night of March' (S, p. 63). In sum, it's always cold outside. Furthermore, fog plays a major part in the narrative of the exterior, as do the small hours, and empty streets generally. Enfield, when he saw Hyde's first outrage, was returning ' "from some place at the end of the world, about three o'clock of a black winter morning, and my way lay through a part of town where there was literally nothing to be seen but lamps" ' (S, p. 31). This story is, of course, related on a Sunday walk down a street normally busy but on that day 'comparatively empty of passage' (S, p. 30). Utterson's nightmare is a nightmare of exteriors ('. . . the more swiftly, and still the more swiftly, even to dizziness, through wider labyrinths of lamp-lighted city . . .' (S, p. 37)), and it comes on the heels of a sleepless night, in which he had 'tossed to and fro until the small hours of the morning began to grow large' (S, p. 37). Utterson's encounter with Hyde is after ten at night: 'the by-street was very solitary . . . very silent. Small sounds carried far . . .' (S, p. 38). The Carew murder takes place after eleven; it is two o'clock, and foggy, before the maid recovers and calls the police (S, p. 47). By nine the next morning, the 'first fog of the season' has arrived (S, p. 48), and Utterson has a surreal ride through 'a marvellous number of degrees and hues of twilight' to Soho (S, p. 48). (As mentioned above, only Utterson's wine has the power to 'set free and to disperse the fogs of London' (S, p. 54).) Twilight is 'premature' on the second Sunday walk (S, p. 60). On the last night, Poole arrives 'after dinner'. As they hurry to Jekyll's house, the wind 'seemed to have swept the streets unusually bare of passengers, besides; for Mr. Utterson thought he had never seen that part of London so deserted' (S, p. 63). The night Hyde visits Lanyon, he arrives after midnight (S, p. 77).

Thus we might summarize the image repertoire as follows:

	speech...	impossibility of speech	
	well-lit interiors	foggy exteriors	JEKYLL'S
WINE	warm fires..................................	wintry cold	POTION
	hearthside company..................	deserted streets	
	evenings	late nights and small hours	

The opposition of these image clusters is, in itself, perhaps not unusual in either of Stevenson's suggested genres: bogy tales or gnomic Gothic. What is more unusual is the singularly reciprocal relationship between catalyser and cluster: wine, as is well-known, literally unlocks speech, usually involves interiors and warmth (in winter), and is generally thought to best serve company and the evening hours (connoting conviviality and temperance). It is, then, as a catalyser, preeminently functional. Because of this, it also has the effect of validating its 'double'—Jekyll's potion—by locating 'the chameleon liquor' so crucially within the image structure of the narrative. Though many critics have found the machinery of metamorphosis unacceptable,[15] it does, undeniably, *belong*, for the overall structure of the story is also one of ineluctable opposites. We should further note the subtlety and unobtrusiveness of this powerful image system within the narrative: the red wine and the blue potion are the arteries and veins of the text, constantly coursing the narrative, omnipresent, yet only occasionally marked.

3

Nabokov next embarks on what we might describe as a spatial reading of another linked opposition in the text: the Jekyll:Hyde:Good:Evil homology mentioned in the lecture summary. To call the homology itself into question is of course nothing new: even the most allegorically-minded of contemporary critics (the anonymous reviewer in the *Rock* of 2, iv, 1886, in an article entitled 'Secret Sin') had to admit of Jekyll that 'there was in his character a certain amount of evil' (Maixner, ed., 1981, p. 225), and critics since have usually made much of this (for example Gwynn, 1939, pp. 130–31; Chesterton, 1929, pp. 69–71; Eigner, 1966, pp. 152–56; Jackson, 1981, pp. 114–16). Nor do Nabokov's diagrams of the Jekyll/Hyde relationship provide any startling insights, though of course they help to clarify matters, by showing visually how Hyde (a small man) is lodged *within* Jekyll (a big man), and thus how the re-agent merely effects a physical separation of these metaphysical components.[16] However Nabokov's 'significant point' about the Jekyll-residue that lurks near Hyde, even in his darkest moments, is well worth noting. Nabokov arrives at this by observing a little remarked but important fact: 'Hyde still wants to change back into Jekyll' (N, p. 184). Although within the compass of narrative events, this is often necessary to escape legal retribution, we know from Lanyon's examination of Jekyll's ledger that Jekyll had been experimenting with hydization for 'a period of many years' (S, p. 76), and by the time the trampling of the little girl takes place (see Jekyll's full statement on p. 87), Hyde already has his Soho address and Jekyll's favourable will (S, p. 86). We can safely assume, therefore, that there was no point at which Hyde wished to remain Hyde *en permanence*, especially after that became a legal option,[17] but that, as Nabokov puts it, parts of the 'acceptable Jekyll' must always have hovered near the 'unacceptable Hyde' (N, p. 184), recalling him (Hyde) to himself (Jekyll). The importance of this is that it further underlines the essential inseparability of the central character as a split subject. This inseparability of the separate is vital for the reader to recognize if he is to activate the fundamental paradoxes of the text, which might be summed up by the anguished coexistence of a conjunction and a verb: Jekyll *and* Hyde; Jekyll *is* Hyde. The former is too often expounded at the expense of the latter—for it is there that Jekyll's tragedy lies.

Nabokov's spatial reading comes into its own, however, when we find analogues of Jekyll's dipsychic nature in the geography of the narrative world. This, in effect, means primarily the geography of Jekyll's house, which, like its owner, has two very different halves—so different, in fact, that even a man like Enfield, who knows the area well, has no idea that the Hyde half is connected to (or, more accurately, part of) the Jekyll half. The Jekyll half (N–S) stands out for its 'wealth and comfort' in a depressed area of 'map-engravers, architects, shady lawyers, and the agents of obscure enterprises' (S, p. 40). The by-street (a left turn a few yards south of Jekyll's front door) containing the Hyde half (E–W), however, 'shone out in contrast to its dingy neighbourhood, like a fire in a forest; and with its freshly painted shutters, well-polished brasses, and general cleanliness and gaiety of note, instantly caught and pleased the eye of the passenger' (S, p. 30). But: 'a certain sinister block of building thrust forward its gable on the street. It was two storeys high; showed no window, nothing but a door on the lower storey and a blind forehead of discoloured wall on the upper; and bore in every feature the mark of a prolonged and sordid negligence' (ibid.). Thus Jekyll's 'hydequarters' disfigure an attractive street, just as the front of his house, the façade he shows to the world, brightens a dingy neighbourhood. Wherever he is situated spatially, Jekyll is out of harmony with his environment: a millionaire among the map-engravers,[18] a beast among the business men.

Wider spatial contexts are more difficult to adduce, as we are not told where Jekyll's house is in London. Lanyon's Cavendish Square residence is but a short walk down Oxford Street from Hyde's Soho address, whereas Utterson's Gaunt Street house is a long way off (near the Elephant and Castle)—and it is Lanyon, not Utterson, that Hyde contaminates with the unutterable, and who subsequently dies. The ability to move about freely in space is significant in the text: Utterson is hardly still for a moment. The Sunday walks with Enfield are mentioned twice; Utterson regularly visits Jekyll, returns incessantly to the by-street when playing Seek to Hyde, visits Lanyon, visits Hyde's Soho address, visits the murder scene 'not far from the river' (S, p. 46), drinks wine with Guest 'by his own hearth' (S, p. 53), and again is much in evidence at Jekyll's at the end. He returns home to read the testaments. Poole, Utterson's latent double,[19] spends the last week 'flying to all the wholesale chemists in town' (S, p. 65). Whereas Jekyll/Hyde becomes increasingly unable to move about in space as the narrative advances, and this cagedness concludes in, and is connected to the ideal of disappearance. Ever since the will was first drawn up, Utterson has been mystified by the linkage between 'the idea of a disappearance and the name of Henry Jekyll' (S, p. 59). After Lanyon's announcement of his own forthcoming death, Jekyll writes to Utterson: ' "I mean from henceforth to lead a life of extreme seclusion. . . . You must suffer me to go my own dark way" ' (S, p. 58). On the last Sunday walk, Jekyll is sitting at the window 'like some disconsolate prisoner' (S, p. 60). ' "You stay too much indoors" ', Utterson tells him. Finally, Jekyll is confined to his 'cabinet'—cabinet used here in its (archaic) sense of 'a private room', every other sense indicating a space far smaller.[20] Jekyll is further confined *to Hyde*—to be obliged to place himself in a body far smaller than his own, which is surely the ultimate denial of space. (With reference to Hyde's space, we might note what Utterson had noted earlier: that Hyde 'had only used a couple of rooms' in his Soho residence (S, p. 49). Hyde's space is not of the 'natural', physical order of spaces: it is primarily unmentionable space, space elsewhere, the space of dark disorder.)

4

Nabokov's third reading, and the reading he devotes most time to, might be broadly described as discursive: a reading of the text's narrative discourse, as defined (with characteristic rigour) by Genette as 'essentially, a study of the relationships between narrative and story, between narrative and narrating, and (to the extent that they are inscribed in the narrative discourse) between story and narrating' (Genette, trans., 1980, p. 29). For Nabokov, lecturing to American undergraduates in the '50s, this highly complex web of reciprocal relationships is most usefully summed up in the more general terms of certain 'artistic problems' of the text. These are what Nabokov returns to throughout (this editorial arrangement of) his lecture, and it is these issues that motivate his extensive quotations.

These 'artistic problems' centre around the 'plausibility' and 'believability' of Jekyll's potion, the transformation, Jekyll's 'adventures'/Hyde's evil, and Hyde's face, with specific reference in each case to the narrative and the characters to whom most of the descriptive effort concerning Jekyll/Hyde is given: Utterson, Enfield, and Poole. It is the problem of grafting onto a Gothic gnome a sufficient quantity of what Barthes calls *l'effet de réel* (the reality effect)[21] to satisfy contemporary literary tastes and Stevenson's own scrupulous standards of craftsmanship. (In Genette's terms, it means primarily the relationship between narrative—the way the story is told—and story itself—the plot, the action, the 'sum total of events to be related in the narrative.'[22])

Nabokov dwells at length here on the stolid, unimpressionable natures of both Utterson (the lawyer) and Enfield (Nabokov extrapolates a 'business man' from Stevenson's 'man about town'): 'matter-of-fact persons' possessed of 'commonplace logic' (N, p. 192).[23] Dr. Lanyon is necessary for the observation of 'scientific detail', which neither Utterson nor Enfield can be expected to note. Nabokov sees the discourse of all three as being essential if the reader is to place any credibility at all in the events that follow: if we cannot trust the perceptions of Utterson, a man of sense, and Lanyon, a man of science, then the story's carefully fastened mimetic armature will slip away. And verisimilitude was something Stevenson was at great pains to achieve: why else use the *risqué* device of the powders, for example, or that of the will? Stevenson also later wrote of the story as 'a fantastic drama' (quoted N, p. 188), and it is noteworthy that it is precisely this combination of verisimilar settings, dialogues and details with 'unreal' subject matter that constitutes the 'classical' fantastic, whose narratives 'assert that what they are telling is real—relying upon all the conventions of realistic fiction to do so—and then . . . proceed to break that assumption of realism by introducing what—within those terms—is manifestly unreal' (Jackson, 1981, p. 34). It is here that the 'subversive' effect of the fantastic is to be found, that subversion that leaves the reader in a limbo of pregnant uncertainty—as to the status of the fiction, and then further of him or herself as a reading subject in relation (or 'realation') to this fiction.

But Nabokov also points out the important factor of the startling effect that Hyde has on the staid 'community of monks' (Gwynn, 1939, p. 130) among whom the story is set. 'I suggest,' says Nabokov, 'that the shock of Hyde's presence brings out the hidden artist in Enfield and the hidden artist in Utterson' (N, p. 193). In other words, Utterson (and to a lesser extent Enfield) 'double' themselves: from being 'cold, scanty and embarrassed in discourse' (S, p. 29), Utterson becomes warm and prolific of discourse, and the role of the imaginary in his conscious life, which we can only assume has been minimal in the past ('long, lean, dusty, dreary'—S, p. 29), plays an important role in the text from the Golo-like nightmare onwards. If we examine the six different descriptions we are given of Hyde's appearance (Enfield p. 31, Utterson pp. 38–40, the maid p. 48, 'common observers' p. 50, Poole p. 68, and Lanyon p. 77) only Lanyon's comes anywhere near Utterson's for imaginative and evocative power. But Lanyon's is vitiated by professional considerations: the 'great muscular activity' and the 'incipient rigor' that Lanyon observes (S, p. 77) have little of the poetry of Utterson's triple question, spoken in soliloquy[24] outside Hyde's entrance to Jekyll's house. ' ". . . Something troglodytic, shall we say? or can it be the old story of Dr. Fell? or is it the mere radiance of a foul soul that transpires through, and transfigures, its clay continent? The last, I think; for, O my poor old Harry Jekyll, if ever I read Satan's signature upon a face, it is on that of your new friend!" ' (S, p. 40). Parallelism, alliteration, assonance, climax, metaphor, autonomasia and erotema all play an important part in this magnificent outburst: the syntax is hardly that of the 'dry lawyer' (S, p. 43), the 'man of a rugged countenance . . . cold, scanty and embarrassed in discourse'

(S, p. 29). In short, it is by doubling Utterson into Seek, and thus generating a new discourse within the text, that Stevenson achieves the remarkable 'reality effect' he does. Utterson is henceforth *both* the dry lawyer and the poet of 'The Face', and both discourses are essential to the text's effective *movement* within the mind of the reader.

It is over the issue of Hyde's face, however, that some of the limitations of Nabokov's reading begin to become apparent, limitations that become still more apparent in the discussion of the evil dimension of Jekyll/Hyde. A consideration of the issue of the face and its description in an 'oblique, imaginative, suggestive way' (N, p. 193) leads Nabokov to consider the opposition of 'nightmare world' to 'reality', and thus to speak disparagingly of the 'vagueness' with which the 'evil' dimension is explored (N, p. 193). 'It was safer for the artist not to be specific and to leave the pleasures of Hyde undescribed. But does not this safety, this easy way, does it not denote a certain weakness in the artist? I think it does' (N, p. 194). And indeed this is the area of the story criticised most recurrently: F. W. H. Meyer's long correspondence with Stevenson is a good example of the widespread feeling that Stevenson was underspecific when dealing with Jekyll's past in/and Hyde's present.[25] There was also considerable discussion of the *nature* of these crimes: sexual or violent?

The point so many critics fail to see here (Nabokov included) is that the indeterminacy of realization that surrounds Jekyll's past adventures, Hyde's chilling physical appearance, and the nature of Hyde's 'unutterable' activities is absolutely essential to the narrative's reception, to a *reading* of the narrative. Indeterminacy, as Iser and the others have pointed out,[26] is a vital part of every reading experience, no matter how detail-encumbered a particular passage might be. Evidence of this is most frequently cited using the 'film of the book' example— specifically the disappointment often experienced when a familiar fictional character's 'indeterminate' appearance (Iser gives the example of Tom Jones) is objectified through concrete realization by a particular actor (Albert Finney in Tony Richardson's 1963 version, for example), provoking the reaction 'that's not how I imagined him'. The work of the imagination in 'picturing' a character or a scene consists of 'concretizing' various details—Hyde's 'displeasing smile' and 'husky, whispering and somewhat broken voice' (S, p. 40)—while leaving the imagination free to fill in the 'gaps' that remain, using intertextual or contextual frames. From the 'hints' we are given as to Hyde's appearance, we build up a picture—a picture essentially imaginary. It is in this 'essentially imaginary' realization of character or setting that the power of fiction resides, for the indeterminate, imagined image is generally immeasurably more powerful than the concrete image.

This is particularly the case with fictions in which abnormal or fantastic states are presented. Here it is the indeterminacies, so important in any case to the reading process, that are foregrounded, almost at the expense of the concrete details: it is not, in fact, Hyde's unpleasant smile or husky voice that we remember so much as Utterson's impressive rhetorical ragout, concocted of the troglodytic, Dr. Fell, Satan's signature, and a foul soul transpiring through, and transfiguring, its clay continent. These stimulatingly 'poetic' metaphors activate the reader's imagination in a much more powerful way than the mere enumeration of facial features ever could. Stevenson was in fact taking the only course open to him if he wished Hyde to affect us as he affected the other characters of the narrative—and the success of the story is testament to the skill with which these indeterminacies are so memorably incorporated in the discourse.

The principle is the same for Jekyll's previous misdemeanours and Hyde's undescribed outrages. It is as important that we *shouldn't* know *exactly* what these are, as it is that we *should* know *vaguely* what they are. We must have 'some idea'—but the idea must be indeterminate, and it must allow the imagination room to manoeuvre. Conjectures as to what Jekyll's '(to say the least) undignified' (S, p. 85) pleasures were, have the variety and attraction that they do for readers, precisely because we can play with various notions—gluttony, excessive drinking, regular brothel trips, orgy and debauchery, homosexuality, sado-masochism, pederasty, rape, pornography, gambling, street fighting, cock fighting—and virtually nothing is ruled out. If we knew that Jekyll had indulged for years in, say, regular brothel trips involving sado-masochism,[27] the story would lose the chief pleasure it offers the reader: its endless power of suggestion.

This is even more important with Hyde's activities, for in Hyde Stevenson wishes to suggest an extract, an essence, a distillation: 'Edward Hyde, alone, in the ranks of mankind, was pure evil' (S, p. 85). Jekyll describes his previous excesses as 'undignified': 'I would scarce use a harder term. But in the hands of Edward Hyde they soon began to turn towards the monstrous' (S, p. 86). Hyde's activities, as was touched upon earlier in the discussion of the image repertoire, are literally 'unutterable', in the fullest sense: to utter that which Hyde engages in, to utter that which Hyde thinks, to utter that which *is* Hyde—is impossible. The edifice of evil that occupies the black heart of this 'dreadful book'[28] would crumble at the merest hint of a name. Hyde's realm is essentially that of the signifier, and his effectiveness in the narrative is reliant upon the free movement of that signifier: *evil*. The enthusiastic *Academy* reviewer of the twenty-third of January 1886 struck the right note when he described Hyde as 'a monster whose play is outrage and murder' (Maixner, ed., 1981, p. 204): one can be no more specific than that particular 'play'. We know that Hyde's abominations were more than merely sexual: 'There is no harm in a voluptuary; and none, with my hand on my heart and in the sight of God, none—no harm whatever—in what prurient fools call "immorality".' Thus wrote Stevenson to John Paul Bocock in November 1887 (Maixner, p. 231). In the same letter he describes 'the beast Hyde—who is no more sensual than another, but who is the essence of cruelty and malice, and selfishness and cowardice . . .'. This play with the signifier 'evil' is the reason for the rather bizarre crimes of which Hyde is actually indicted: the trampling of the little girl and the murder of Carew. As Gerard Manley Hopkins wrote to Robert Bridges, the 'trampling-scene is perhaps a convention: he was thinking of something unsuitable for fiction.'[29] This *abuse* of a little girl is symbolic, a token, a 3 a.m. event on a crossroads en route from the end of the world. And the second crime is 'archetypical' to the narrative in the same way: instead of a little girl, we have a frail old man on his way to the postbox. There is moonlight all around; a lonely maidservant is indulging in romantic reverie. Into this idyll erupts Hyde, clubbing and trampling with ape-like fury, the Rue Morgue murderer at large in Lambeth. There is of course no motive or *raison* for either act: they are both gratuitous, and unlikely withal, and so much the better. Stark acts: 'insensate cruelty' (S, p. 47). It is the string of periods they leave in the mind of the reader, suggesting other acts in other places, that are the real justification for their existence. Hyde's real crimes must always be other, and elsewhere. To wish for a more concrete account surely denotes a certain weakness in the critic.

5

Thus we might summarize the merits of Nabokov's lecture as aperient: he opens up a number of new ways of reading a text previously clogged by a small number of 'frozen' readings. The lecture has, of course, its faults: the notes Nabokov's editor was working with were the least 'finished' of all those used for *Lectures on Literature*, and the quotations—in a book and not a lecture hall—seem unnecessarily lengthy. Some of the aspects of the story—the good/evil relationship that Nabokov diagrammatizes, for example—get much more space than they deserve, while other important aspects are totally ignored (see below). But Nabokov as a teacher and critic was, to use John Simon's words, 'learned, meticulous, fascinating, erratic and frustrating'[30]—and in that peculiar mix (the list could be lengthened) lay his particular appeal.

But what of Stevenson? The very fact of his inclusion— between Flaubert and Proust—is salutary, even if it does provoke remarks like 'quite a comedown' and 'this section reads at times like an uneasy apologia' from reviewers.[31] But it is perhaps to be regretted that so much of the Stevensonian context, and the wider literary context, is missing. There is missing, with reference to the former, the background of Calvinism and the backdrop of Edinburgh, both omnipresent in this a-religious London narrative (see Chesterton, 1929, pp. 68–84). *Deacon Brodie* is missing (1864, rewritten and revised with W. E. Henley, 1879): Stevenson's earlier, dramatic, attempt to plumb the depths of the 'double life'; and of course *Markheim* (1885) and the destroyed story *The Travelling Companion* (see Swearingen, 1980, p. 62), each of which provides (or might have provided) subtle analogues and variants on one of the principle concerns of 'Jekyll and Hyde': to chart the anfractuous progress of the signifiers *good* and *evil*—in relation to the self, a troubled self: 'that damned old business of the war in the members' (Stevenson to J. A. Symonds, in Stevenson, ed. Colvin, 1899, Vol. 2, p. 23). A reading of the later *Fables* (1895, though some were written considerably earlier), and later stories like 'The Bottle Imp' (1891) and 'The Waif Woman' (1892, pub. posth. 1914) reveal a dissolution of the insistence with which these signifiers are ordered and used into the more richly complex issues of *relationships* between these two major signifiers and others: the innocent and the experienced, the material and the immaterial. Language, too, takes on a new and more intense role in these later texts.

Nabokov also leaves unturned another boulder: the issue of the double, *qua* double. By this is meant primarily the literature of what Rogers calls the manifest double (see footnote 19)—though, should one wish to extend the term to include latent doubles, Stevenson's other work is again of great interest. Dick Shelton and Richard of Gloucester, Alan Breck and David Balfour, Loudon Dodd and Jim Pinkerton, Henry and James Durie, Archie and Adam Weir are all latent doubles of major importance—see Eigner, 1966 throughout for an informed discussion of this issue. Stevenson is certain to have known occurrences of the double motif in Whitman, Poe ('William Wilson', 1840), James Hogg (*Confessions of a Justified Sinner*, 1824), Musset ('La nuit de décembre', 1835, and elsewhere), and Balzac (*La peau de chagrin*, 1831); and it is likely he knew Dostoevsky's short novel on the theme (*The Double*, 1846). Hoffmann's stories (*c.* 1813–22), de Chamisso's 'Peter Schlemihl' (1832), and Hawthorne's 'Monsieur du Miroir' (1837) Stevenson possibly knew. Maupassant's 'He' (1884) and 'The Horla' (1887) were written at about the same time as 'Jekyll and Hyde', and Oscar Wilde's *The Picture of Dorian Gray* (1891), James's 'The Jolly Corner' (1908) and Conrad's 'The Secret Sharer' (1913) were all written later. As were, of course, Nabokov's *The Eye* (1930), *Laughter in the Dark* (1931), *Despair* (1934), *Lolita* (1955), *Pale Fire* (1962), and *Ada* (1969), all of which involve considerable play on, in and around doubles. However Nabokov was always, superlatives aside, cagey about his own work; and in an interview with Alfred Appel, to whom he was prepared to give more than to most, he was asked: 'Would you care to comment on how the *Doppelgänger* motif has been both used and abused from Poe, Hoffman, Andersen, Dostoevsky, Gogol, Stevenson, and Melville, down to Conrad and Mann? Which *Doppelgänger* fictions would you single out for praise?' (Nabokov, 1973, p. 83). The full reply was succinct, if nothing else: 'The *Doppelgänger* subject is a frightful bore' (ibid.).

This is a shame; little else. Suffice it to say here that Stevenson's contribution to this literature is major, both in 'Jekyll and Hyde' and in other, less overt, instances of latent doubling. The widely held view that 'doubles are among the facile, and less reputable devices in fiction'[32] is becoming increasingly untenable, as questions of self and subjectivity in fiction grow in importance and relevance to our own contemporary readings of ourselves. The contribution of 'Jekyll and Hyde' is distinguished here in three ways. Firstly it offers an extremely colourful and stereoscopic realization, in terms of narrative setting and locale, of the problem of the other within the self. It is far from being a masterpiece in monochrome, *à la* Dostoevsky: the image repertoire, the subsidiary character groups, and the spatial dynamics of the story all help to authenticate and substantiate, as well as contrast with, the split subject at the text's centre. Secondly, 'Jekyll and Hyde' offers a carefully wrought and elaborated plot schema for the type of the manifest double, to which the 'crude' popular image of the story does little justice. Dr. Jekyll and Mr. Hyde share one body, one brain. There is, in fact, no separation at all: the chemicals merely effect an oscillation of *forms*, a replacement of one form by another within it. (In this sense, the title of the piece, though striking, is misleading and inaccurate.) Once this basic 'given' is realized, the plot takes on a subtlety and formal fitness seldom appreciated, particularly in relation to the artfully layered narrative frames, which emphasize the increasing isolation of Jekyll/Hyde and the incomprehension of the community. Thirdly, 'Jekyll and Hyde' realizes the essential ambiguity and unknowableness of the self and its double(s). It accomplishes this by exploring the underbelly of the self (so evident in nearly all of the literature of the double) with substantial success, a success that is due to the enormous narrative energy Stevenson invests in suggestiveness and indeterminacy. This indeterminacy takes hold with reference to Jekyll and Hyde's 'otherwhere' activities, and the suggestiveness by using the environment and the image repertoire of the text to generate atmosphere and duplicate the basic paradigmatic polarity at every coign and turn of the narrative.

Thus, when we come to lay down Henry Jekyll's full statement, we know all, and we know nothing. The whole we think we know is but a shadowy half, a merely narrative half, and all that remains of the other is the fog in our nostrils and the memory of empty streets—together, of course, with more reading, and more readings.

NOTES

1. The others included *Anna Karenin*, 'The Death of Ivan Ilyich', *Dead Souls*, 'The Greatcoat', *Fathers and Sons*, *Madame Bovary*, *Swann's Way*, 'The Metamorphosis', and possibly some Chekhov. See Nabokov, 1980, pp. vii–viii.

2. This coupling is returned to almost obsessively throughout *Lectures on Literature*: '. . . a work of fiction or a work of science (the boundary line between the two is not as clear as is generally believed)' (p. 3); 'the best temperament for a reader to have, or to develop, is a combination of the artistic and the scientific one' (pp. 4–5); 'That little shiver behind [the shoulder blades] is quite certainly the highest form of emotion that humanity has ever attained when evolving pure art and pure science' (p. 64); 'What is the joint impression that a great work of art produces upon us? . . . The Precision of Poetry and the Excitement of Science' (p. 123); 'After all, there are other thrills in other domains; the thrill of pure science is just as pleasurable as the pleasure of pure art' (p. 382).

3. Though the widely known 'Happy Thought' shows that Stevenson was by no means immune to the 'serendipitous' detail:

> The world is so full of a number of things,
> I'm sure we should all be as happy as kings.

Robert Louis Stevenson, *A Child's Garden of Verses* (London: Longman's, 1885), reprinted in *Collected Poems*, ed. Janet Adam Smith (London: Hart-Davis, 1950), pp. 361–411, poem p. 375.

4. The two are further amalgamated in the following remark in *Lectures on Literature*: 'It seems to me that a good formula to test the quality of a novel is, in the long run, a merging of the precision of poetry and the intuition of science' (p. 6).

Dr. Jekyll and Professor Nabokov: Reading a Reading

5. As Steiner points out of Nabokov, 'whereas so many other language exiles clung desperately to the artifice of their native tongue or fell silent, Nabokov moved into successive languages like a travelling potentate. Banished from Fialta, he has built himself a house of words' (George Steiner, 'Extraterritorial' in *Extraterritorial* (London: Penguin, 1975), pp. 14–21, quotation p. 18).

Stevenson perhaps moved less swiftly among languages than Nabokov—though he had fluent French and learnt Samoan—but he travelled much further and faster than Nabokov ever did, living at various times at Menton, Fontainebleau, Monterey (California), Bournemouth, Davos (in the Swiss Alps), Hyères (near Nice), Saranac Lake (in the Adirondack mountains), the Marquesas, Hawaii, the Gilbert Islands, and of course Samoa. There can be no doubt that this affected his writing: with reference to this, Peter Keating wrote recently of Stevenson's 'chronic state of uncertainty about the kind of reading public he was reaching', as a consequence of his incessant 'movement from country to country'. According to Keating, this uncertainty is reflected in 'the frequently piecemeal composition' and the 'restless imagination constantly testing out different literary forms' (*Times Literary Supplement*, 26 June 1981, 715).

6. Stevenson admired Scott, of course, and was aware of the great debt he owed him. What I have in mind here, however, are comments like 'With the map before him, he will scarce allow the sun to set in the east, as it does in *The Antiquary*. With the almanac at hand, he will scarce allow two horsemen, journeying on the most urgent affair, to employ six days, from three of the Monday morning till late in the Saturday night, upon a journey of, say, ninety or a hundred miles, and before the week is out, and still on the same nags, to cover fifty in one day, as may be read at length in the inimitable novel of *Rob Roy*' (Stevenson, 1893; reprinted 1907, p. 376).

Nabokov's disparagement of Dostoevsky—he usually referred to him as 'Dusty'—was unswerving: he once graded all the great Russian authors for his students, and some way below Tolstoy's A-plus and Pushkin and Chekhov's A's (and even Turgenev's A-minus and Gogol's B-minus) trailed Dostoevsky with 'C-minus. (Or was it D-plus?)' Hannah Green, 'Mr. Nabokov', in Peter Quennel, ed., *Vladimir Nabokov— A Tribute* (London: Weidenfeld and Nicolson, 1979), p. 37.

7. Compare this with Nabokov's remarks on style at the end of his lecture on *Mansfield Park*: 'Style is not a tool, it is not a method, it is not a choice of words alone. Being much more than all this, style constitutes an intrinsic component or characteristic of the author's personality. Thus when we speak of style we mean an individual artist's peculiar nature, and the way in which it expresses itself in his artistic output' (N, pp. 59–60).

8. 'Jekyll and Hyde' has passed into the vocabulary of (English) popular allusion in a way that, for example, William Wilson, or Yakov Golyadkin, or the young captain and Leggatt have not.

9. *Fabula* is the Russian formalist term for the 'basic story stuff', the sum

total of events to be related in the narrative—in a phrase, the "material for narrative construction"' (Seymour Chatman, 'Towards A Theory of Narrative' in *New Literary History*, VI, No. 2, Winter 1975, 295). Thus a *fabula*-bound reading is a reading *for the story alone*, a reading that regards the narrative discourse as transparent.

10. Conan Doyle regarded Stevenson's 'The Pavilion On The Links' as 'the first story in the world' and 'so complete in itself, and so symmetrically good, that it is hardly conceivable that it should ever be allowed to drop out of the very first line of English literature' (see Maixner, ed., 1981, p. 14).

11. An a-generic reading—in a broad sense—is impossible of course. In order to make 'sense' of any work of art, we need to 'bring it within the modes of order which culture makes available . . .' (Jonathan Culler, *Structuralist Poetics*, London: Routledge and Kegan Paul, 1975, p. 137). 'It is indeed this word (novel, poem) placed on the cover of the book which (by convention) genetically produces, programmes, or "originates" our reading. We have here (with the genre "novel", "poem") a *master-word* which from the outset reduces complexity, reduces the textual encounter, by making it a function of this reading already implicit in the law of this word' (Marcelin Pleynet, 'La poésie doit avoir pour but . . .' in *Théorie d'ensemble* (Paris: Seuil, 1968), pp. 95–6; cited and trans. in ibid., p. 136).

However Nabokov urges that we 'should always remember that the work of art is invariably the creation of a new world, so that the first thing that we should do is to study that new world as closely as possible, approaching it as something brand new, having no obvious connection with the worlds we already know' (N, p. 1).

12. It's possible, however, that Stevenson was merely being disparaging about the piece. This seems unlikely in the light of the qualification Stevenson makes: '. . . but the gnome is interesting, I think, and he came out of a deep mine, where he guards the fountain of tears. It is not always the time to rejoice' (Stevenson, ed. Colvin, 1899, Vol. II, p. 11).

13. '(Oddly enough, there is no other of all his books where his kindly feeling for vintages makes itself so often felt)' (Gwynn, 1939, p. 130).

14. So much can be made of the names in the text that it seems hard to imagine that they were not chosen carefully. Nabokov's assertion that the names Jekyll and Hyde 'are of Scandinavian origin' and 'that Stevenson chose them from the same page of an old book on surnames where I looked them up myself' seems primarily designed to forestall other (Freudian or psychological) interpretations. *Hide*, 'a haven', and *Jökulle*, 'an icicle', are rather disappointing, even compared with Nabokov's own offering of the 'symbolic meanings' his students should avoid: 'that Hyde is a kind of hiding place for Dr. Jekyll, in whom the jocular doctor and the killer are combined' (N, p. 182).

In fact it is nearly impossible to avoid the obvious connotations of Hyde: Hyde is hidden in Jekyll and his past, Jekyll hides in Hyde, goes into hiding, or goes out Hyde-ing on the town. And Hyde hides Jekyll. Hyde is the hidden of society, and of man in society. The most convincing account of Jekyll corresponds to this reading: Je-kill, both I kill (as in Hyde's violence) and the killing of the *je*, the I. (In Lacanian theory, the *je-idéal* is 'the ideal self . . . to which the subject tries to conform, and with which (s)he tries to coincide, since it constitutes his or her identity' (Jackson, 1981, p. 89).) When Jekyll Hydes, he is killing himself, his *je*, in an act of dis-appearance ('here again were the idea of a disappearance and the name of Henry Jekyll bracketed' (S, p. 59)). The day on which Jekyll becomes Hyde involuntarily for the first time forces Jekyll to effect a separation of personal pronouns: 'He, I say—I cannot say, I' (S, p. 94). That is the point at which the *je* is killed, and from then on the Hidden is in the ascendant. (It should be remembered, of course, that Stevenson's French was fluent. Though as a qualification it might also be added that according to Richard Aldington, Stevenson pronounced Jekyll's name Jeekyl (Richard Aldington, *Portrait of a Rebel*, London: Evans, 1957, p. 183). The case stands, however, as the story is to be read silently rather than retailed orally; and Stevenson always spoke English with a Scots accent, in which Jeekyl is a more likely pronunciation.)

Utterson is the other major name in the narrative, and see below for the significances of this name.

15. See for example E. T. Cook's *Athenaeum* review in Maixner, ed., 1981, 202–3, or F. W. H. Meyer's long correspondence with Stevenson (ibid, pp. 212–22).

16. Perhaps this diagrammatic reification is the reason for Nabokov's omitting from the lecture the lepidopterological material he had sketched out on metamorphosis, which is a radically transformative process, and one that—introduced as a metaphor—would falsify the essential *projection* of Jekyll into Hyde.

17. In narrative terms. Many critics have of course pointed out (even to Stevenson, a qualified lawyer) the impossibility of the terms of the will, among them Rider Haggard (in a letter to Stevenson of 26 January 1886) and E. T. Cook in the above mentioned review.

18. Jekyll's 'quarter of a million sterling' (S, p. 48) would be worth well over a million in present day terms.

19. Robert Rogers, in his book *The Double in Literature* (Detroit: Wayne State University Press, 1970) makes the distinction between *manifest* doubles, which are overt doubles: two separate characters, one the *alter ego* of the other—Jekyll and Hyde, the two Golyadkins in Dostoevsky's *The Double*, or the young captain and Leggatt in Conrad's 'The Secret Sharer'. *Latent* doubles are implicit doubles, and may in fact be multiple, more than two: Rogers cites the examples of the four brothers Karamazov, Macbeth and Lady Macbeth, and Hamlet's father, Claudius and Polonius. In the case of latent doubles, their personalities are such that they complement each other, making a whole within the narrative. It is in this sense that Poole doubles with Utterson: upstairs and downstairs, they are the talkers, the act-ers, the movers of the text.

20. The *Oxford English Dictionary* also lists the revealing sixteenth-century and seventeenth-century meaning of 'a den or hole of a beast' (*The*

Compact Edition of the Oxford English Dictionary, 2 Vols. (Micrographic), Volume I, p. 312).

21. Roland Barthes, 'L'effet de réel' in *Communications*, 11 (1968), 84–9.

22. Seymour Chatman, *Story and Discourse* (Ithaca: Cornell University Press, 1978), p. 19. The distinction is derived from the Russian Formalists' *fabula/sjužet* distinction, for which see note 9, and, for example, Boris Tomashevsky, 'Thematics', in Lee T. Lemon and Marion J. Reis, eds., *Russian Formalist Criticism* (Lincoln: University of Nebraska Press, 1965), pp. 66–8; or P. N. Medvedev/M. M. Bakhtin, *The Formal Method in Literary Scholarship*, trans. Albert J. Wehrle (Baltimore: Johns Hopkins University Press, 1978), p. 106.

23. Though the characterization is open to question in the case of Enfield: the text seems to imply that his character was in some ways the opposite of Utterson's, even though on their walks together they both appear 'singularly dull' to observers (S, pp. 29–30). What was Enfield doing, after all, 'at the end of the world, about three o'clock of a black winter morning'? (S, p. 31). Nabokov is, perhaps, thinking of p. 38: 'unimpressionable Enfield'.

24. Utterson 'enjoyed the theatre'—though he 'had not crossed the doors of one for thirty years' (S, p. 29).

25. See Maixner, ed., 1981, pp. 212–22, especially pp. 214–15 and 217.

26. See Wolfgang Iser, *The Implied Reader: Patterns of Communication in Prose Fiction from Bunyan to Beckett* (Baltimore: Johns Hopkins University Press, 1974), pp. 282–83, and Wolfgang Iser, *The Act of Reading* (London: Routledge and Kegan Paul, 1978), pp. 170–79. Also Roman Ingarden, *The Literary Work of Art*, trans. George C. Grabowicz (Evanston: North Western University Press, 1973), and Roman Ingarden, *The Cognition of the Literary Work of Art*, trans. Ruth Ann Crowley and Kenneth R. Olsen (same publication details as previous work).

27. As so many Victorian gentlemen did: see Steven Marcus, *The Other Victorians* (London: Corgi, 1969), Chapter 6.

28. J. A. Symonds's deeply-felt description in a letter to Stevenson: 'it touches one too closely' (Maixner, ed., 1981, pp. 10–11). See also the following footnote.

29. We might also note that Hopkins told Bridges 'You are certainly wrong about Hyde being overdrawn: my Hyde is worse' (Maixner, ed., 1981, p. 229). Hopkins, of course, was a Jesuit priest.

30. John Simon, 'The Novelist At The Blackboard', *Times Literary Supplement*, 24 April 1981, 457.

31. Ibid.

32. Cited (and partially expressed) by Ralph Tymms, *Doubles in Literary Psychology* (Cambridge: Bowes and Bowes, 1949), p. 1.

Dr. Jekyll and Professor Nabokov: Reading a Reading
APPENDIX

A Brief Summary of Nabokov's Lecture on 'The Strange Case of Dr. Jekyll and Mr. Hyde'

(Nabokov's lecture on Stevenson exists 'in what can [be] described only as rough notes; hence the present ordering of its material is almost entirely the responsibility of the editor'—Fredson Bowers, 'Editor's Foreword', in Vladimir Nabokov, *Lectures on Literature* (Weidenfeld and Nicolson, London: 1980), p. ix.)

Nabokov begins (in this editorial arrangement) by enjoining his audience to see Stevenson's work as 'a phenomenon of style' rather than as 'some kind of a mystery story, a detective story, or movie'. He then considers three 'important points . . . completely obliterated by popular notions about this seldom read book': these are all to do with the widely accepted four-term homology Jekyll: Hyde: Good: Evil. 'Jekyll is not pure good, and Hyde . . . is not pure evil . . .', and Nabokov devotes considerable space to diagrammatic analysis of the exact relationship between each term. Nabokov then relates this to the geography of Jekyll's house.

He then considers the 'difficult artistic problem' of the story, which might be summarized as the general problem of rendering Gothic plausible. This includes the character of Utterson (and Enfield) in relation to events and narrative; Hyde's face; the setting of the story; the exact nature of Jekyll's, and Hyde's, misdemeanours; and the 'epoch-making scene' of the transformation. Nabokov concludes by noting the thematic link between Stevenson's own last words—'Do I look strange?'—and 'the fateful transformations in his most wonderful book'. The lecture as printed also includes a facsimile page of notes on the metamorphosis of butterflies omitted from Nabokov's lecture. Stevenson's story is not mentioned in these notes.

SELECT BIBLIOGRAPHY

Calder, Jenni, *RLS: A Life Study* (London: Hamish Hamilton, 1980).

Chesterton, G. K., *Robert Louis Stevenson* (London: Hodder and Stoughton, 1927).

Eigner, Edwin M., *Robert Louis Stevenson and Romantic Tradition* (Princeton: Princeton University Press, 1966).

Genette, Gerard, *Narrative Discourse*, trans. Jane E. Lewin (Oxford: Basil Blackwell, 1980).

Gwynn, Stephen, *Robert Louis Stevenson* (London: Macmillan, 1939).

Jackson, Rosemary, *Fantasy: The Literature of Subversion* (London: Methuen, 1981).

Robert Louis Stevenson

Maixner, Paul, ed., *Robert Louis Stevenson: The Critical Heritage* (London: Routledge and Kegan Paul, 1981).

Nabokov, Vladimir, *Lectures on Literature*, ed. Fredson Bowers (London: Weidenfeld and Nicolson, 1980).

Nabokov, Vladimir, *Strong Opinions* (New York: McGraw-Hill, 1973).

Stevenson, Robert Louis, *Dr. Jekyll and Mr. Hyde and Other Stories*, ed. Jenni Calder (London: Penguin, 1979).

Stevenson, Robert Louis, 'A Gossip on Romance', *Longman's Magazine* 1, November 1882, 69–79. Reprinted in *Memories and Portraits* (London: Chatto and Windus, 1920), pp. 151–67.

Stevenson, Robert Louis, 'My First Book—*Treasure Island*', *The Idler* 6, August 1894, 2–11. Reprinted in *The Works of Robert Louis Stevenson* (Pentland Edition), Vol. V (London: Cassell and Co., 1907), pp. 367–77.

Stevenson, Robert Louis, 'A Note on Realism', *The Magazine of Art*, 7, November 1883, 24–8. Reprinted in Ibid., 262–68.

Stevenson, Robert Louis, 'On Some Technical Elements of Style in Literature'. Originally published as 'On Style in Literature: Its Technical Elements' in *The Contemporary Review* 47, April 1885, 548–61. Reprinted in Ibid., 269–88.

Stevenson, Robert Louis, *The Letters of Robert Louis Stevenson to his Family and Friends*, selected and edited by Sidney Colvin, 2 Vols. (New York: Charles Scribner's Sons, 1899).

Swearingen, Roger G., *The Prose Writings of Robert Louis Stevenson: A Guide* (London: Macmillan, 1980).

3

Landscape with Figures

by JAMES WILSON

The painter John Everett Millais told the critic Sidney Colvin at a dinner party that he considered Stevenson 'the very first of living artists. I don't mean writers merely,' he said, 'but painters and all of us. Nobody living can see with such an eye as that fellow, and nobody is such a master of his tools.'[1]

This was more than convivial politeness or a casual, social compliment. The Pre-Raphaelite Millais had been endowed with an extraordinary and precocious talent which he had compromised in the service of a paying public, and his tribute touched on an aspect of Stevenson's equally extraordinary ability (Henry James called it 'the note of visibility')[2] which is displayed at least as much in his travel writing as it is in his fiction. He was a meticulous and practised observer with an obsessive attention to detail that can be seen in a letter he wrote to Colvin describing a painting by Jacob van Ruysdael in the National Gallery of Scotland.

> I think it is one of the best landscapes in the world; a grey still day, a grey still river, a rough oak wood on one shore, on the other chalky banks with very complicated footpaths, oak woods, a field where a man stands reaping, church towers relieved against the sky and a beautiful distance, neither blue nor green.[3]

The details of the description are exact and can be verified in the gallery, and—implicit in their listing—is an aesthetic principle shared with the painter: all objects are treated with the same care, the same seriousness.

Stevenson was writing to Colvin in the spring of 1875 and was newly back in Edinburgh after a visit to France. He had stayed in Barbizon, a village on the western fringe of the forest of Fontainebleau which had given its name to a school of painters inspired by the naturalism of Ruysdael and his seventeenth-century Dutch contemporary, Meindert Hobbema. For Stevenson, travel writing was landscape painting in words, and—like Jean François Millet, who is buried in the graveyard at Barbizon—he saw landscape as a background for people.

No one can know for certain what experiences Stevenson had in mind when he told his step-son Lloyd Osbourne that writers like himself had been muzzled like dogs 'and condemned to avoid half the life that passes us by'.[4] What we do know is that, because of that muzzling, the travel book which may be his most enduring, as it is certainly his most powerful and uncompromising, remained unpublished in his lifetime and was not to appear in its entirety for more than seventy years after his death.

It is worth remembering that he was a travel writer before he became a story-teller. His first essay to be published and paid for was called 'Roads', and in it he argued that we have to guard against 'the dazzle and accumulation of incongruous impressions . . .'.

His second published essay, 'Ordered South', is an invalid's view of Mentone in southern France—'Here, at his feet, under his eyes,' he tells us, 'are the olive gardens and the blue sea'[6]— but the invalid has only what Stevenson calls head-knowledge of this landscape and that is divorced from enjoyment. As he looks at the scene, he remembers the wintry streets of Edinburgh.

> The hopeless, huddled attitude of tramps in doorways; the flinching gait of barefoot children on the icy pavement; the sheen of the rainy streets towards afternoon; the meagre anatomy of the poor defined by the clinging of wet garments. . . . If only the others could be there also; if only those tramps could lie down for a little in the sunshine, and those children warm their feet, this once, upon a kindlier earth; if only there were no cold anywhere, and no nakedness, and no hunger; if only it were as well with all men as it is with him![7]

This is the writer who said to Colvin, perhaps defensively, that his 'Forest Notes', written after that visit to Fontainebleau, were 'too sweet to be wholesome'.[8] Colvin accepted the assessment and so, by and large, have succeeding generations of critics. It is revealing therefore to go back to the essay itself, for it is another example of a landscape with figures.

> A blue-clad peasant rides home, with a harrow smoking behind him among the dry clods. Another still works with his wife in their little strip. An immense shadow fills the plain; these people stand in it up to their shoulders; and their heads, as they stoop over their work and rise again, are relieved from time to time against the golden sky.[9]

That could have been the work of a Barbizon painter, but Stevenson superimposed a second, contrasting image—as he did at Mentone.

> These very people now weeding their patch under the broad sunset, that very man and his wife, it seems to us, have suffered all the wrongs of France. It is they who have been their country's scapegoat for long ages. . . .[10]

Perhaps the over-sweetening came when he went on to say that the peasants had come into their reward now that the castle was empty and green creepers were growing over its broken balustrades.

> Out on the plain, where hot sweat trickles into men's eyes, and the spade goes in deep and comes up slowly, perhaps the peasant may feel a movement of joy at his heart when he thinks that these spacious chimneys are now cold. . . .[11]

'Forest Notes' came out in 1876, and in September of that year Stevenson began the journey which he called *An Inland Voyage*, his account of a canoe trip in Belgium and France. This was his first book and there was an admiring but unsigned review of it in a short-lived magazine called *London*. The editor was Stevenson's friend W. E. Henley, and he himself was a contributor.

Readers were advised that the author

> flatly declines to look at the world as it is used to be looked at . . . he dares (and his audacity is unconscious: a quite

remarkable circumstance) to stand on his own legs, to decline precept and example from any and everybody, to keep his heart and his intelligence for that alone which interests him . . . and in questioning nothing to be master of everything.[12]

Sidney Colvin was Slade Professor of Fine Art at Cambridge when *An Inland Voyage* was published, and he described it as

> like the landscape-painting of the Japanese, setting down this or that point that happens to have made itself vividly felt, and leaving the rest; so that another traveller might go the same journey and scarcely notice any of the same things. . . .[13]

Stevenson had made the point himself in an essay called *An Autumn Effect*.

> Any man can see and understand a picture; it is reserved for the few to separate anything out of the confusion of nature, and see that distinctly and with intelligence.[14]

He carried a sketch-book and used it to supplement his written notes. He was also interested in photography—'We expose our mind to the landscape (as we would expose the prepared plate in the camera)'[15]—and reminds us by his method, as the photographer does, that we are always looking at relationships: between people and places, between one object and another, between ourselves and the subject, and between past, present and future.

An Inland Voyage was a geographic, artistic and personal exploration. It was followed in 1879 by the increasingly assured *Travels with a Donkey in the Cevennes* and in 1880 by *The Amateur Emigrant*, although this was not to be published for another fifteen years. *The Silverado Squatters* came out, belatedly, in 1884 and was, effectively, the last of the travel books. It seemed that Stevenson had gone too far, both literally and metaphorically. He had begun to invite, if not to ask, uncomfortable questions.

In January 1880 he wrote to Colvin, who had made no bones about his unfavourable response to the first part of *The Amateur Emigrant*, 'a somewhat wordy and spiritless record of squalid experiences'.[16] He wondered whether Colvin had to be so eloquent in his dispraise. 'I know I shall do better work than ever I have done before,' he said; 'but, mind you, it will not be like it. My sympathies and interests are changed. There shall be no more books of travel for me.'[17]

But let us back-track. From the beginning, Stevenson had included himself as a figure in the landscape. That unsigned review in *London* described *An Inland Voyage* as 'charming in itself, and charming in an even greater degree by reason of the glimpses it affords of its author's personality'.[18] For many readers this was an attractive device, but for others it was disturbing and would become more so. The fact remains that for Stevenson his presence 'in the picture' was necessary to his purpose. As he said,

> It is one thing to describe scenery with the word painters: it is quite another to seize on the heart of a suggestion and make a country famous with a legend.[19]

An Inland Voyage had shown him how quick his critics could be to take offence, for he was accused of laughing at religion. There was always something to see about a church, he had said—'whether living worshippers or dead men's tombs; you find there the deadliest earnest, and the hollowest deceit.'[20] It made no difference that he had also said that mankind was never so happily inspired as when it made a cathedral.

The trouble was that he contrasted elegance and soaring splendour with the nondescript and the shoddy, and his eye had picked out and followed an old woman who was making her lonely, conscientious way from altar to altar.

> To each shrine she dedicated an equal number of beads and an equal length of time. Like a prudent capitalist with a somewhat cynical view of the commercial prospect, she desired to place her supplications in a great variety of heavenly securities.[21]

He was criticized by much the same people in much the same way for *Travels with a Donkey*. 'The book has the same fault as *An Inland Voyage*,' his father told him, 'for there are some three or four irreverent uses of the name of God which offend me and must offend many others.'[22]

The words 'style' and 'charm' were freely invoked by his admirers—double-edged compliments which suggested, among others connotations, decoration and superficiality. Yet, as far as style was concerned, Stevenson believed in pruning. Alfred Noyes quoted him as saying, 'Give me a blue pencil and I will make an epic out of a daily newspaper.'[23] Style meant selection—the selection of the significant detail, the significant word, the significant cadence. As for charm, if it implied an attempt to ingratiate he could be singularly careless in its employment. Take, for example, his treatment of the donkey he called Modestine: he procured a wooden goad with a pin an eighth of an inch long and flailed the animal until her legs were raw and bleeding. It is a story that reflects badly on Stevenson and he knows it, but he tells it against himself.

As with all the travel books, his method of working was to keep a diary and, if necessary, add to it later. *The Cevennes Journal*, published in 1978, revealed that Stevenson and his donkey came together in a bad week when the animal was in heat: she was understandably difficult and he was understandably exasperated. He tells us, nevertheless, that she had 'a patience, *une endurance*, beyond that of saints'.[24] He makes nothing of his own endurance, but he must have walked close to 150 miles[25] in twelve days. That was in difficult country with an animal whose dilatoriness made it impossible to find a rhythm. On top of that, he had to discipline himself to keep his journal, and he did this to such polished effect that much of it was carried over, unaltered, to the published text. Re-tracing the route, one has to ask: how is it that he works his magic? How is it that he captures the essence, the so-called 'genius' of the place?

Stevenson's father complained that there was too much scene-painting, but time and again it is the figures that define the landscape—people seen in the distance kneeling on the steps of a church, a giggling girl sticking out her tongue, a white-robed monk struggling with a barrow-load of turfs, a crippled old shepherd hobbling on a pair of sticks, a woman singing plaintively among the chestnut trees.

He rarely wrote about architecture and this also was misunderstood. When he was in Monastier, the place to visit was the abbey church named after an eighth-century martyr, and a French critic complained that he seemed not to appreciate the beauty of the building. He questioned whether he had even visited the church. Well, we know from the journal that he did. He took notes, but made no use of them. Instead, in a billiard-room, he gave us the disreputable Father Adam who sold him his donkey for sixty-five francs and a glass of brandy, then disconcertingly shed a tear that 'made a clean mark down one cheek'.[26]

The secret was the freshness and vividness of his reporting and the fact that nothing was allowed in the picture

> that did not serve, at once, to complete the composition, to accentuate the scheme of colour, to distinguish the planes of distance, and to strike the note of the selected sentiment. . . .[27]

The prose is best appreciated when it is re-read, for it has the texture and density of poetry. Stevenson has no need to dissect or analyse or even explain; he reveals people who, by their appearance and behaviour, give scale and significance to the setting. It was a gift that he had displayed from the beginning. For instance, there is a fragment called 'Cockermouth and Keswick' which begins with a comment on the painter's trick of half-closing his eyes 'so that some salient unity may disengage itself from among the crowd of details . . .'.[28]

He tells how he walked up a street in Cockermouth, felt lonely at the sight of young lovers, then spotted a hat-maker's sign that diverted him: the name was Smethurst, the hats were of Canadian felt. The next day he met Mr. Smethurst who was standing at his door brushing one of the hats with more of them stacked on his head, waiting their turn. The hatter had seen him pass by the night before and was happy to talk— about walking and fishing and convalescence—and, because of the pleasure to be found in little things, he told Stevenson that he was going to lend him his boat.

> It ought to have been very nice punting about there in the cool shade of the trees, or sitting moored to an overhanging root; but perhaps the very notion that I was bound in gratitude specially to enjoy my little cruise, and cherish its recollection, turned the whole thing from a pleasure into a duty.[29]

The twist, the tying of the knot that makes the story worth telling, is beautifully managed. It is done with a sleight-of-hand dexterity when he tells us that, being ashamed of not having enjoyed Mr. Smethurst's treat sufficiently, he had to go further up the river to find some other, roundabout way back into

Cockermouth, always remembering that he had to be in time for dinner.

Both *An Inland Voyage* (made in appalling weather) and *Travels with a Donkey* (undertaken too late in the year)—both of these were planned so that a book could follow; but to say that is to say very little. More interestingly, *Travels with a Donkey* was the book with which Stevenson proved himself to be a committed and professional writer. He was in love, he was 27, and he was filled with the anguish of separation; it was a farewell to his youth, a rueful acceptance of responsibility, a last adventure (as he thought) deliberately undertaken to shape his thoughts on life and the future. As for his writing, he was already a master of lean and muscular prose as can be seen from the second sentence of the first chapter, his laconic description of his starting place. 'Monastier', he tells us, 'is notable for the making of lace, for drunkenness, for freedom of language and for unparalleled political dissension.'[30] He tells how

> The tide of prosperity came and went, as with our northern pitmen, and left nobody the richer. The women bravely squandered their gains, kept the men in idleness, and gave themselves up, as I was told, to sweethearting and the merry life.[31]

If the departments of English literature refuse to learn from that, perhaps the schools of journalism might pay attention to the weight and placing of the words. There is the mastery and flexibility of the first person narrative, the skilful introduction of comment and supposition, the ways in which he achieves fluidity by varying the length of his sentences, his characteristic final clause drawn out and elegantly shaped to achieve an effect of musical resolution; then, elsewhere, there are his changes of tense, shifts in time and space, and—not least skilful—his persistent use of verbs of movement attached to objects which are themselves motionless. He is the master of the active sentence.

Stevenson said of *Travels with a Donkey* that lots of it was mere protestations to the woman he loved,[32] and he makes repeated reference to the need for companionship. His journey was made in the autumn of 1878 and the book was published in the summer of 1879—a speed of production that must arouse the envy of present-day writers and the admiration of their publishers.

The Amateur Emigrant, the account of his journey to California to join Fanny Osbourne, was written in August and September 1879 and revised in 1880. It fell naturally into two parts, and the first of these—*From the Clyde to Sandy Hook*—was his record of the voyage across the Atlantic; the second part told of a dismally uncomfortable crossing of the United States by rail.

Colvin was disappointed and thought the book 'quite unworthy'.[33] Henley shared this opinion, finding it 'feeble, stale, pretentious'.[34] Nevertheless, it was accepted for publication. It was Stevenson's father who swung the balance decisively, and in August 1880 the book was withdrawn. Nothing that Stevenson had written had been attacked so fiercely by family and friends. As we have noted, the first part was not, in fact, published until after his death, and even then there were revealing omissions. The second part—*Across the Plains*—appeared in Longman's Magazine in 1883 and was reprinted, in shortened form, in 1892. It was not until 1966 that we were given an unexpurgated edition.[35] 'I think it not only the worst thing you have done, but altogether unworthy of you,'[36] his father had told him. He was speaking of what Richard Aldington a lifetime later called 'the most mature piece of work Stevenson had yet produced'.[37]

It is worth looking again at what Stevenson wrote. He admitted that, for the first time, he understood what he called the prolonged and crushing series of defeats suffered by the British working classes in the nineteenth century—whole streets of houses standing deserted, homeless men, closed factories, useless strikes, starving girls.

He was no longer alone and apart as he had been in the mountains of the Cevennes, and he sensed that he was the better for it; but it was a bitter experience. He discovered that if you travel steerage—or, as he did, associate with those who do—people treat you differently. Sailors called him 'mate', officers addressed him as 'my man', his comrades—Stevenson's word—accepted him as one of themselves. His accent, his clothes, his paper-smooth, uncalloused hands made no difference. The saloon passengers gave him 'a hard, dead look, with the flesh about the eye kept unrelaxed'.[38] Thinking about women, he speculated at what stage a man became invisible to what he called the well-regulated female eye. 'My height seemed to decrease with every woman who passed me, for she passed me like a dog.'[39]

'The steerage conquered me,' he tells us.

> I conformed more and more to the type of the place, not only in manner but at heart, growing hostile to the officers and cabin passengers who looked down upon me.[40]

It has to be emphasized that he was no stranger to prejudice or misunderstanding. A rural postman in the France of 1876 had assumed, and would not be dissuaded, that he was a pedlar of pornographic photographs. Worse than that, he had been arrested for lack of identification, stripped of his possessions and locked in an underground cell. Less frightening, but nevertheless upsetting, he and his friend Walter Simpson (his companion on *An Inland Voyage*) had been refused food or lodging or even shelter one pouring night when an inn-keeper mistook them for tramps. They had been lucky to find hospitality elsewhere.

So it had been in the Cevennes. Stevenson had slept in the open, and indoors had been grateful to share a room with strangers—once with a young cooper and his wife and child, on another occasion with five surveyors working for the railway. He was living rough and staying, when he could, in what were called hedge-inns where you were expected to eat with your own knife and where you had your meal in the kitchen which also served as the only washroom. None of these experiences prepared him for the *S.S. Devonia*.

He has a chapter in which he relates how he and two other passengers found an elderly man lying helpless in the scuppers. The man was able to tell them he had seen the ship's doctor twice, but had been given nothing for the cramp in his stomach. Stevenson and one of his shipboard friends went for help and learned for themselves how indifferent both officers and crew could be to the fate of the people in steerage. In the words of the bo's'n, 'They wouldn't mind if they saw you all lying dead one upon the top of another.'[41]

The heart of the story was cut from the version that

eventually appeared after Stevenson's death, but his journal tells us that the man had been sick and his head was in his vomit. Stevenson and his companions tried to lift the man clear of the deck and the filth, but this was difficult—'for he fought in his paroxysms like a frightened child, and moaned miserably when he resigned himself to our control.'[42]

Stevenson warned one of the others to watch where he kneeled; his own knee was in the sickness. The journal goes on:

> I thought the patient too much occupied to mind our observations; but he heard me, relaxed his struggles, and began to twist in a new way with his arm across his body. I could not imagine what he was at; till suddenly forth came a coloured handkerchief; and he held it out to me, saying 'Wipe your knee wi' that.'[43]

As Stevenson intended, the story reflects on what he called the unaffected courtliness of a good heart. It also reflects on those who muzzled him, as he said, like a dog.

Much of the trouble must have lain in the false expectations of his admirers, and the extent of these can be gauged from an announcement which appeared in *The Athenaeum* in February 1880, stating that the author was preparing what it called 'a third set of charming *impressions de voyage*'. So much for charm! Eight months later the magazine carried another announcement. It said that 'Mr. R. L. Stevenson has determined to suppress his *Amateur Emigrant*, announced by us some little time ago, and has withdrawn it from his publishers' hands.'

If he had shown stoicism in the Cevennes, he drove himself almost to the point of death on his journey to California. When he landed, his body was a mass of sores, all of them itching, and he was soaked to the skin in New York so that he had to jettison the clothes he was wearing, because he could neither dry them nor pack them wet. After that, there was still more rain and he had to brush himself dry when, finally, he found a corner on a train heading west out of Jersey City. He had numerous changes to make along the way until he reached what was called the Pacific Transfer Station on the eastern bank of the Missouri. The Union Pacific ran an emigrant train from there with wooden benches for the passengers and a long line of baggage-waggons. Stevenson hired a board and three straw cushions and made a bed of sorts which he shared with a Pennsylvania Dutchman. He shared the price of washing materials with two others—a tin bowl, a towel and a block of soap. They filled the bowl at a water filter and took it out to the platform of the car where they could kneel and make an uncomfortable shift at washing face, neck and hands. Stevenson said it was cold, insufficient and, if the train was moving fast, somewhat dangerous.

'I died a while ago,' he wrote to Colvin; 'I do not know who it is that is travelling.'[44] Crossing the plains of Nebraska, he sat on top of a waggon roof wearing nothing but an unbuttoned shirt and a pair of trousers. He wrote another letter, this time to Henley. It was, he said, a strange vicissitude that had taken him from the Savile Club to the desolation of the prairie; as for his body, it was 'all to whistles'.[45]

For better and for worse, it was mostly his fellow-countrymen he had met on the *Devonia*. On the emigrant train he encountered what he called the 'Despised Races', and in Pittsburgh he was served, for the first time, by a coloured man. 'I had come prepared to pity the poor negro,' he reported,

> to put him at his ease, to prove in a thousand condescensions that I was no sharer in the prejudice of race; but I assure you I put my patronage away for another occasion, and had the grace to be pleased with that result.[46]

He also spoke up for the Chinese who were the subject of endless abuse from the other passengers, and for the American Indians. 'For my own part,' he said, 'I could not look but with wonder and respect on the Chinese. Their forefathers watched the stars before mine had begun to keep pigs.'[47]

As for the Indians,

> If oppression drives a wise man mad, what should be raging in the hearts of these poor tribes, who have been driven back and back, step after step, their promised reservations torn from them one after another as the States extended westward, until at length they are shut up into these hideous mountain deserts of the centre—and even there find themselves invaded, insulted and hunted out?[48]

He was writing eleven years before the massacre at Wounded Knee and only three years after the battle of the Little Bighorn.

The words 'Out of my country and myself I go' had appeared in quotation marks in *An Inland Voyage*[49]; they reappeared in *The Amateur Emigrant*,[50] and the likelihood is that they were Stevenson's own. (There are six lines of 'attributed' poetry in *Travels with a Donkey* which were later included in his collected poems.) What at first may have been little more than a conceit had taken on a new and poignant meaning.

He worked on the galley proofs of *The Amateur Emigrant* at Silverado where he and Fanny spent their unconventional honeymoon, accompanied by Fanny's son, the young Lloyd Osbourne, and a mongrel dog called Chuchu. His thoughts were turning to fiction, but he was also keeping the journal which was to be the first draft of *The Silverado Squatters*.

The *Emigrant* was written in a style appropriate to the subject, the *Squatters* likewise. The Californian book reflected a partial recovery in health, a more contented spirit and an appeasement of those sexual longings which he had expressed in his Cevennes journal, longings for 'the woman a man has learned to love wholly, in and out, with utter comprehension'.[51] Nevertheless, it was open to the same criticism as the first two volumes—that it might seem, to some readers, to be about nothing very much. The setting, after all, was at that time a remote and little-known part of northern California where he and Fanny had chosen, for economy's sake, to stay in the shattered bunkhouse of an abandoned silver mine perched high on the shoulder of a mountain. It could also be said—and, as usual, he anticipated the criticism—that he was attempting to pour new wine into old bottles. He had to hope that laying it down would improve the quality, and it was two years before he completed the revision of the journal at Davos in Switzerland.

Going over the ground in California, as in the Cevennes, one sees the landscape differently because of him. His view of it becomes our view, and for many people who live there—and for many who visit—he has made the Napa valley and Mount Saint Helena famous with a legend. Perhaps because he was not continually on the move, there is more detailing of the human figures and he brings more of them into the foreground.

He was not a tourist, and—as he had said nothing about the church he was expected to admire in Monastier—so he dismissed a petrified forest that was regarded as one of the

85

curiosities of Sonoma County. 'Doubtless the heart of the geologist beats quicker at the sight,' he conceded, 'but for my part I was mightily unmoved. Sight-seeing is the art of disappointment.'[52]

Instead, he found what for him was a much more delightful curiosity. The sign on the gate had identified the proprietor, Charles Evans, and this man—Petrified Charley, as he was called locally—turned out to be a 'brave old white-faced Swede'[53] who had discovered a graveyard of giant redwoods which had been buried under volcanic ash and turned to stone six million years before. Mr. Evans had been a seafaring man, an unsuccessful prospector and a hard drinker. He had come into the valley 'bent double with sciatica, and with six bits in his pocket and an axe upon his shoulder',[54] and he was as ready-made for Stevenson as Mr. Smethurst, the hat-maker of Cockermouth, whose sign had caught his eye in the Lake District.

> When I mentioned I was from Scotland, 'My old country,' he said; 'my old country'—with a smiling look and a tone of real affection in his voice. I was mightily surprised, for he was obviously Scandinavian, and begged him to explain. It seemed he had learned his English and done nearly all his sailing in Scottish ships. 'Out of Glasgow,' said he, 'or Greenock; but that's all the same—they all hail from Glasgow.' And he was so pleased with me for being a Scotsman, and his adopted compatriot, that he made me a present of a very beautiful piece of petrifaction—I believe the most beautiful and portable he had.[55]

The ironic twist is still there, although used in a different place, but there is a manipulation that was not apparent in the story of Mr. Smethurst. It seems that, in *Silverado*, Stevenson is trying—as never before—to be all things to all men. Nevertheless, it is a memorable landscape and the figures it contains come vividly to life, sometimes in less than a line. If we look to the corners and the background of the picture, we find people who are becoming self-consciously aware of their own reflected image—the spitting, gum-chewing layabout with his unheroic vanity, the equally self-admiring hunter with his suit of fringed buckskin, the Chinese gambler, the consumptive school teacher and—not least—'the ogling, well-shod lady with her troop of girls'.[56]

It was a world that was looking both backwards and forwards—back to stage-coaches and highwaymen, forward to the railroad and the new-fangled telephone. Stevenson dropped in one night to Cheeseborough's hotel in Calistoga and was asked if he would like to speak to one of the already legendary stage-drivers. He said that he would because he had heard tales of this man, but was then disconcerted to find himself with one object thrust at his ear, another at his mouth, and nothing in the world to say, for he had never in his life used a telephone.

> So it goes in these young countries; telephones, and telegraphs, and newspapers, and advertisements running far ahead among the Indians and the grizzly bears.[57]

Vineyards appealed to him more than petrifaction, and there was nothing cagey about his admission—his boast perhaps?—that he tasted eighteen varieties in the winery of Jacob Schram.

> I tasted all. I tasted every variety and shade of Schramberger, red and white Schramberger, Burgundy Schramberger, Schramberger Hock, Schramberger Golden Chasselas, the latter with a notable bouquet, and I fear to think how many more.[58]

Jacob Schram had the oldest vineyard in the valley and Stevenson was fascinated to hear that he had started out as a penniless barber, and even after he had begun to plant and cultivate the vines had

> continued for long to tramp the valley with his razor. Now, his place is the picture of prosperity; stuffed birds in the verandah, cellars far dug into the hillside, and resting on pillars like a bandit's cave—all trimness, varnish, flowers, and sunshine, among the tangled wildwood. Stout, smiling Mrs. Schram, who had been to Europe and apparently all about the States for pleasure, entertained Fanny on the verandah while I was tasting wines in the cellar.[59]

The use of his wife's name was a breach of Victorian literary convention and added an extra touch of spontaneity and attractively unguarded enthusiasm. What was not included, perhaps understandably, was a further reference to Mrs. Schram.

> Her one trouble, worthy woman, is a question of clothing. Mr.
> Schram wishes her to wear corsets; God help me, in this hot
> weather; she has to wear them when she goes to pay a visit,
> hence pays no visits, hence as she says, 'people hate her.'[60]

That deleted remark was first published as part of 'The
Silverado Diary' in the Vailima and Tusitala editions in the
1920s, and it was not until 1954 that the complete *Silverado
Journal* was published in the United States. The additions that
were made by Stevenson in Europe, as opposed to the
deletions, were mainly to do with the organization and
'modelling' of the material, and this in turn often had to do
with seeing and hearing. 'The seeing imagination',[61] as Henry
James called it, is nowhere more vividly displayed than in the
journal; but it may be supplemented. There is, for instance,
Stevenson's description of the cabin at night when, sometimes,
he would go outside and walk about on what had been the
platform of the mine. The others would be in bed but still
awake, and he could hear their voices. The light indoors came
from a single candle in the neck of a bottle, and yet—

> It shone keen as a knife through all the vertical chinks; it struck
> upward through the broken shingles; and through the eastern
> door and window it fell in a great splash upon the thicket and
> the overhanging rock.[62]

Afterwards, he added another picture in which he is both
observed and observing. This was when the squatters made
their way from what had been the assayer's office to the
bunkhouse—

> moving bedwards round the corner of the house, and up the
> plank that brought us to the bedroom door; under the immense
> spread of the starry heavens, down in a crevice of the giant
> mountain, these few human shapes, with their unshielded
> taper, made so disproportionate a figure in the eye and mind.[63]

It may be that Stevenson's greatest gift is in that glorious
disproportion, in that intensely visual evocation of figures in a
landscape. By contrast, his hearing imagination sometimes
seems to belong more to the study. He savours again a place-
name like Chimborazo which he had invoked in at least three
of the earlier essays—'The Ideal House', 'The Stimulation of

the Alps' and 'Roads'. Then there is his trick of expressing emotion and a sense of loss while at the same time listing faults and deficiencies. It is not over-sweetening; rather, it is the adding of salt to taste. He had used the effect in his *Edinburgh: Picturesque Notes* which he completed in Monastier before setting off with his donkey. He varied it in another passage about his homeland in *The Silverado Squatters.*

> There is no special loveliness in that grey country, with its rainy, sea-beat archipelago; its fields of dark mountains; its unsightly places, black with coal; its treeless, sour, unfriendly-looking cornlands; its quaint, grey, castled city, where the bells clash of a Sunday, and the wind squalls, and the salt showers fly and beat. I do not even know if I desire to live there; but let me hear, in some far land, a kindred voice sing out, 'O why left I my hame?' and it seems at once as if no beauty under the kind heavens, and no society of the wise and good, can repay me for my absence from my country. . . . I will say it fairly, it grows on me with every year: there are no stars so lovely as Edinburgh street-lamps.[64]

Students of style may perhaps consider the artifice with which the phrase 'O why left I my hame?' is placed in the text, and that also had been used before—in his account of life among the emigrants in Steerage No. 1 of the *Devonia.*

Henry James said of *The Silverado Squatters* that it was perhaps less vivid, as it was certainly less painful, than the account of the railway journey *Across the Plains* to San Francisco.

> He has never made his points better than in that half-humorous, half-tragical recital. . . . It is much to be regretted that this little masterpiece has not been brought to light a second time, as also that he has not given the world—as I believe he came very near doing—his observations in the steerage of an Atlantic liner.[65]

That was the judgement of the writer who was to prove the most understanding of Stevenson's friends, the shrewdest and most helpful of his critics. In his letters, James made repeated reference to Stevenson's gift for the 'visible'. He said that he missed it in *Catriona* and in a privately printed edition of the South Seas essays. He called it 'the personal painter-touch'. When he wrote about *The Amateur Emigrant*, he said—'Here, as always, the great note is the heroic mixture—the thing he *saw*, morally as well as imaginatively.'[66]

We remember Stevenson's own comment that it was reserved for the few to see 'distinctly and with intelligence'. He may also have known that the Dutchman Ruysdael literally starved for his art; it could even have been in his mind when he told Lloyd Osbourne that starvation was a weapon used by the bourgeoisie.

> If as a writer or artist you run counter to their narrow notions they simply and silently withdraw your means of subsistence.[67]

Skeletal at the best of times, he lost fourteen pounds in weight on that Atlantic voyage. A week and a half of travelling by rail made matters even worse, and he came close to death in the Santa Lucia mountains where he 'lay out under a tree in a sort of stupor'[68] for two nights. He survived to take on new and worrying responsibilities and the example that he was forced to follow was of that other Dutch landscape artist, Hobbema, who had been admired and imitated by the Barbizon School. Hobbema did not starve like Ruysdael: he gave up the struggle.

Did Stevenson regret the abandonment of a form that was so congenial to him? It is certainly possible, for he wrote to Henry James in the summer of 1893 that he was in one of his moods 'of wholesale impatience with all fiction and all verging on it'. His problem, he said, was how to get over, how to escape, its 'besotting particularity'.[69]

Travel writing had been, and might have remained, a means of getting over that particularity. It was a form that he could adapt to his own purposes, his own situation. It allowed him to explore both inner and outer worlds of experience; it offered possibilities that were denied to him in fiction; it freed him from those limitations of theme and subject that were imposed by the literary essay. He could look at the world as he found it—morally, and with intelligence. Not least, he could—in reflection—reveal himself; he could be a figure in every landscape. The travel books and the letters allowed him his nearest approach to autobiography, to a full-length self-portrait. His assertion was (and this had been implicit in those seventeenth-century Dutch paintings) that only the concrete and the visible could tell us anything that was worth the trouble of comprehension.

One feels, on the other hand, that Stevenson, the travel

writer, did not understand—could not bring himself to understand—the workings of society, and he admitted as much on the *Devonia*. There was little enough illumination in Steerage No. 1, but—like the light from the candle in the Silverado bunkhouse—it must have seemed like a conflagration in the surrounding darkness. The men in steerage were in no doubt that politics, which is to say society, was about money or the lack of it. But they went further than that. For some of them at least, it was 'a question which should long ago have been settled by a revolution'.[70] Stevenson repudiated this and accused the working classes of laziness, and yet—even as he did so—he showed an understanding of the bleakness of their prospects and had to admit that, in their place, he would have been no different. He was trapped as they were—by upbringing, by education, by circumstance.

In May 1880, after his marriage, his parents told him that he could count on £250 a year. Two months later he agreed to the withdrawal of the *Emigrant* and his father compensated the publisher for the financial loss. It has been argued that, although deeply hurt, Stevenson accepted the criticisms as valid; but the awkward fact is that when times had changed Colvin suggested that the book should be included in the Edinburgh edition of the collected works. It seemed to him then (in 1894) that the four travel books would make up nicely—two in one volume, two in another—and Stevenson agreed.

Now that we can read it as it was written, *The Amateur Emigrant* stands even further apart from the other travel books because of its directness and absolute honesty of response. 'Why left I my hame?' was a maudlin song that came, weakly, from an emigrant in steerage and 'a pertinent question in the circumstances', said Stevenson, for the setting was a foul-smelling, shadowy place. It was followed by an English song on the death of Nelson, equally maudlin, and the singing, as feeble as the songs themselves, was 'to the accompaniment of plunging, hollow-sounding bows and the rattling spray-showers overhead'.[71] The emigrants were in the nose of the ship, constantly pitched up and down and beaten about by the hammer blows of the ocean. Little wonder that Stevenson saw some heroism in the singing, for, as he said—

All seemed unfit for conversation; a certain dizziness had interrupted the activity of their minds; and except to sing they were tongue-tied.[72]

In *Silverado*, those same words—'Why left I my hame?'— are used for calculated literary effect. The coolness of Ruysdael has gone, greyness is not enough, the painting has been re-touched. Put another way, in terms of the hearing imagination it is a note that belongs with the public sentimentality of a Harry Lauder.

Stevenson described *The Silverado Squatters* as 'an example of stuff worried and pawed about, God knows how often',[73] and the writing and re-writing that he undertook in Europe meant that, before it was finished, the first version of *Treasure Island* had been dispatched and serialized.

Lloyd Osbourne said he did not doubt that Stevenson turned to romance with immense relief.

> Here he could escape from those voices coming to him out of the darkness; from the thought, always so persistent, that a comparative handful of mankind was keeping fellow millions in a state of poverty, ignorance and subjection.[74]

Were some of those voices from emigrants in the fetid darkness of Steerage No. 1, from tramps in Edinburgh door-ways, from blue-clad peasants working early and late in the fields around Barbizon? Certainly, it is a far cry from the reality of the *Devonia* to the romance of the *Hispaniola*. The descent into steerage was a descent into hell. 'The stench was atrocious . . . the merest possibilities of health or cleanliness were absent.'[75] Not so on the *Hispaniola*. On that ship

> Double grog was going on the least excuse; there was duff on odd days, as, for instance, if the squire heard it was any man's birthday; and always a barrel of apples standing broached in the waist, for anyone to help himself that had a fancy.[76]

Treasure Island delighted his father's heart—'it was *his* kind of picturesque'[77]—but there is an imaginative truth that will not remain buried. It thrusts upwards to the surface, like stones hidden in the earth, for there are powerful and dis-concerting elements imbedded in the story—unthinking folly on the upper deck and rebellion down below; violence put down by equal violence; and, at the end, the threat that cannot be forgotten, the voice that cannot be shut out, the narrator's recurring nightmare that he has communicated, with hypnotizing eloquence, to the reader.

No writer of his time created more vivid pictures for the mind's eye; none, as Millais said, was such a master of his tools—but there were unexplored continents of the imagination, journeys out of himself that would never be made. The 'realist' in Stevenson was sorely beaten in 1880—by worries about money and the future, by the responsibilities of marriage, and (most devastatingly) by what he called the 'venom' of his family and friends. The anger and the frustration must have flickered and flared around Vailima in the last years of his life; for—in an image used by Graham Greene—the granite was coming through.

> It is at that point, where the spade strikes the edge of the stone, that the biographer should begin to dig.[78]

The letters and the travel writing are the inner biography: we know from these sources that Stevenson had no doubt about his talent for the depiction of reality, that he compromised it and was afraid of it. 'It is strange,' said Lloyd Osbourne,

> how many of Stevenson's strongest opinions failed to find any expression in his books. He was emphatically what we would call today a 'feminist'. Women seemed to him the victims alike of men and nature. . . . It was the same with social reform. Both on this subject and his views about women, Stevenson was far ahead of his times—so far ahead, indeed, that I imagine he thought there was no audience for such opinions.[79]

The wound (for that was what it was) never healed, and there was a lingering, gall-like bitterness which Stevenson expressed more and more openly towards the end of his life. He insisted that he was more than a story-teller and had started differently, but said he was well aware that his other work was regarded with indifference and—worse that that— aversion. Not long before he died, he spoke to Osbourne about the books he might have written, given freedom. 'But,' he said, 'they give us a little box of toys and say to us: "You mustn't play with anything but these." '[80]

Truth, as Thoreau said (and Stevenson quoted him often)—truth has to be heard as well as spoken.

NOTES

1. *The Works of Robert Louis Stevenson* (Tusitala Edition, London, 1924), Vol. XXXI, pp. xiv–xv.
2. *Henry James and Robert Louis Stevenson—A Record of Friendship and Criticism*, ed. Smith (London, 1948), p. 258.
3. Tusitala, Vol. XXXI, p. 228.
4. Ibid., Vol XVI, p. viii.
5. Ibid., Vol. XXV, p. 183. Stevenson re-phrases the same thought in *A Humble Remonstrance*, Tusitala, Vol. XXIX, p. 135. The reference is to 'the dazzle and confusion of reality'.
6. Ibid., p. 63.
7. Ibid., p. 64.
8. Ibid., Vol. XXXII, p. 23.
9. Ibid., Vol. XXX, p. 117.
10. Ibid., pp. 117–18.
11. Ibid., p. 118.
12. *Robert Louis Stevenson—The Critical Heritage*, ed. Maixner (London, 1981), p. 48.
13. Ibid., p. 50.
14. Tusitala, Vol. XXX, p. 70.
15. Ibid., p. 67.
16. Ibid., Vol. XXXII, p. 98.
17. Ibid., pp. 99–100.
18. *The Critical Heritage*, p. 47.
19. Tusitala, Vol. XXIX, pp. 123–24.
20. Ibid., Vol. XVII, p. 95.
21. Ibid., pp. 95–6.
22. *The Critical Heritage*, p. 64.
23. *Robert Louis Stevenson—His Work and His Personality* (London, 1924), p. 212. Another version—'A man who knew how to omit would make an Iliad of a daily paper'—is in a letter to R. A. M. Stevenson. Tusitala, Vol. XXXII, p. 271.
24. *The Cevennes Journal* (Edinburgh, 1978), pp. 95–6.
25. Stevenson said 'upwards of a hundred and twenty miles', but this seems not to allow for mistakes and detours. Tusitala, Vol. XVII, p. 253.
26. Tusitala, Vol. XVII, p. 148.
27. Ibid., Vol. XXVIII, p. 73.
28. Ibid., Vol. XXX, p. 57.
29. Ibid., p. 62.
30. Ibid., Vol. XVII, p. 145.
31. Ibid., p. 132.
32. An unpublished letter to R. A. M. Stevenson quoted by Graham Balfour in his *Life* London, 1901), Vol. I, p. 160.

33. Unpublished letter, Beinecke collection.
34. Ibid.
35. *From Scotland to Silverado*, ed. Hart (Cambridge, Mass., 1966).
36. Unpublished letter, Beinecke collection.
37. *Portrait of a Rebel* (London, 1957), p. 109.
38. Tusitala, Vol. XVIII, p. 56.
39. Ibid.
40. Ibid., p. 58.
41. Ibid., p. 37.
42. Ibid., p. 35.
43. *From Scotland to Silverado*, p. 49.
44. Tusitala, Vol. XXXII, p. 73.
45. Ibid., p. 75.
46. Ibid., Vol. XVIII, pp. 87–8.
47. Ibid., p. 117.
48. Ibid., p. 199.
49. Ibid., Vol. XVII, p. 88.
50. Ibid., Vol. XVIII, p. 55.
51. *The Cevennes Journal*, p. 81.
52. Tusitala, Vol. XVIII, p. 166.
53. Ibid., p. 164.
54. Ibid.
55. Ibid., pp. 165–66. (This edition uses the form 'Scotch ships'.)
56. Ibid., p. 220.
57. Ibid., p. 161.
58. Ibid., p. 171.
59. Ibid., pp. 170–71.
60. Ibid., pp. 257–58.
61. *A Record of Friendship and Criticism*, pp. 198, 239.
62. Tusitala, Vol. XVIII, p. 246.
63. Ibid.
64. Ibid., pp. 172–73.
65. *A Record of Friendship and Criticism*, p. 148.
66. Ibid., p. 258.
67. Tusitala, Vol. XVI, p. viii.
68. Ibid., Vol. XXXII, p. 77.
69. Ibid., Vol. XXXV, pp. 67–8.
70. Ibid., Vol. XVIII, p. 60.
71. Ibid., p. 19.
72. Ibid., pp. 19–20.
73. Ibid., Vol. XXXII, p. 285.
74. Ibid., Vol. I, p. xvi.
75. *From Scotland to Silverado*, pp. 52 & 22.
76. Tusitala, Vol. II, p. 64.
77. Ibid., p. xxvii.
78. *Collected Essays*, Graham Greene (London, 1969), p. 82.
79. Tusitala, Vol. I, p. xv.
80. Ibid., Vol. XVI, p. viii.

4

Robert Louis Stevenson and the Romance Form

by HONOR MULHOLLAND

> The artistic result of a romance, what is left upon the memory by any really powerful and artistic novel is something so complicated and refined that it is difficult to put a name upon it, and yet it is something as simple as nature. . . . It is not that there is anything blurred or indefinite in the impression left with us, it is just because the impression is so very definite after its own kind, that we find it hard to fit it exactly with the expressions of our philosophic speech. . . . One might almost number on one's fingers the works in which such a supreme artistic intention has been in any way superior to the other and lesser aims. . . . At the present moment we can recall one man only, for whose works it would have been equally possible to accomplish our present design: and that man is Hawthorne. There is a unity, an unwavering creative purpose in some at least of Hawthorne's romances that impresses itself on the most indifferent reader; and the very restrictions and weaknesses of the man served perhaps to strengthen the vivid and single impression of his works.[1]

This definition of the romance and Stevenson's identification of Hawthorne as the major romance writer of the age provide a useful starting-point for a consideration of Stevenson's own use of the romance form.

In 'The House of Eld'[2] Stevenson is dealing with the type of moral dilemma which absorbed Hawthorne's attention. Like Hawthorne, Stevenson was deeply conscious of the influence of Puritanic inflexibility on social and personal behaviour, and in this tale he follows through the fate of a boy who, confronted with irrational, puritanical norms, subjects them to scrutiny and attacks the falsity which he perceives at their root. In his essay 'Victor Hugo's Romances' Stevenson identifies moral significance as being the essence of the romance, and the moral significance of this tale concerns the paradox inherent in benevolent and courageous iconoclasm which leads Jack to question the underlying assumptions of his own society. Questioning these assumptions, and questioning the faith on which they are based, Jack is assured by authorities outwith his society that its constraints are imposed and maintained by a sorcerer—that the underlying force of the order imposed on his world is superstition. With courage and sincerity Jack leaves his village to find the sorcerer, as a means both of testing the truth of his own culture's beliefs and the allegations that those beliefs are based on fraud. Jack's quest leads him to the sorcerer who appears to him in the shape of the boy's uncle, his father and finally his mother, each of whom the boy attacks with the village's ceremonial sword, believing them to be no more than the sorcerer disguised in these shapes. When Jack returns home he discovers first of all that the people of his village have replaced the fetters from which he had released them with another set of constraints which are equally enslaving. Finally he discovers that the shapes he had struck were in fact those of his parents and uncle, all of whom are dead. Jack's quest for the truth and his determination to release his people from the tyranny of superstition have resulted in his destroying those people dearest to him, and, ironically, the community he wanted to set free has immediately adopted an alternative and very similar restrictive orthodoxy.

The idea on which the tale is based and its moral significance are simple: man's good intentions are invariably subverted by forces outwith himself and by his own limited vision and knowledge, and the consequences of that reversal generate anguish compared with which the original wrong he intended to put right becomes insignificant. The theme is a commonplace one, involving archetypal patterns of growth from innocence through experience to knowledge and guilt, symbolized by a journey from home to the unknown and back home—a home which is so radically changed as a result of the seeker's behaviour as to make it a totally new place laden with sorrow and guilt unknown before the seeker's departure. The use of the journey outward and back is also an archetypal convention depicting the psychological growth from childhood to adulthood with its inevitable but unanticipated burden of responsibility including guilt for the very process of gaining that adult responsibility.

Stevenson's reliance upon convention both in the theme and structure of this moral fable draws attention to the particular way in which he handles those conventions. The directness of the opening establishes the tone of the story. No explanation is given as to what the gyve is or by whom it was riveted. We are brought to the narrative in mid-stream and the abruptness of this thrust generates and sustains the emotional detachment which is central to the romance's moral significance. The choice of vocabulary—'grown folk', 'unhandy', 'many strangers began to journey through that country'[3]—establishes in the first few paragraphs the slightly antiquated, perhaps even biblical, note which reinforces the detached stance of the narrator to whom the world Jack inhabited is alien and upon which he can look dispassionately. The detachment of the narrator and the use of this slightly alien and alienating vocabulary appropriately reflects the state of mind of the child, Jack, as he confronts an increasingly incomprehensible world, interpretable only in the language of the catechist whose rhetorical speech patterns conform to conventional religious platitudinizing. Throughout the tale Jack's language retains this rhetorical tone, thus emphasizing the enigmatic nature of his, or any, quest for truth and meaning when the only way of finding that truth is by using the language of the conventions under scrutiny.

Once Jack sets out on his journey events assume the clarity and disconnectedness of dream sequences. This reinforces the distancing necessary for the romance: character, coherency of sequence and emotional involvement in the plot are subordinated to the abstract idea. The intangible meaning and essence of the events are more important than the events themselves, so the reader does not identify with the protagonist but simply observes a series of ritual steps in a progression from innocent dependency to self-determination, experience, knowledge and the guilt and sorrow inherent in that growth.

Stevenson gives a credible portrayal of Jack's growth. The child questions the need to wear the gyve and perfectly logically wishes that he was not one of the chosen: 'upon my word, I could wish I had been less fortunate . . . for if I had been born benighted, I might now be going free'. His uncle's warning that such thoughts are dangerous and that the heathens 'are vile, odious, insolent, ill-conditioned, stinking brutes, not truly human—for what is a man without a fetter—and you cannot be too particular not to touch or speak with them' is sufficient to convince the child, and for a time Jack 'would never pass one of the unfettered on the road but what he spat at him and called him names'.[4] When he was 15, however, he discovered one of the boys from the village dancing in the woods without his fetter. Jack was shocked, but the incident demonstrates the inaccuracy of the catechist's claim that if he ever took off the gyve he 'would be instantly smitten by a thunderbolt'.[5] The belief which Jack has so far accepted is dismissed as being 'an old wives' tale . . . only told to children', and so Jack is filled with doubt, not simply because of the discomfort of the painful fetter, but because 'he loved the less to be deceived or to see others cheated'[6] and so he starts to seek out and question strangers. He is told that wearing of the gyve is not a command of Jupiter's but

> the contrivance of a white-faced thing, a sorcerer, that dwelt in the Wood of Eld. He was one like Glaucus that could change his shape, yet he could be always told; for when he was crossed, he gobbled like a turkey. He had three lives; but the third smiting would make an end of him indeed; and with that his house of sorcery would vanish, the gyves fall, and the villagers take hands and dance like children.[7]

Consistent with his earlier probing of evidence, Jack does not impulsively set about exposing the belief as fraud. He tries to find out about the credibility of his informants by seeking information about their own homes. He does not get completely satisfactory answers, but accepts that no place is entirely happy and makes the fairly logical deduction that if a perfectly happy place did exist, the inhabitants would not have any cause to leave it and so he would be unlikely to meet them. He can therefore place qualified credence in the information given by these outsiders and this, added to the evidence of the boy in the wood, provides Jack with adequate grounds to put that combined evidence to the test.

In this first phase of the story Stevenson has established the character of Jack by narrating a series of incidents in which the boy's character can be adduced from his actions. By making use of a slightly archaic rhetorical style in the voice of an impersonal narrator, Stevenson avoids the sentimentality or patronizing condescension which could easily surround such a narrative. The reader remains detached from the boy's experience but, at the same time, a clear picture of his character as a serious and unimpetuous youth is carefully and rapidly constructed. The basis for the voyage of discovery is therefore set on this pragmatically sound foundation which, outwith the bounds of the tale, has psychological credibility in its depiction of the growth from childhood to adolescence. The force of this first part of the fable is intensified by the resemblance between the uncle's bigoted rhetoric and the unreasoned tirades against unorthodoxy which typified much of the Presbyterian rhetoric of the Scotland Stevenson knew. The dependence on fear of such attacks shaped Stevenson's own childhood, and it can be seen to influence Jack in his acceptance of his uncle's warning. The anomalous counter-productiveness of such tactics can be seen in the behaviour of the boy in the wood, who dismisses the beliefs of his society, happily breaks its rules but is terrified in case the catechist is informed of his misdemeanour. In the wider context Stevenson is making a scathing attack upon the fear-based conformity which was so prevalent in his own society.

The second phase of the fable assumes the lucidity and disconnectedness of a dream. Jack took the 'sword of heavenly forgery' which was only used in the temple, and set off at night to seek the sorcerer. 'All night he walked at a venture' and when day came he asked the way of strangers who gave him conflicting directions until he realized he was being deceived and 'showed the bright sword naked.' The effect of this was that the gyve on the stranger's ankle rang and Jack got a proper answer, although not without being abused and attacked by the people he questioned. Stevenson does not elaborate on this, simply observing that 'his head was broken'[8] and moving on to the next stage of his journey which brought him to the Wood of Eld and sorcerer's house. The dreamlike description of the house conveys both a sense of its weirdness and the young man's acceptance of all experience as a manifestation of a new world in which everything is equally normal. His observation of detail recalls the boy's earlier cautious approach to the problems confronting him. The weirdness of the house, 'where funguses grew, and the trees met and the steaming of the marsh arose about it like a smoke'[9] conforms to conventional gothic settings for witchcraft and sorcery. The oddness is accepted by the boy in the way that inconsistencies in a dream are accepted:

> some parts of it were ancient like the hills, and some but of yesterday and none finished; and all the ends of it were open, so that you could go in from every side. Yet it was in good repair and all the chimneys smoked.[10]

The fact that 'he was aware of a house'[11] and that he finds a plausible explanation for its quaking beneath every step reinforces the surreal dreamlike nature of the journey. It also is consistent with psycho-analytic journeys into the subconscious, but it is important to notice that Stevenson presents these sequences without elaboration and this serves both as a means of sustaining the courageous and literal character of the boy already established, and avoids the sentimentality into which such a tale could easily degenerate.

The journey through the house discloses an interior which in the ordinary world would be dismissed as hallucination, but has credibility in the dream world which has already been established in the fable. Jack began to be hungry and at first was afraid to eat the food which was set out in the house. Being cautious, he made use of the magical sword to determine whether or not the food was wholesome—'by the shining of the sword, it seemed the food was honest'—and so he ate it, and 'was refreshed in mind and body'.[12] At this point 'there came into the room the appearance of his uncle.' As in a dream there is no explanation of how the uncle came to be there but the simple acceptance that he was. Jack was afraid because he had taken the sword, but the uncle was kind and friendly towards him and encouraged him to return home. Only when Jack points out that the hospitality of the house 'is no proof that a man should wear a gyve on his right leg'[13] does the appearance of his uncle gobble like a turkey and Jack realizes that this is the sorcerer. One further piece of evidence is thus gained in support of the allegations made about the basis of the constraints imposed on his society. Jack struck down the appearance with the sword and 'a little bloodless white thing fled from the room.'[14] As in a dream the boy felt fear and revulsion at what he had done but recognized that he must go on and finish what he had started. He pursued the 'bloodless white thing' which appeared first in the shape of his father, whom Jack struck through the heart, and then in the shape of his mother, whom he cut through the middle. All this murderous violence is reported with the same detached candour as was used in the early part of the tale. It is stressed at each stage that it is 'the appearance' of the uncle, father and mother that Jack struck; the surreal non-sequiturs of the dream world help to distance the boy's behaviour from normal moral judgement. It is significant that Stevenson does not portray the boy, even within this surreal world, as being without a moral conscience. At each attack he is horrified at what he sees he must do, even when he is convinced that it is the appearance and not the reality of his family that he is striking. Stevenson conveys this without sensationalizing the boy's dilemma by the brevity of the description of the event: 'His hand held back and his heart failed him for the love he bore his uncle',[15] and again, 'The blood ran backwards in his body and his joints rebelled against him for the love he bore his father'[16]; and finally when he had struck down his mother the narrator simply reports that 'He never knew how he did that.'[17]

As soon as he had struck his mother the house disappeared and the gyve was loosened from his leg and Jack was alone, the dreamlike aura gives way to weariness touched with Jack's characteristic pragmatism: 'Let me get forth out of the wood, and see the good I have done to others'.[18] Ironically, he is the first of those freed from the gyve to take it up voluntarily, and on his way back to the village he meets the people wearing the fetter on their left leg because 'that was the new wear, for the old was found to be a superstition'.[19] Perceiving the futility and irony of his action, Jack seeks God's forgiveness—his realization of 'original sin'. When he reaches home the bodies of his uncle, father and mother are lying dead bearing the wounds Jack had inflicted, 'And he sat in the lone house and wept beside the bodies.'[20]

'The House of Eld' is very short, less than 3,000 words in length, and in its compressed intensity Stevenson achieves the 'unity and unwavering creative purpose'[21] he admired in Hawthorne's romances. This tale resembles in its theme, its dreamlike tone, its psychological credibility and its detached rhetorical mode, Hawthorne's tale 'My Kinsman Major Molyneux', in which Robin's assured innocence confronts disconnected, confusing events with relative equanimity, only to be brought from that innocence to adulthood and an enigmatic knowledge of the world through surreal and incomprehensible experience. Hawthorne's tale is much more complex than Stevenson's, but the similarity in the theme of the boy growing to adulthood and the disjunctive sequence of dreamlike events, together with the tone, call to mind that tale and Stevenson's admiration for Hawthorne.[22]

The unity of 'The House of Eld' is sustained by Stevenson's use of the passive narrator, whose story-telling voice retains sufficient anonymity by the use of biblical rhythms and slightly archaic language to avoid being identified as that of the author. In the tale every detail is necessary: the boy's early discussion with his uncle does more than merely carry on the narrative. It discloses the character of the society, showing its bigotry and its dependence upon fear. It shows the little boy's logical perception but also shows the power of fear to subvert that logic for a time. Again, the incident in the wood not only re-awakens Jack's doubts about the gyve and furthers the narrative; it also exposes the falsity produced by the society which bases its authority on intimidation. It indicates the joylessness of such a society, and allows Stevenson to strike a blow at the very similar paralysing imposition of respectability and misery which characterized his own society. Similarly Jack's encounters with the strangers reveal information about the sorcerer which is necessary to the narrative, but they also reinforce the characteristics in Jack's personality which make him a credible protagonist in such a tale: he is not an impulsive boy—at each stage he seeks rationally acceptable evidence on which to proceed and finds plausible reasons for not being able to establish absolute proof. It is important for the psychological coherence of the tale that the protagonist is not seen simply as a rash adolescent rebel, but as a cautious and caring young man meticulously preparing his way before undertaking the scrutiny of the foundations of his world.

Having set this basis for Jack's quest, the supernatural world which he enters with such coolness is acceptable to the reader because it has been prepared for both by the narrative and by the psychological coherence of his growth towards maturity. The dream world of his journey is appropriate, not only because it is an accepted convention of the romance form and compatible with the supernatural subject-matter, but because it is an apt reflection of, and medium for, Jack's entry into the unknown of adulthood. The vanishing of the sorcerer's house coincides with the vanishing of the surreal aura in the tale, just as it coincides with the disappearance of Jack's guiltless childhood. The tone thereafter is, as at the beginning of the story, one of dispassionate narration: normality and logical sequence have returned to the world, but for Jack it is a new and unspeakably more painful world than the one he had left.

In his charming *Edinburgh: Picturesque Notes* Stevenson relates the legend of two maiden sisters who quarrelled 'on some point of controversial divinity belike' and remained living in the same room, sleeping in the same bed, without ever again speaking to each other. 'A chalk line drawn upon the floor separated their two domains'; and they continued to live together 'in a hateful silence'. Stevenson draws a parallel between this legend and Scotland's ecclesiastical history, pointing out the irony of the race's capacity as 'wonderful patient haters for conscience' sake'. What is of particular interest about his comment on the legend is that Stevenson rightly saw in it elements of a characteristic Hawthorne tale:

> Here is a canvas for Hawthorne to have turned into a cabinet picture—he had the Puritanic vein, which would have fitted

him to treat this Puritanic horror; he could have shown them to us in their sicknesses and at their hideous twin devotions, thumbing a pair of great Bibles, or praying aloud for each other's penitence with marrowy emphasis; now each, with kilted petticoat, at her own corner of the fire on some tempestuous evening; now sitting each at her window, looking out upon the summer landscape sloping far below them towards the firth, and the field-paths where they had wandered hand-in-hand; or, as age and infirmity grew upon them and prolonged their toilettes, and their hands began to tremble and their heads to nod involuntarily, growing only the more steeled in enmity with years.[23]

This is certainly a theme Hawthorne would have relished, and Stevenson's description could have fitted, in both theme and tone, into Hawthorne's *Notebooks*. However, his suggested conclusion to such a tale reveals a misinterpretation of Hawthorne's mode which provides some insight into Stevenson's own tales. He suggests that Hawthorne would have resolved the tale by saying of the two sisters that

one fine day, at a word, a look, a visit, or the approach of death, their hearts would melt and the chalk boundary be overstepped for ever.[24]

Now this is precisely what Hawthorne would not have done. At their most optimistic Hawthorne's romances end in enigma; a theme such as this would have been more likely to conclude, like 'The Minister's Black Veil', 'Rappaccini's Daughter' and 'Ethan Brand', in unambiguous foreboding or tragedy. Stevenson's handling of conflict and enigma in 'The House of Eld' show that he did perceive the tragic consequences of his own vision and his comment on the legend of the two sisters:

Alas! to those who know the ecclesiastical history of the race . . . this will seem only a figure of much that is typical of Scotland . . . a figure so grimly realistic that it may pass with strangers for caricature.[25]

indicates that he was not unaware of its tragic implications and unremitting consequences. Nor would Hawthorne have been unaware of them. But this vignette, fine as it is in its context, exemplifies the gap which existed between Stevenson's fiction and that of those creative talents within the romance form which he admired and chose to emulate. 'The Merry Men',[26] dealing with puritanical fanaticism and the supernatural, once again calls to mind the themes and preoccupations which are central to Hawthorne's vision.

Stevenson described 'The Merry Men' in letters to Sidney Colvin and to W. E. Henley in July 1881 as 'a fantastic sonata about the sea and wrecks',[27] and in August of that year he elaborates further in a letter to Henley: 'My uncle is not the story as I see it only the leading episode of that story. It is really a story of wrecks as they appear to a dweller on the coast. It's a view of the sea.'[28] As 'a view of the sea' the tale is freighted with the superstitions and supernatural conventions traditionally associated with the precarious life of fishing and sea-faring communities. Gordon Darnaway, the uncle in the tale, is pathologically obsessed by the terrors of the sea. He is described as 'a man whom ill-fortune had pursued',[29] scraping a meagre existence on a remote and inhospitable island and 'biting his nails at destiny'.[30] His inner misery and discontent is compounded by a fanatical and loveless religious observance centred on judgement, and the fear—in the literal sense—of the Lord. His terror of the sea is expressed in terms of his religious preconceptions:

> . . . if it wasnae prentit in the Bible, I wad whiles be temp'it to think it wasnae the Lord, but the muckle black deil that made the sea. There's naething good comes oot o't but the fish; an' the spectacle o' God riding on the tempest—But, man, they were sair wonders that God showed to the Christ-Anna—wonders do I ca' them? Judgements, rather: judgements in the mirk nicht among the draggons o' the deep. And their souls—to think o' that—their souls, man, maybe no prepared! The sea—a muckle yett to hell![31]

The man's hysterical obsession with the sea is bound up with his notions of supernatural punishment; all forms of threat and fear, all the manifestations of dreaded supernatural intervention in man's destiny, are attributed to the sea as a living and malign force: 'the sea's like the land but fearsomer,[32] he says and goes on:

> . . . ye would hae learned the wickedness o' that fause, saut,
> cauld, bullering creature, and of a' that's in it by the Lord's
> permission: lobsters an' partans, an' sic like, howking in the
> deid; muckle, gutsy, blawing whales; an' fish—the hale clan o'
> them—cauld-wamed, blind-ee'd, uncanny ferlies.

The man's frenzy explodes in a terrified cry 'the horror—the
horror o' the sea'.[33] Later suspecting his nephew's scepticism
'with a kind of exultation', he cried out 'I'll tell ye, man! The
deid are down there—thick like rattons!'[34]

Gordon Darnaway's manic terror is convincing as a depiction of the influence of the sea on the people whose lives were
governed by it. The hysteria of his outbursts, however, suggests
to his nephew and to the reader that he is demented not solely as
a result of the sea's very real threat. It emerges that, despite his
fanatically moralistic religious notions, he had not only profited
from the sea's destructive force by looting a wrecked ship, he
had also murdered the sole survivor of the wreck. Part of his
frenzy then arises from the fear of what he regards as inevitable
and just retribution for his actions. In the light of this
information, it appears that the terror and horror attributed to
the sea are projections onto the outside world of the inner terror
inspired by the man's own guilt. As a romance, the moral
significance transcending character or incident in this tale is the
working out of retributive justice in which Gordon Darnaway
believes, as do the other characters in the tale. Briefly, this
justice is effected by a second storm blowing up in which
another ship is wrecked. Gordon Darnaway is transformed into
a fanatical but joyous observer revelling in the sea's destructive
power. Questioned by his nephew about this transformation he
explains:

> . . . if it wasnae sin, I dinnae ken that I would care for't. Ye see
> man, it's defiance. There's a sair spang o' the auld sin o' the
> world in yon sea; it's an unchristian business at the best o't; an'
> whiles when it gets up, an' the wind skreighs—the wind an' her
> are a kind of sib, I'm thinking—an' thae Merry Men, the daft
> callants, blawin, and lauchin', and pair souls in the deid-thraws
> warstlin' the leelang nicht wi' their bit ships—weel it comes'
> ower me like a glamour. I'm a deil, I ken't. But I think naething
> o' the puir sailor lads; I'm wi' the sea, I'm just like one o' her ain
> Merry Men.[35]

History appears to repeat itself, as once again there is a sole survivor, a black man. Gordon Darnaway is driven out of his mind by the emergence of this man, whom he evidently regards as the man he had murdered come back to life. Darnaway flees, is chased, and the following day, after it had proved impossible for the stranger to leave the island, is inadvertently cornered and chased by the black man into the sea and both men are drowned.

Gordon Darnaway's fate is, in his own terms, just: it is entirely in keeping with his perception of natural justice that retribution should be meted out for his evil deeds. There is a grandeur and inevitability in his meeting that fate by drowning in the sea which was both the centre of his obsessive natural terror and the source of his demonic transformation. The inversion of Christian values which Darnaway himself recognizes—'I'm a deil, I ken't'—is carried by Stevenson beyond the purely narrative stratum of the tale. There is a thread of inverted paracletian imagery running through the romance: the obvious allusion in the name of the sunk Spanish galleon, the *Espirito Santo*, is carried on in the image of the Merry Men leaping up from this submerged source of material, as opposed to spiritual, gifts. In keeping with the inversion, the leaping element is water, not tongues of fire as in the biblical imagery, and the Merry Men leap up while the tongues of fire descended. The giddy and incomprehensible babble of the Merry Men, frequently referred to in terms of voices and laughter, inverts the Pentecostal notion of the paraclete descending and giving the power to communicate. The principal gift of the spirit at Pentecost was to confer courage and banish the fear which had paralysed the Apostles since the Ascension; in this inversion, the abject terror of Gordon Darnaway and the timidity of the narrator, Charles, are evidence of the apposite converse of those gifts. Charles had descended to the depths of the sea in search of material treasure; Gordon had descended to moral depths to satisfy his greed by the murder of the survivor of the *Christ-Anna*; these descents, inverting the Ascension, are rewarded in the case of Gordon by self-destructive terror, alienation from the self, demonism and death, while in Charles's case, since the intended 'sin' was not in fact enacted, the punishment is not so severe: he is merely restrained by his timidity, and his subsequent existence is governed by fragments of superstition and smug judgementalism.

This network of paracletian imagery and allusion fails in 'The Merry Men' and that failure is symptomatic of the failure of the tale as a whole. The name of the sunk vessel is so obviously allusive, and Stevenson takes up the biblical connotations in such a mechanically conspicuous way in the elaboration of the story that it cannot be ignored. Yet the tale does, in the end, not sustain the weight of its allusions. The celebration of sin and Gordon Darnaway's declaration that he is 'a deil'[36] is consistent with Stevenson's attempt to create a coherent pattern of inverted biblical images. It is compatible also with Gordon Darnaway's transformation from a miserable but God-fearing christian to his gleeful identification with the sea which he believes to be the power of evil. The murder of the survivor; the paradoxical insistence on using the 'grand braws'; his drunkenness and his lust for the sea's destructiveness: all these are inversions of orthodox Christian behaviour emanating from his initial reversal. However, despite the consistency in the imagery, Stevenson appears not to work out fully the implications of the elaborate range of inversion images he creates.

As 'The Merry Men' is a romance, the question of its moral significance must be faced. And it is here that the failure of the elaborate pentecostal allusions epitomizes the wider failure of the tale, for, at the end of 'The Merry Men', what is the moral significance? From Charles Darnaway's smug point of view the drowning of his uncle was a regrettable but inevitable consequence of his demonism. But what about the black man? Stevenson has explained the man's presence perfectly plausibly: he had been left behind when his companions returned to the schooner. The foreigner communicates by mime, eats the food given to him, sleeps, responds normally to events and is very conspicuously not a ghost. His drowning therefore is not a supernatural intervention punishing only Gordon Darnaway although, not surprisingly, the uncle reacts to his appearance as if he were the murdered man risen up to exact vengeance. By emphasizing his natural existence Stevenson prevents the reader from accepting that the black man is a spirit, yet his melodramatic emergence from the sea could have sustained that meaning if such conspicuous efforts had not been made to demonstrate his normality.

The romance is not clear at this point: is the black man really a sprite—another pentecostal inversion, rising from the sunk *Espirito Santo*, not to save, but to destroy Gordon Darnaway? If so, Charles Darnaway's bland literalism has prevented him from recognizing this so he has self-righteously offered hospitality to a demon and has precipitated his uncle's destruction. If Charles Darnaway is correct in perceiving the man simply as a chance survivor, how can Stevenson allow him to be drowned simply to enact the retributive justice due to Gordon Darnaway? The romance does not clarify which of these interpretations is intended and, no matter which one is correct, the moral fate of Charles Darnaway remains unresolved.

In 'The House of Eld', the action leads Jack through a sequence of experiences culminating in a new view of the world for the protagonist. In 'The Merry Men' there is a confusion as to who the protagonist is. If, as Stevenson said, it is 'the sea and wrecks', there is a great deal of entirely superfluous material in the tale which diverts attention from the central theme. In such an interpretation, the introduction of the Spanish historian and his appearance on the island is quite unnecessary: it would have been sufficient for any ship to have been involved in the storm. If Stevenson intended to show that the schooner with the historian on board was sunk as 'a judgement' for the greed involved in seeking the treasure of the *Espirito Santo*, it is inconsistent that Charles Darnaway should not have met a similar fate, for he too had intended to retrieve the wealth. He gave up not on specifically moral grounds—although he did use that as a justification after the event—but on superstitious grounds engendered by revulsion at finding a human bone. If Gordon Darnaway is the protagonist whose moral growth is central to the romance, then once again there is no need for many of the strands of the story which remain extraneous to his fate. The moral coherence is obscured by the drowning of the black man and by the distraction of so much extraneous narrative detail. If Charles Darnaway, the narrator, is the protagonist whose moral growth is being scrutinized, then, once more, unnecessary material obstructs perception of that growth. Charles Darnaway's character is the most carefully developed in the tale: if he is not central to it, why did Stevenson build such an elaborate character? If he is central to the moral significance of the romance, why do two other characters and the men on the schooner die, while the fate of the protagonist is merely to intensify his smug self-righteousness, generate in him a restraining timidity along with superstition and reinforce his judgementalism.

The calm and conventionally lyrical ending of the romance is in itself a distraction from what the tale has exposed. It is in conflict with the evidence of the evil and greed for which Gordon Darnaway is punished. The ending is in the words of Charles Darnaway, and as such, they suggest that either Stevenson wished to evade the logical and aesthetic consequences of his own creation, or, alternatively, he wished to portray the weak, evasive face of Charles Darnaway as a manifestation of evil just as destructive of life as the active self-destructiveness of Gordon Darnaway. If this latter interpretation is correct—and it seems to me to be a more satisfying one—then Stevenson has consistently diverted attention from his central theme by superfluous and distracting themes and has failed to apply the inverted pentecostal imagery to the area of the romance where it would reveal most—that is, to Charles Darnaway himself.

Despite some superb writing 'The Merry Men' fails as a romance because, having set up the machinery for a morally significant fable, Stevenson either loses the central theme in excessive detail, or he simply fails to allow the moral significance of his own imaginative creation to be taken to its logical conclusion and diverts it into a lyrically peaceful cul-de-sac devoid of moral significance. The inconsistency in the conclusion parallels Stevenson's misrepresentation of Hawthorne's mode, manifested in the passage quoted from *Edinburgh: Picturesque Notes*. That Stevenson had the capacity to handle the subtlety of the romance is evident in 'The House of Eld', and there are moments in *Edinburgh: Picturesque Notes* which have the clarity and atmosphere of Hawthorne's portrayals of New England. More often, however, he draws together the spiritual and moral elements characteristic of the romance and then dissipates the images thus created in evasions which emasculate the imaginative force in the tale. Nowhere is this more true than in 'The Beach of Falesá',[37] a tale dealt with in this collection in Peter Gilmour's essay 'Robert Louis Stevenson: Forms of Evasion'. In his letters Stevenson disclosed a great deal about the writing of this tale and it is worth considering his comments for what they reveal about its development.

In November 1890 Stevenson wrote to Sidney Colvin:

> My long and silent contests in the forest had had a strange effect on me. The unconcealed vitality of these vegetables, their exuberant number and strength, the attempts—I can use no other word—of lianas to enwrap and capture the intruder, the awful silence, the knowledge that all my efforts are only like the performance of an actor, the thing of a moment and the wood will silently and swiftly heal them up with fresh effervescence; the cunning sense of the tuitui, suffering itself to be touched with wind-swayed grasses and not minding—but let the grass be moved by a man, and it shuts up; the whole silent battle, murder, and slow death of the contending forest; weigh upon the imagination. My poem the 'Woodsman' stands; but I have take refuge in a new story, which just shot through me like a bullet in one of my moments of awe, alone in that tragic jungle.[38]

The new story was 'The Beach of Falesá'. Stevenson's comments in the letter on the terror of the jungle and the apparently conscious hostility of Nature to man which had so gripped his imagination in the forest suggests that it was those characteristics which were uppermost in the vision which shot through him 'in that tragic jungle'. Ten months later he wrote again to Colvin:

> . . . the story is so wilful, so steep, so silly—it's an hallucination I have lived through, and yet I never did a better piece of work, horrid, and pleasing, and extraordinarily *true*; it's sixteen pages of the South Seas; their essence. What am I to do? Lose this little gem—for I'll be bold, and that's what I think it—or go on with the rest, which I don't believe in, and don't like, and which can never make ought but a silly yarn? Make another end to it? Ah, yes but that's not the way I write; the whole tale is implied; I never use an effect, when I can help it unless it prepares the effects that are to follow; that's what a story consists in. To make another end, that is to make the beginning all wrong . . . well I shall end by finishing it against my judgement.[39]

It is true that 'the whole tale is implied' in the first chapter. The fabric of the romance is formed by the interplay of images of the extremes of good and evil established in the first chapter, but that fabric disintegrates when the carefully constructed imagery of evil explodes into sensationalist farce in which Wiltshire's violence belongs to schoolboy, bloodthirsty fantasy:

> ' "That's for Underhill! And that's for Adams! And now here's for Uma, and that's going to knock your blooming soul right out of you!" With that I gave him the cold steel for all I was worth. His body kicked under me like a spring sofa; he gave a dreadful kind of a long moan, and lay still.
>
> . . . When I came to myself . . . the first thing I attended to was to give him the knife again a half a dozen times up to the handle. I believe he was dead already, but it did him no harm and did me good.[40]

In the same letter to Colvin written some days later he says:

> The High Woods are under way, and their name is now the 'Beach of Falesá', and the yarn is cured. I have about thirty pages of it done; it will be fifty to seventy I suppose. No supernatural trick at all; and escaped out of it quite easily; can't see why I was so stupid for so long.[41]

By 'curing' the yarn he has in fact evaded the evil his original vision presented. The effect of this on the earlier imaginative construction is to render the grotesque images of Randall, of Case's vision of Adams's death, of Tarleton's description of Underhill's death, all entirely gratuitous. Had the evil been dealt with in the imaginative resolution of the romance these hideous images would have remained part of the fabric of the extreme evil. As it is, they fail in credibility because they are not part of the imaginative necessity of the tale. Because the moral implications of Case's evil are not confronted, his phoney demonic shrine is the most superfluous of all the grotesque images in the tale. If the real conflict is simply commercial rivalry, there was no need for Case to use such an elaborate device to exert control over a people who are, in the tale—and also in the colonial stereotype—depicted as gullible innocents whom he could have duped and intimidated without any of this sophisticated trickery.

It is interesting that late in September 1891, a few weeks

after the letter quoted above, Stevenson wrote to Colvin about 'The Beach of Falesá' which was then rewritten.

> . . . One of the puzzles is this: it is a first person story—a trader telling his own adventure in an island. When I began I allowed myself a few liberties, because I was afraid of the end; now the end proved quite easy, and could be done in the pace; so the beginning remains about a quarter tone out (in places); but I have rather decided to let it stay so . . . There is a vast deal of fact in the story, and some pretty good comedy. It is the first realistic South Sea story; I mean with real South Sea character and details of life. Everybody else who has tried, that I have seen, got carried away by the romance, and ended in a kind of sugar candy sham epic, and the whole effect was lost—there was no etching, no human grin, consequently no conviction. Now I have got the smell and look of the thing a good deal . . . the yarn is good and melodramatic, and there is quite a love affair—for me; and Mr. Wiltshire (the narrator) is a huge lark, though I say it. But there is always the exotic question, and everything, the life, the place, the dialects—trader's talk . . . the very trades and hopes and fears of the characters, are all novel and may be found unwelcome to that great, hulking, bullering whale, the public.[42]

Almost a year later he wrote—again to Colvin—that this tale was 'in some ways my best work; I am pretty sure, at least, I have never done anything better than Wiltshire.'[43]

The character of Wiltshire is carefully developed and he has greater diversity than the characters of Gordon or Charles Darnaway in 'The Merry Men'. As a personality he has greater potential range and complexity than Jack in 'The House of Eld', but the blunt, comic figure cannot be credible as both 'a huge lark' and a vicious murderer, nor as 'a huge lark' and the paralysed figure presented at the end of the tale: the 'human grin' is an inane perversion of the beginning of the tale. That promised a rich and complex insight into the power of evil and the power of an otherwise 'ordinary' human being to combat that force. It offered an insight into the complex relationships involved in imperialism and colonialism. Yet these images are squandered in the tale which fails to face the consequences of the images which it has formed.

Stevenson's letters show that in 'The Beach of Falesá' he did

lose the 'little gem' and turned it into a 'silly yarn', but the
yarn and the evasions in it have substantial implications for
any estimate of Stevenson as a writer. The 'Moral' at the end
of 'The House of Eld' may provide a summary explanation of
why, in two romances which have many of the qualities of
excellent fiction, Stevenson has dissipated elaborate and significant images into unsatisfactory and trivial conclusions.

> Old is the tree and the fruit good,
> Very old and thick the wood.
> Woodman, is your courage stout?
> Beware! the root is wrapped about
> Your mother's heart, your father's bones
> And like the mandrake comes with groans.[44]

In 'The House of Eld' the Moral serves as a moving and
poignant commentary upon Jack's experience. But in the
other tales examined here it seems as if the essence of that
Moral has acted as an inhibiting force in the tale. In both
cases Stevenson has perceived the existence of real evil in the
world but, recognizing the anguish consequent upon confronting the nature of the evil, has shied away from the issue and
has presented the reader with a moral and aesthetic impasse:
it is as if Jack, at the point of realizing that his uncle was the
sorcerer, had put up his sword and gone meekly home to the
village. In both tales the moral evasion is itself embodied in
formal and imaginative inconsistencies which, as can be seen
in 'The House of Eld', Stevenson did have the creative ability
to resolve. There is a strong temptation to look on Jack's
experience in 'The House of Eld' as autobiographical and see,
in Stevenson's artistic evasions, his will not to offend either his
family or the public in general. Aesthetically this is an unacceptable proscription, and places Stevenson's romances outside the framework where rigorous comparison can be made
with writers of the calibre of Hawthorne. It is an added
frustration in dealing with such tales that they frequently bear
a resemblance, in theme and occasionally in tone, to Hawthorne's incisive stories. In his little masterpiece 'The House of
Eld' Stevenson demonstrated as early as 1874 his ability to
sustain the romance form and use it to confront serious
spiritual and moral dilemmas. His later tales fail as romances

because they evade the consequences of their inspiration; equally they fail as adventure stories because they start off with the burden of serious issues which remain unassimilated in the resolution of the tale.

NOTES

1. 'Victor Hugo's Romances' in *Men and Books* in the Swanston Edition of *The Works of Robert Louis Stevenson*, Vol. III (London, 1911), pp. 26, 27.
2. The text used is 'The House of Eld' in *Weir of Hermiston and Other Stories*, ed. Paul Binding (London: Penguin, 1979).
3. Ibid., p. 287.
4. Ibid., pp. 287, 288.
5. Ibid., p. 287.
6. Ibid., p. 288.
7. Ibid.
8. Ibid., p. 289.
9. Ibid.
10. Ibid.
11. Ibid.
12. Ibid., p. 290.
13. Ibid.
14. Ibid.
15. Ibid.
16. Ibid., p. 291.
17. Ibid.
18. Ibid., p. 292.
19. Ibid.
20. Ibid.
21. 'Victor Hugo's Romances', p. 27.
22. Ibid. and *The Letters of Robert Louis Stevenson* in four volumes edited by Sidney Colvin (1911; rpt. Greenwood Press, New York, 1969), Vol. I, p. 339; hereafter referred to as *Letters*.
23. *Edinburgh: Picturesque Notes* in the Pentland edition of *The Works of Robert Louis Stevenson*, Vol. I (London, 1906), pp. 312, 313.
24. Ibid., p. 313.
25. Ibid.
26. The text used is 'The Merry Men' in the Colinton Edition, *The Works of Robert Louis Stevenson*, Vol. XIII (London, n.d.).
27. *Letters*, Vol. II, p. 48.
28. Ibid., p. 51.
29. 'The Merry Men', p. 1.
30. Ibid., p. 2.
31. Ibid., p. 17.

32. Ibid., p. 19.
33. Ibid., pp. 19, 20.
34. Ibid., p. 25.
35. Ibid., p. 59.
36. Ibid.
37. The text used is 'The Beach of Falesá' in *The Strange Case of Dr. Jekyll and Mr. Hyde and Other Stories*, ed. Jenni Calder (London: Penguin, 1979).
38. *Letters*, Vol. III, p. 238.
39. Ibid., p. 335.
40. 'The Beach of Falesá', pp. 165, 166.
41. *Letters*, Vol. III, p. 341.
42. Ibid., pp. 342, 343.
43. Ibid., Vol. IV, p. 111.
44. 'The House of Eld', p. 292.

5

The Master of Ballantrae: An Experiment with Genre

by CAROL MILLS

The Master of Ballantrae shares an unfortunate characteristic with several of Stevenson's mature works, in that a well-constructed story ends in an unsatisfactory manner. The work appears to disintegrate at the end, and the event which ought to be the climax of the plot—the simultaneous death of the two brothers—happens in circumstances which are difficult to accept on the evidence of the rest of the story. The story is apparently flawed at a fundamental level; the high point is the central climactic episode of the nocturnal duel (seen by Stevenson himself as 'the real tragedy'[1]) and the latter part never reaches these dramatic heights. The curious thing about this structural problem is that Stevenson was aware of it before he had even written the novel, but he nevertheless went on to write it in the flawed form. The purpose of this essay is to explore the reasons for this; and to suggest that they arise from Stevenson's conception of romance genre.

Stevenson's gifts as a writer (and a 'fine writer', whose polished prose is lucid and uncontrived) allowed him to attempt many different forms of literature, but his major creative efforts were romances, of which *The Master of Ballantrae* is the most ambitious. He defends romance in 'A Humble Remonstrance', and attempts to analyse its appeal in 'A Gossip on Romance', where he also indicates what, to him, characterizes the romance genre. In particular, he sees the incidental descriptions, the scene-setting and the 'atmosphere' in the romance as essential to the narrative and central to the romantic nature of the story. In 'A Gossip on Romance' the seminal nature of place and time in the construction of a romance is noted. The suggestibility of place is remarked[2]:

> there is a fitness in events and places . . . it is thus that tracts of young fir, and low rocks that reach into dark surroundings, particularly torture and delight me. Something must have happened in such places . . .; and when I was a child I tried in vain to invent appropriate games for them as I still try, just as vainly, to fit them with the proper story. Some places speak distinctly. Certain dark gardens cry aloud for a murder; certain old houses demand to be haunted; certain coasts are set aside for shipwreck.

Places can suggest kinds of romance and be the source of inspiration, and Stevenson goes on to instance the Hawes Inn as a major inspiration for *Kidnapped*.[3] The distinctive nature of the David Balfour novels is owed, in part, to Stevenson's exploitation of the 'fitness of places' in his creation of mood by, for example, the descriptions of Glencoe, of Erraid, and of Gullane Sands.

Equally, romances *require* an appropriate setting. If the events are unusual, or fantastic, their impact is heightened by the appropriateness of the setting—its 'fitness' amplifies and reflects the events taking place. The emphasis which Stevenson places on the fitness of setting for a romance is strikingly similar to more recent theories of genre, notably that of Northrop Frye.[4] Frye distinguishes 'the sense of unity of mood' as part of the controlling and co-ordinating power producing the creative work. The specific generic form of romance is defined as much by its peculiarities of time and place—generally exotic, and either past or future—as by differences of characterization, narration, or plot. Romance transports the reader into a fantasy—it is always escapist.

The Master of Ballantrae was written 'to carry the reader to and fro in space over a good half of the world, and sustain his interest in time through the extent of a generation'.[5]

Stevenson's extensive correspondence contains many references to his writing, although these are frequently flippant, and he tends to strike poses, affecting even an inability to distinguish popular success from literary achievement. The genesis of *The Master of Ballantrae* is well documented and on the whole the comments appear considered; in letters from Saranac Lake to the *Scribner's Magazine* publisher G. L. Burlingame, to Sidney Colvin, and to Henry James it is obvious that his enthusiasm is fired by the project. He writes to Colvin on Christmas Eve, 1887[6]:

> [I] . . . have fallen head over heels into a new tale, *The Master of Ballantrae*. No thought have I now apart from it, and I have got along up to page ninety-two of the draft with great interest. It is to me a most seizing tale: there are some fantastic elements; the most is a dead genuine human problem—human tragedy, I should say rather. It will be about as long, I imagine as *Kidnapped*.

Dramatis personae

(1) My old Lord Durisdeer
(2) The Master of Ballantrae *and*
(3) Henry Durie, his sons.
(4) Clementina, engaged to the first, married to the second.
(5) Ephraim Mackellar, land steward at Durisdeer and narrator of most of the book.
(6) Francis Burke, Chevalier de St. Louis, one of Prince Charlie's Irishmen and narrator of the rest.

Beside these, many instant figures, most of them dumb or nearly so: Jessie Brown the whore, Captain Crail, Captain McCombie, our old friend Alan Breck, our old friend Riach (both only for an instant), Teach the pirate (vulgarly Blackbeard), John Paul and Macconochie, servants at Durisdeer. The date is from 1746 to '65 (about). The scene, near Kirkcudbright, in the States, and for a little moment in the French East Indies.

Subsequent revisions changed the detail of the novel—in particular, some of the 'instant figures' play a more substantial part than this resumé would imply, notably Jess Broun. However, the central battle between the brothers, the use of Mackellar as narrator, and the shifting of the scene to distant locations are all present in this initial resumé and in the final version.

Stevenson clearly felt that it was important to record the genesis of the story for posterity, presumably because he was so taken with it initially. In a note originally intended for *Scribner's* but unfinished[7] he indicates the main source of inspiration for the story. The note has the benefit of hindsight, being written in Samoa some years later, but is consistent with the evidence of letters written at the time. Accordingly to this note, the plot was inspired by a similar historical episode:

> It was the case[8] of the Marquis of Tallibardine [*sic*] that first struck me; the situation of a younger brother succeeding in this underhand, irregular fashion, and under an implied contract of seniority, to his elder's place and future, struck me as so full of bitterness and the mental relations of a family thus circum-stanced so fruitful of misjudgement and domestic animosity, it took my fancy then as a drama in a nutshell, to be solved between four persons and within four walls.[9]

The essentials of the novel are apparent from this story. In addition, the *Note* goes on to relate what Stevenson felt he could add to the fictional version of the tale:

> . . . with my new incident and with my new aim I saw myself, and rejoiced to be, committed to great voyages and a long evolution of time. But in the matter of the characters involved, I determined to adhere to the original four actors. With four characters . . . I was to carry the reader to and fro in space over a good half of the world, and sustain his interest in time through the extent of a generation.

Thus there are two matters central to the novel; one, the plot, taken and developed from historical fact; and two, the expan-sion of the plot on a wider stage both in space and time. This extension of the original idea is mentioned in the correspon-dence of winter 1887–88, as in the letter to Colvin, ibid., and to Burlingame.[10] It is a fundamental aspect of his initial con-ception of the story, that it should take place both in Scotland and in more exotic places.

The extension of time and place accords well with his conception of the central theme of the novel as related to Henry James in the well-known letter written in March 1888.[11] In it he reflects on the manner of the development of the relationship of the brothers.

I got the situation; it was an old taste of mine: the older brother goes out in the '45, the younger stays; the younger, of course, gets title and estate and marries the bride designate of the elder—a family match, but he (the younger) had always loved her, and she had really loved the elder. Do you see the situation? Then the devil and Saranac suggested this dénouement and I joined the two ends in a day or two of constant feverish thought, and began to write. And now—I wonder if I have not gone too far with the fantastic? The older brother is an Incubus; supposed to be killed at Culloden, he turns up again and bleeds the family of money; on that stopping he comes and lives with them, whence flows the real tragedy, the nocturnal duel of the brothers (very naturally and, I think, inevitably arising) and second supposed death of the elder. Husband and wife now really make up, and then the cloven hoof appears. For the third supposed death and the manner of the third reappearance is steep; steep, sir.

He starts with a potentially disastrous decision (determined by a malevolent chance) taken for the political protection of the family, like the Atholl incident, and explores its tragic implications for the private relationships involved. In the process of developing the character of the elder son he returns to the exploration of moral evil in human nature which he has treated elsewhere; and in doing so he moves from the naturalistic to the 'fantastic', from events grounded in fact to events which are ridiculous, unless interpreted on another level of truth.

How, with a narrator like Mackellar, should I transact the melodrama in the wilderness? How . . . attack a passage which must be either altogether seizing or altogether silly and absurd?[12]

The clash between the settings obviously worried him even before the story was in its final form. He is unsure of the acceptability of the ending on a commercial level, as he writes to Burlingame[13]:

It is a howling good tale—at least these first four numbers are; the end is a trifle more fantastic, but 'tis all picturesque.

To James, he is more self-critical[14]:

Five parts of it are sound human tragedy; the last one or two, I regret to say, not so soundly designed; I almost hesitate to write them; they are very picturesque, but they are fantastic; they shame, perhaps degrade, the beginning.

He has not yet written those final parts at this stage (it was a serial publication); why, then, did he not carry out a fundamental revision of the story?

He clearly found revision onerous. He was easily exhausted by the effort and a rethinking of the dénouement would have required a fundamental recasting greater than the chapter by chapter revision he was undertaking. However, he was entirely serious about the novel, and it is unlikely that he had a frivolous attitude to the ending. There is no doubt that he was under pressure from Burlingame for the work, having signed a contract with *Scribner's* for literary articles as well as for the serial publication of the novel. However, the pressure of deadlines *per se* cannot have been the only factor determining the quality of the latter parts of the book. The conclusion must be that Stevenson's original inspiration was such that he was *unable* as well as unwilling to alter the story; the Master's character *demanded* the changes of location and the fantastic events in these locations. He regrets their necessity; but they *are* necessary, for 'that was how the tale came to me however'.[15] The fantastic events and settings are unalterable; it is his task to tell the tale well and in particular to make the fantastic plausible. He is therefore setting himself a huge task. He is attempting to fit into novel form a story which from the start is fixed. The plot, the story line, and the locations cannot be changed; he has to use all his skill to 'tame' them into a novel which will both hold the reader's attention and convince the reader of its underlying truthfulness. In part, he attempts to solve the problem by using the device of an unreliable narrator—Mackellar filters the events and in so doing relates the very different types of event, from the evening before James goes 'out' to the exhumation in the wilderness, in a unifying plain style. However, the story he tells is a hybrid—the Scottish events a recognizable historical romance, and the rest an adventure yarn. He attempts, using Mackellar as his link, to merge specific types of romance in order to draw upon all his resources as a writer. The book is indeed 'daring in its design'[16]; at a fundamental level it is experimental, intermingling the two sub-genres in the manner of a collage. The initial tale recalls the romances of Scott and Emily Brontë, but its characters are displaced into another world entirely, which disturbs the basic

123

'unity of mood' (in Frye's phrase). The changes in the reader's terms of reference—the pace, the types of activity, and the behaviour of the central characters—call into question the 'world' of the story, forcing the reader to readjust, like the characters, to new values and new realities.

The form of the narrative and the setting of the novel for most of its length place it firmly in the tradition of the Scots historical romance. The heavy emphasis on the relationship of the brothers obviously differentiates it from the romances of Scott, which nevertheless are an influence on it. The story of the brothers is told with a concentration that does not allow for diffuseness; there is no exploration of the political issues involved in the period; and Stevenson is not interested in presenting a view of Scottish history. These are all unnecessary to the purpose of exploring the relationship; he uses the tradition as a backdrop to their struggle. He evokes the *world* of the historical romance—its settings, its atmosphere, its evocation of a semi-feudal society—and links it to the central struggle by showing how it reflects and intensifies the differences between the brothers.

The beginning of the novel is recognizably in the tradition of Scott. The narrator journeys from Edinburgh to the south-west—this and several other features recall *Redgauntlet*. The ominous presence of the sea and the shadowy presence of pirates brood over both. In Scott, the descriptions of the Solway, the salmon fishers, and the gypsies are occasions for baroque prose; Stevenson's economy is notable in comparison. Scott's description of men on the sands runs thus[17]:

> The whole was illuminated by the beams of the low and setting sun, who showed his ruddy front, like a warrior prepared for defence, over a huge battlemented and turreted wall of crimson and black clouds, which appeared like a immense Gothic fortress, into which the Lord of day was descending. His setting rays glimmered bright upon the wet surface of the sands and the numberless pools of water by which it was covered, where the inequality of the ground had occasioned their being left by the tide.
>
> The scene was animated by the exertions of a number of horsemen who were actually employed in hunting salmon . . . they chased the fish at full gallop, and stuck them with their

barbed spears, as you see hunters spearing boars in the old tapestry.

Stevenson puts his beach scene in an entirely different context.[18]

> One day, I remember, we were late upon some business in the steward's room. This room is at the top of the house, and has a view upon the bay, and over a little wooded cape, on the long sands; and there, right over against the sun, which was then dipping, we saw the free-traders, with a great force of men and horses, scouring on the beach. Mr. Henry had been staring straight west, so that I marvelled that he was not blinded by the sun; suddenly he frowns, rubs his hand upon his brow, and turns to me with a smile. 'You would not guess what I was thinking' says he. 'I was thinking I would be a happier man if I could ride and run the danger of my life with these lawless companions.'

The Scott passage is a pastoral observed by an aesthete; the 'Mackellarese' of Stevenson's description strips the prose bare, and it is used, not as a set piece, but as an episode to illustrate Mr. Henry's character. This use of detail to amplify a character trait or to contradict can also be observed in the description of Durisdeer, where the gardens strongly resemble those of Mount Sharon in *Redgauntlet*[19]:

> . . . The father of the present proprietor had a considerable taste for horticulture which had been inherited by his son, and had formed these gardens, which with their shaven turf, pleached alleys, wildernesses, and exotic trees and shrubs, greatly excelled anything of the kind which had been attempted in the neighbourhood.
>
> . . . the house most commodiously built in the French fashion, or perhaps Italianate, for I have no skill in these arts; and the place the most beautified with gardens, lawns, shrubberies, and trees I have ever seen. The money sunk unproductively here would have quite restored the family; but, as it was, it cost a revenue to keep it up.

Mackellar has no time for lengthy descriptions (the description of Mount Sharon goes on for several pages)—he only sees the cost—and the pretensions of the family. The situation of the house comes as a surprise to Mackellar, who has been guided to the place by a 10-year-old scallywag with 'more ill tales upon his tongue than ever I heard the match of'; a child surely related to the 'impudent urchin', Benjie, who performs a not dissimilar function for Darsie Latimer and the Quaker. Further echoes of *Redgauntlet* may be found in the Master's reference to Wandering Willie on leaving Durisdeer for the last time; and Stevenson may have remembered the name Mackellar from the Jacobite gathering in Crackenthorpe's inn. However, the principal characteristics of *The Master of Ballantrae* as a Scots romance are not just distillations of a favourite Scott novel; the landscape is used continually to provide the appropriate atmosphere. He exploits weather, particularly if cold and frosty, and time of day; the sunset observations of smuggling operations are a recurring motif; the rough nature of the landscape from the start, a countryside of bogs and scaurs. The sea is ever-present, a bringer of bad news and evil from afar. The hostile populace, gullible, changeable and ignorant, are symbolized by the 'instant figures' detailed earlier—the cameo of Jess Broun, in particular, illustrating the point. It is notable that no members of the local gentry feature in the novel; Stevenson uses the minor characters merely to illustrate the main theme and to isolate the household in a claustrophobic loneliness. The subordinate characters of whore and free-traders are part of the malevolent world surrounding Durisdeer, intensifying the gloom. The Master's past actions have wronged them; his present exactions are wronging them even now; but the family (for whom his inheritance was forfeit) suffer the penalty. The fine clothes and expensive possessions of the Master are no mere Jacobite frippery either; he is revenging himself on his brother through wasting his substance. The details continually focus on the brothers and the destructive effect of their relationship, which goes far deeper than any in an orthodox historical romance.

Several years ago Eigner[20] pointed out the similarities of approach between Stevenson's work and that of Emily Brontë. There, too, an equally intense relationship dominates other characters, landscape, and time. There is in both the element of the fantastic; but *Wuthering Heights* remains in the one location, unified by that and by the isolation from the rest of the world. The *Master* combines the Scots romance setting with a narrative of passionate intensity; it is, in Frye's terms, a true

'Northumbrian romance'. The intensity is, if anything, strengthened by the involvement of a further element—the brothers' relationship with Alison Graeme and their father. It is principally through this relationship that the attractive nature of James is portrayed. He is, according to her, 'the soul of generosity'; on his return the spell is cast even over Mackellar[21]:

> . . . turning about for a pleasant word with John, fondling his father's hand, breaking into little merry tales of his adventure, calling up the past with happy reference—all he did was so becoming, and himself so handsome, that I could scarce wonder if my lord and Mrs. Henry sat about the board with radiant faces, or if John waited behind with dropping tears.

It appears, from all the evidence, that James is subject only to the censure of Mackellar and Mr. Henry—neither of whom are impartial. The introduction of the narrative of Chevalier Burke further complicates the evidence. His story is inset into the Durisdeer narrative, in the tradition of romance, as a contrast to the main narrative. Its principal purpose is to give further evidence on James Durie's character; evidence which, coming from a third party, helps to corroborate the internal evidence so far assembled of his amorality, his lack of compassion, and, indeed, his lack of generosity. It strengthens the suspicion that the man has extraordinary power to dominate and deceive; he easily gains control of the pirate ship; he has a kind of natural authority which he exercises with destructive force. The tale which is told has the same theme, but it is told from an entirely different viewpoint and in an entirely different context. Burke's narrative removes the story from its Scottish setting in one location. The erstwhile enclosed narrative opens out into an after-dinner adventure story, full of action and moving at a breathless pace. The Master and his companion are never still for long. They journey over sea, involve themselves with pirates, travel to a hostile wilderness and bury treasure, surrounded by danger. The changing scene recalls 'A Gossip on Romance':

> A friend of mine preferred the Malabar coast in a storm, with a ship beating to windward, and a scowling fellow of Herculean proportions striding along the beach; he, to be sure was a pirate. This was further afield than my own homekeeping fancy

127

loved to travel, and designed altogether for a larger canvas than
the tales that I affected.

The journey, the changing action, and the excitement provide
a clear contrast with the static frustrating world of Durisdeer.
The lives of the adventurers are filled with 'brute incident';
but just as the trappings of Scots romance are used to illustrate
the characters of Henry and the absent or dissembling James,
so the 'incident' is used to illustrate James in his own element.
He gains control of the pirate ship; *he* disposes of Dutton; he is
a veritable embodiment of opportunism. But here his amorality
and his untrustworthiness are more apparent since Burke is
under his spell, and not prejudiced against him. Although
essentially sympathetic to the Master, Burke notes his ani-
mosity with Alan Breck Stewart; his self-seeking departure from
Scotland; the matter of Dutton; and his reliance on chance,
symbolized by the toss of the coin which is particularly
significant in the light of the origin of the story. He acts, and acts
in an entirely arbitrary way, devoid of human feelings, but
admired by those with the feelings he lacks. The Master's world
is one of action, chance, and death; to evoke it requires a new
approach like Burke's.

In telling of the Master's wanderings Stevenson attempts to
elevate the adventure story into a vehicle for a more serious
intent. As he uses the Scots historical genre earlier, so here he
illustrates the Master's amorality through action. In the
'Gossip' he characterizes the search for 'a certain type of
incident' as a feature of boyhood reading, explaining the
popularity of the 'yarn'. An action story has no underlying
message, for the interest is in event, not motive:

> There is a vast deal in life and letters both which is not immoral,
> but simply non-moral; which either does not regard the human
> will at all, or deals with it in obvious and healthy relations; where
> the interest turns not upon what a man shall choose to do, but on
> how he manages to do it.

There are a number of techniques which emphasize the
suspense and the vicarious danger of the adventure, among
them the presentation of events as a series of problems to be
solved by decisive behaviour; the device of the journey, which
allows the author to emphasize change as a solution to

problems of plot, and also allows him to vary the pace of events; and the use of the narrator as confidant of the protagonist, which allows the author to draw character through event. All of these elements are present in Burke's narrative—and at the same time Stevenson uses Burke's own reflections on the Master's behaviour and the unstable nature of their relationship to make a moral point. The reader is encouraged to identify—how will they survive the next setback?—and the continuous action comes as a relief from the apprehensive, static atmosphere of the Durisdeer story. However, the character of the Master as revealed by his behaviour in this adopted milieu is unchanged. He is an agent of destruction; the motives for his destructiveness are pride and avarice; and, the adventure reveals a love of power over others and, more importantly, effortless exercise of that power. The adventure story has a moral dimension (*pace* the 'Gossip'), and focuses on the Master's character more than ever.

Burke's narrative is a tale within a tale—and as an inset adventure in a historical romance it succeeds. The narrative is interrupted, but then continues in the anchor location as before. The final flight of the family from Durisdeer is a shift of more significance. The characters of the romance are transported into the adventure mode—the world of the Master. He succeeds in uprooting them—and from that point is the victor. It is a strategic withdrawal, an attempt by Mackellar and Mrs. Henry to stave off the inevitable final confrontation. However, it is a mistake. They leave behind their world, their true element—the place to which they travel is peopled by traders, merchants and adventurers, those of the Master's acquaintance. They keep up the pretence of gentility, which is undermined by the Master's behaviour[22]:

> The public disgrace of his arrival—which I sometimes wonder he could manage to survive—rankled in his bones; he was in that humour when a man ... will cut off his nose to spite his face; and he must make himself a public spectacle in the hopes that some of the disgrace might spatter on my lord.

Henry plots with the very thugs and assassins who have been the Master's companions on his adventures. He no longer cares about calumny and ill-feeling (which has followed them to their refuge)—he has lost the dignity which was an important feature of his behaviour at Durisdeer. Henry starts behaving like an adventurer himself; freed from the constraints of the Scots milieu, he rouses himself to murderous action. In leaving behind the closed world of Durisdeer, Henry leaves behind any remaining scruples—the mutual hatred of the brothers is all that matters to both of them and the final confrontation must take place. Henry is reduced to the same moral level as his brother—and thereafter operates in the Master's world entirely. He journeys away from civilization into the wilderness of Burke's adventure story; the creation of a fantasy world of ice and snow aims to intensify our awareness of the evil surrounding the characters, made palpable by the Indian hostility apparent from Mountain's narrative. Clearly, Stevenson wishes to create an 'atmosphere' of danger and evil; however, the execution is poorly done, and the 'atmosphere' does not establish itself. The pretext for Henry's foray is a weakly defined 'diplomatic expedition' which exists mainly to discover the Master's grave. The trader Mountain's 'narrative' is not as carefully characterized as is Mackellar's or Burke's, where the teller's approach is an important element in deciding the reader's reaction to events. Mountain is merely a means of filling a difficult gap and Mackellar doctors the evidence. The element of suspense, which is necessary to engage the reader's attention, is lacking. The passivity of Henry's approach to murder contrasts with the drama of the earlier duel in the shrubbery at Durisdeer—he remains a surrogate killer, several removes from action. The crucial difference, however, is the lack of close focus on the Master, whose behaviour until this point has been the main interest. He is seen fleetingly, from a distance; he confides only in his servant, and he dissembles all the time[23]:

> It's possible he hoped to repeat the business of the pirate ship and be himself, perhaps, on hard enough conditions, elected leader. But, the rock he split upon was Hastie, who remembered and applied what he had learned. Indeed, he had not proceeded very far, when the Master rolled carelessly upon one side, which was done (in Mountain's opinion) to conceal the beginnings of despair upon his countenance.

There is no accomplice in whom he confides his despair; we are unsure whether he was in reality despairing. The focus is fuzzy, and the credulous acceptance of the Master's death by the assassins is unconvincing. The narrative is sloppy else-where—for instance, compare the difficulty of the assassin's journey and return with the ease with which the second party reached the spot. Because of these deficiencies, the concentration on the two brothers, which is central to Stevenson's purpose, dissipates in a welter of pedestrian detail. It is thus that the 'daring design' comes to grief. He has removed the confrontation of the frailty of 'average' morality with dynamic evil from an orthodox context—the historical romance—into adventure story: in doing so he has contradicted his own definitive of adventure as 'non-moral'.[24] He is using the adventure mode as a vehicle for a relationship etc. This adventure study has a moral aspect—the final dissolution of Henry stems from his adoption of James's opportunism. The success of this approach depends on the final narrative being well-knit and well-motivated.

Thus the change of mode is the principal cause of the book's disunity. It is not the innate nature of the plot which is flawed, but the execution; the plot is 'given' in the terms of Stevenson's original creative impetus, and demands that the undiluted hatred of the brothers be brought to its ultimate conclusion in their destruction. It is the disorientation brought about by the switch to adventure story which worried Stevenson, and the unfortunate lapse in creative power in the composition of that story justifies his anxiety. Had he given more consideration to the wilderness narrative, he might well have pulled it off, and his experiment with genre would have been a success. As it is, it is a noble failure. He succeeds in establishing a strong base with the Durisdeer narrative, and the inset Burke narrative, but the attempt to shift the entire story into the adventure mode is less carefully constructed and results in an ending which is un-satisfactory. His gamble in violating the principle of unity of mood fails; as the author says elsewhere 'the right sort of thing should fall out in the right kind of place'. Henry does not belong in the icy landscape of New England and he is diminished by the change. One cannot help wondering whether the author's own experiences and the sojourn at Saranac have had this deleterious effect; after all, he is attempting to portray the situation of the family in New England as exotic and fantastic—a situation at the time more real to him, at Saranac, than the Scotland he had left behind. In some ways, Stevenson was living an adventure story, and it was the prosaic which he found strange. 'The devil and Saranac' have something to answer for; he might have been advised to ignore their suggestions.

NOTES

1. Letter to Henry James, March 1888, in *Letters*, ed. Colvin, vol. II, pp. 98–9.
2. 'A Gossip on Romance', *Works*, vol. XIII, pp. 24–5. References are to the Vailima edition.
3. 'The Old Hawes Inn at the Queen's Ferry makes a similar call upon my fancy. There it stands, apart from the town, beside the pier, in a climate of its own, half inland, half marine. . . .'
4. Northrop Frye, 'Theory of Genres' in *Anatomy of Criticism* (Princeton, 1957).
5. 'A note on *The Master of Ballantrae*', *Works* (Vailima Edition) vol. XXIV, pp. 479–81.
6. To Sidney Colvin, 24 December 1887, in *Letters*, ed. S. Colvin, vol. II (London, 1900).
7. 'A Note on *The Master of Ballantrae*', op. cit., pp. 479–81.
8. The case referred to concerns the family of the first Duke of Atholl (1660–1724). The family was thrown into turmoil by the first Jacobite rebellion of 1715. The Duke had been an outspoken critic of the Union of Parliaments in 1707 and was under some suspicion of disloyalty to the Crown. His surviving heir, the Marquis of Tullibardine, went 'out' in 1715 and in 1716 he was dispossessed of his inheritance by an Act of Parliament obtained by his father. This meant that should the Duke die, the estates would not be forfeit as they would have been as the heir was subject to an Act of Attainder. The effect was to vest the estates in the Duke's second surviving son, who was a senior officer in the Royal Scots and loyal to the Hanoverians. The further ramifications of this episode in the history of the Murrays of Atholl are detailed under the family name in *The Scots Peerage*, ed. J. Balfour Paul (Edinburgh, 1904), I, 478–88.
9. These are noted as 'two brothers, a father, and a heroine' later in the *Note*.
10. 'The scene of the romance is Scotland—the States—Scotland—India—Scotland—and the States again; so it jumps like a flea' (to G. L. Burlingame, *Letters*, op. cit., II, pp. 90–1).
11. To Henry James, March 1888, *Letters*, op. cit., II, pp. 98–9.

12. *Note*, ibid.
13. To G. L. Burlingame, op. cit., pp. 90–1.
14. *Letters*, ibid.
15. To Henry James, ibid.
16. To Henry James, ibid.
17. *Redgauntlet*, Ch. 4.
18. *Master of Ballantrae*, Ch. 2.
19. *Redgauntlet*, Ch. 7; *Master of Ballantrae*, Ch. 2.
20. E. M. Eigner, *Robert Louis Stevenson and Romantic Tradition* (Princeton, 1966).
21. *Master of Ballantrae*, Ch. 4.
22. Ibid., Ch. 10.
23. Ibid., Ch. 11.
24. Ibid., 'Gossip', see p. 128.

6

Highland History and Narrative Form in Scott and Stevenson

by ANDREW NOBLE

And I have read the *Castle of Otranto* and find it to be rubbish. Yet it was epoch-making, was it not? But some of these epoch making books succeeded by virtue of new and interesting matter in spite of a poor form, for instance Ossian and in the main the Waverleys; of which last I hold, subject to wider reading and your better judgement, that, though they contain a mass of good reading and scattered literary excellences, yet as wholes they are scarcely to be called works of art and have been and are over-rated. They seem to be the products of a fine and gentle character, a fertile memory, and a flowing talent and to have even touches of genius in certain incidents, strokes of true invention; but in the general texture of them genius seems to be quite wanting. I think Robert Lewis (sic) Stevenson shows more genius in a page than Scott in a volume.

—*Gerard Manley Hopkins*

People read history and then they seem to feel that everything has to conclude in their own time. 'We have read history, and therefore history is over,' they appear to say.

—*Saul Bellow*

Stevenson's desire to write a history of the Highlands considerably preceded his undertaking of a Highland historical novel. Exile always caused his thoughts to turn homeward and in letters from Davos in the winter of 1880, to his father and to Sidney Colvin, he outlined his proposed work. To Colvin he wrote:

> No. I do not think I shall require to know the Gaelic; few things are written in that language, or ever were; if you come to that, the number of those who could write, or even read it, through almost all my period, must by all accounts, have been incredibly small. Of course, until the book is done, I must live as much as possible in the Highlands, and that suits my book as to health. It is a most interesting and sad story, and from the '45 it is all to be written for the first time. This, of course, will cause me a far greater difficulty about authorities; but I have already learned much, and where to look for more. One pleasant feature is the vast number of delightful writers I shall have to deal with: Burt, Johnson, Boswell, Mrs. Grant of Laggan, Scott. There will be interesting sections on the Ossianic controversy and the growth of the taste for Highland scenery. I have to touch upon Rob Roy, Flora MacDonald, the strange story of Lady Grange, the beautiful story of the tenants of the Forfeited Estates, and the odd, inhuman problem of the great evictions. The religious conditions are wild, unknown, very surprising.[1]

Physically it was a wildly false hope. The damp Highland climate was utterly incompatible with Stevenson's respiratory problems. Mentally his relationship to the North was more ambiguous. There is some condescension, the oral element apart, in his dismissal of Gaelic literature. On the other hand, there is a desire to deal with the crucial social problem of the Clearances, which had been largely avoided by Scott and totally evaded by subsequent best-selling Scottish Victorian novelists who wrote on Highland themes, such as William Black and James Grant. Writing to his father, he asserted an even stronger desire to write not only a firmly factual but a radical kind of Scottish history:

> Thanks for your notes; that fishery question will come in, as you notice, in the Highland Book, as well as under the Union; it is very important. I hear no word of Hugh Miller's *Evictions*; I count on that. What you say about the old and new Statistical is

odd. It seems to me very much as if I were gingerly embarking on a *History of Modern Scotland*. Probably Tulloch will never carry it out. And, you see, once I have studied and written these two vols., *The Transformation of the Scottish Highlands* and *Scotland and the Union*, I shall have a good ground to go upon. The effect on my mind of what I have read has been to awaken a livelier sympathy for the Irish; although they never had the remarkable virtues, I fear they have suffered many of the injustices of the Scottish Highlanders.[2]

Stevenson's Irish sympathies were reversed by subsequent rural Irish terrorism, to which he responded with a madcap but fortunately transient plan to install himself and his family on an Irish farm and seek martyrdom in order to expose the nature of their political violence. Despite this evidence of Stevenson's sympathy for the unjustly dispossessed, his dislike of Europe's economic imperialism is frequent and convincing in his *factual* writing. His witness to the conditions prevailing in the Pacific provoked in him deep and sincere hostility to it. Indeed, his knowledge of the South Sea islanders ('the natives are the next thing conceivable to Highlanders before the forty-five') led him to an intensified awareness of the unjust fate of his Gaelic fellow-countrymen.[3] Hence, his Highland history unwritten, he returned to it as a still possible book eleven years later while resident in Samoa. 'Now,' he wrote to Colvin, 'what am I to do next? Lives of the Stevensons? *Historia Samoae*? A History for Children? Fiction? I have had two hard months at fiction; I want a change.'[4] These kind of erratic impulses and this kind of generic compartmentalization is disconcertingly characteristic of Stevenson. In particular it points to the core of the present essay; the complex, troubling question regarding his discrimination between the art of the novelist and that of the historian. Continuing his discussion of a history for children he wrote:

Now the difficulty is to give this general idea of main place, growth and movement; it is needful to tack it on a yarn. Now Scotch is the only history I know; it is the only history reasonably represented in my library; it is a very good one for my purpose,—owing to two civilisations having been face to face throughout—or rather Roman civilisation face to face with our ancient barbaric life and government, down to yesterday, to

1750 anyway. But the *Tales of a Grandfather* stand in my way; I am teaching them to Austin now, and they have all Scott's defects and all Scott's hopeless merit. I cannot compete with that; and yet, so far as regards teaching History, how he has missed his chances! I think I'll try; I really have some historic sense, I feel that in my bones. Then there's another thing. Scott never knew the Highlands; he was always a Borderer. He has missed the whole, long, strange, pathetic story of our savages, and, besides, his style is not very perspicuous to childhood. Gad, I think I'll have a flutter.[5]

The epistolary evidence of writers less whimsical than Stevenson is problematical enough. This is intensely difficult to interpret. Did he mean that, unlike his novels, which many now assume to be a profound examination of the clash of these two cultures, Scott failed when writing history as such? Or, even more worryingly, did he mean that the novel, as entertainment, was no place for such actual, historical collisions? At worst, such an attitude would allocate fiction as escapist role for both author and reader, with historical content supplying little more than cosmetic heightening. This comment on *Tales of a Grandfather* was made between the writing of *Kidnapped* and *Catriona*. Earlier comments on Scott do not diminish the ambiguity. As with all paternal figures, Stevenson's relationship with Scott was deeply ambiguous. As James remarked, we find in him 'the filial relation quite classically troubled'.[6] Careful stylist that he was, he stringently criticized Scott on this ground: 'it is undeniable that the love of the slap-dash and the shoddy grew upon Scott with success.'[7] Yet he also admitted Scott as a direct influence on his own Highland writing. Of 'The Merry Men' he wrote that 'there is a little of Scott's *Pirate* in it, as how should there not? He had the root of romance in such places.'[8] Scott appears to him in 1874 as both personally admirable and politically wrong-headed:

> Scott again, the ever delightful man, sane, courageous, admirable; the birth of Romance, in a dawn that was a sunset; snobbery, conservatism, the wrong thread in History, and notably in that of his own land.[9]

This, along with his other sympathetic remarks about the Highlanders, would lead us to anticipate in Stevenson's fiction a very different political and moral vision of Scottish history to that found in Scott. As will be seen, this is not so. Although there is a greater congruence between his anti-imperialist Pacific reportage and his island stories, we can discern there, too, a troubling disparity between radical aspirations and conventional fictional conclusions. A repeated Stevensonian theme is that of the young man who cannot break with often corrupt established authority and is, indeed, often broken by it. This pattern, albeit in comic form, is repeated in *Kidnapped* and *Catriona*. Like the fathers in his fiction, Scott was to impose his will. It is 'Highland' history moulded by Scott's fictional conventions on which *Kidnapped* and *Catriona* are essentially based.

Although the last few years of his life saw Stevenson, he himself believed unsuccessfully, trying to use fictional form as a means of the fullest engagement with reality rather than an evasion of it, his earlier aesthetic remarks seem to deny the ability of the novel so to do. In 1883, worried by his father's deepening depression, he wrote to him:

> I have just finished re-reading a book, which I counsel you above all things *not* to read, as it made me very ill, and would make you worse—Lockhart's *Scott*. It is worth reading, as all things are from time to time that keep us nose to nose with fact; though I think such reading may be abused, and that a great deal of life is better spent in reading of a light and yet chivalrous strain. Thus no Waverley novel approaches in power, black-ness, bitterness, and moral elevation to the diary and Lock-hart's narrative of the end; and yet the Waverley novels are better reading for everyday than the life. You may take a tonic daily, but not phlebotomy.[10]

Escapism into 'reading of a light yet chivalrous strain' from such biographical pain cannot inspire hope that the nature of historical suffering will not be so treated. Stevenson was typically Victorian, at least in this instance, of valuing Scott's historical fiction for its anodyne power.

This use of art as an artificial antidote to life—a disease primarily and, indeed, definitively diagnosed early in Steven-son's career by William Archer—had, then, considerable potential for harm with regard to dealing with history.[11] This was especially true when the history concerned the destitution and even destruction of whole communities. Some of Stevenson's historical fiction was knowingly escapist. 'Tushery' was the word that he and Henley invented for such armour and horse-opera. Stevenson considered his *The Black Arrow* in direct line of descent from the Ivanhoe side of Scott's work. His motives in writing such a book were both self-indulgent and commercial:

> So, as my good Red Lion Counter begged me for another Butcher's Boy—I turned me to—what thinkest 'eu?—to Tushery, by the mass! Ay, friend, a whole tale of tushery. And every tusher tushes me so free, that may I be tushed if the whole thing is worth a tush. *The Black Arrow: A Tale of Tunstall Forest* is his name: tush! a poor thing![12]

While *Kidnapped* and *Catriona* are manifestly not of this order, more sophisticated reservations are provoked by them. In both there is, perhaps, the ultimate literary critical problem regarding Stevenson: the degree to which he was able not only to parody the adventure story but employ it for higher moral and social purposes. Further, there is the whole question of how the conflict between two civilizations and, more, the tragic collapse of one of them, can be embodied in an essentially comic plot. David Balfour, by way of Scott, has the essential characteristics of the hero of the eighteenth-century English comic novel. He is the young man who, after a series of adventures, discovers both his identity and his inheritance and then, of course, marries the right girl. Is such private felicity compatible with public sorrow? Can such a personal biography be properly symbolic of a national history? Is there an inherent contradiction in the Scottish Highland story Stevenson seemed to wish to tell and the Scott-derived narrative form he adopted to do so?

Stevenson's most considered account of the relationship of the art of fiction to the art of history is to be found in his essay, 'A Humble Remonstrance', which was written in response to James's fine celebration of the freedom and potency of the novel, 'The Art of Fiction'. In his essay James had argued powerfully for the congruence of the activities of historian and novelist: 'as the picture is reality, so the novel is history.'[13] Countering the insidious late nineteenth-century argument that the 'make-believe' novel was less factually or morally sound than the art of history, he wrote:

> It implies that the novelist is less occupied in looking for the truth than the historian, and in doing so it deprives him at a stroke of all his standing room. To represent and illustrate the past, the actions of men, is the task of either writer, and the only difference that I can see is, in proportion as he succeeds, to the honour of the novelist, consisting as it does in his having more difficulty in collecting his evidence, which is so far from being purely literary.[14]

Stevenson did not deny the relationship between the novelist and the historian. His qualification of the manner in which the novelist employed narrative form to his subject matter compared to the historian was, however, anti-Jamesian in its stress on the inevitable disparity between the orderly, pleasurable artifice of such fabricated forms and the crude, painful disorder of reality. The historian was for Stevenson closer to life—he totally disavowed James's notion that they both 'compete' with life—but that was only a matter of relative representational success:

> The art of narrative, in fact, is the same, whether it is applied to the selection and illustration of a real series of events or of an imaginary series . . . it is in every history where events and men, rather than ideas, are presented—in Tacitus, in Carlyle, in Michelet, in Macaulay—that the novelist will find many of his own methods most conspicuously and adroitly handled. He will find besides that he, who is free—who has the right to invent or steal a missing incident, who has the right, more precious still, of wholesale omission—is frequently defeated, and, with all his advantages, leaves a less strong impression of reality and passion. Mr. James utters his mind with becoming fervour on the sanctity of truth to the novelist; on a more careful examination truth will seem a word of very debatable propriety, not only for the labours of the novelist, but for those of the historian. No art—to use the daring phrase of Mr. James—can successfully 'compete with life'; and the art that seeks to do so is condemned to perish *montibus aviis*. . . . No art is true in this sense: none can 'compete with life': not even history, built indeed of indisputable facts, but these facts robbed of their vivacity and sting; so that even when we read of the sack of a city or the fall of an empire, we

are surprised, and justly commend the author's talent, if our pulse is quickened. And mark, for a last differentia, that this quickening of the pulse is, in almost every case purely agreeable; that these phantom reproductions of experience, even at their most acute, convey decided pleasure; while experience itself, in the cockpit of life, can torture and slay.[15]

That formal licence leads to loss of intensity of content and meaning is perhaps more troublingly true of Stevenson as a novelist than of the novel as creative form and force. With regard to this problem of fiction and history, it would be convenient if he and James could be offered as polar opposites. They are not wholly so. James was not the least fastidious of men. Not all history was grist to his creative mill. His historical imagination had certain reservations about full frontal confrontation. With particular regard to the history of his 'own dear native land' he was often remarkably evasive. Indeed, one could go further and say that James fled America because of its history or, to put it in his own terms, because of its lack of a history. In his early, stimulating and often wholly unfair study of his ancestor Nathaniel Hawthorne, James wrote that 'the moral is that the flower of art blooms only where the soil is deep, that it takes a great deal of history to produce a little literature, that it needs a complex social machinery to set a writer in motion'.[16] To provide material plastic enough for the novelist to work into the stuff of profound, subtle character, James believed that a culture had to have matured for centuries in the mould of established institutions. It may shock our emancipated souls, but James saw the class system as necessary both to civil life and great fiction. It was the shallowness of America's roots and the partial consequent vacuity of its populist social life which led James (Eliot was to do likewise) to leave America and live in England. He may, of course, have been misled in thinking that Europe provided him with a real alternative to America. Pound, after all, saw Mussolini as a demi-god compared to a demonic F.D.R.

At the heart of James's vision of the novelist as historian, then, is the fact that the cultures which had the ripest material to offer the novelist did so by virtue of the longevity of their national life and the relatively undamaged nature of their traditions. Such cultures tend to be historically unself-conscious. Their past is to a considerable extent their present. This leads to a paradox. It is societies without this organic, temporal connection which tend to write historical novels. T. S. Eliot, agreeing with James's diagnosis of the deprivation of the American present, also agreed that this was what had forced Hawthorne to make its Puritan, colonial history his so frequent subject. 'The only dimension', he wrote, 'in which Hawthorne could expand was the past, his present being so narrowly barren. It is a great pity, with his remarkable gift of observation, that the present did not offer him more to observe.'[17] This, of course, is by no means the whole truth of the matter. Hawthorne saw the early events of American history as archetypal: 'sins of the fathers' which, differently disguised, would recur. James and Eliot's aesthetic response concerning their New England ancestor came from a mixture of admiration and fear of his profound historical sense. Hawthorne, as historical novelist, turned to the past to explore the hidden, unconscious wounds of his fellow countrymen. This communal analysis might be seen as analogous to the nature of psychoanalysis of the individual. Both forms are concerned with unstable senses of identity and look to an exploration of the past to discern and, hopefully, make good prior traumatic damage. The historical novel, as written by Hawthorne, can be a profound form of communal therapy. Of course, like psychoanalysis, historical fiction can be merely escapist and self-indulgent. The nineteenth-century historical novel and contemporary psycho-analysis are arguably both products of a wealthy, leisured middle class with a histrionic taste for exotic fantasy and eager to rehearse the new, narcissistic nomenclature for what they thought and think excites and ails them. Perhaps in both modes we see the manipulation of the past in order to justify present irresponsibility. Determinism, pseudo-science, can be a major source of temporary consolation.

James, who, in any case, tended consistently to believe the grass on the Eastern side of the Atlantic was greener, did not see Scotland as disconnected from its past in the manner of America. His actual experience of the country was slight. Like Hawthorne, his knowledge of Scotland was largely based on Scott. Unlike Hawthorne, he did not usually perceive an alarming discrepancy between Scott's fiction and his experience of the real nation.[18] James's deep personal friendship with Stevenson led him to ponder Stevenson's roots in both Scottish life and literature. At times this led him to see, as in his own happy self, the best of both worlds in the Scotsman:

> If it is a good fortune for a genius to have had such a country as Scotland for its primary stuff, this is doubly the case when there has been a certain process of detachment, of extreme secularization. Mr. Stevenson has been emancipated—he is, as we may say, a Scotchman of the world.[19]

This is perhaps a questionable compromise between his national and international elements but, in the main, James was unequivocal in seeing a direct connection not only between Stevenson and his Scottishness but also with Scott:

> His descent and origin all contribute to the picture, which, it seems to me, could scarce—since we speak of 'endings'—had a better beginning had he himself prearranged it. Without his having prearranged it, indeed, it was such a matter could never be wasted on him, one of the innumerable things, Scotch and other, that helped to fill his romantic consciousness. Edinburgh, in the first place, the 'romantic town', was as much his 'own' as it ever was his great precursor's whom in *Weir of Hermiston* as well as elsewhere, he presses so hard. . . .[20]

This congruence of Scott, Stevenson and an inherently 'romantic' Scottish history—particularly that embodied in Edinburgh—recurs in James's vision of these writers. Unlike his own experience of America, he felt Scottish roots nourished them. Hence the happy experience of the young Stevenson:

> How must it not have beckoned on the imagination to pass and repass, on the way to school, under the Castle rock, conscious acutely, yet familiarly, of the grey citadel on the summit lighted up with the tartans and bagpipes of Highland regiments! Mr. Stevenson's mind, from an early age, was furnished with the concrete Highlander, who must have had much of the effect that we nowadays call decorative.[21]

It is an odd Highlander (even in an Edinburgh context) who is both concrete and decorative. Perhaps he is akin to a character from Skelt's Juvenile Drama who is boldly coloured but two-

dimensional. James had hardly any experience of the Highlands. In 1878, however, he spent a weekend at Tillypronie in
Aberdeenshire. There he performed the rituals of the Victorian
tourist. He rambled through the heather to a ruined castle,
visited a Highland games and went to a ball where, unlikely as it
may seem, the Master danced two polkas. All this he reported
to his invalid, house-bound sister, Alice:

> But don't envy me too much; for the British country house has at
> moments, for a cosmopolitanized American, an insuperable
> flatness. On the other hand, to do it justice, there is no doubt of
> its being one of the ripest fruits of time—and here in Scotland,
> where you get the conveniences of Mayfair dove-tailed into the
> last romanticism of nature—of the highest results of civilization.
> Such as it is, at any rate, I shall probably have a little more of it.[22]

Here we certainly see an image of the evolution of civilized life
as predicted both in the economic theories of the Scottish
Enlightenment and in Scott's fiction. In this Victorian upper-
class affluence we see the 'romantic' past happily decanted
into highly serviced, neo-Gothic forms. The 'primitive' is no
longer a hidden, caged beast but has been affluently domesti-
cized. Notwithstanding such creature comforts, James had
moments of severe boredom. He had other moments when the
self-imposed mask of conventional visitor dropped and the
piercing eye of the artist looked out. If he did not quite see a
pattern in this Highland carpet, disconcerting figures emerged
on the dance floor:

> At the ball was the famous beauty Mrs. Langtry, who was
> staying in the house and who is probably for the moment the
> most celebrated woman in England. She is in sooth divinely
> handsome and it was 'extremely odd' to see her dancing a
> Highland reel (which she had been practising for three days)
> with young Lord Huntly, who is a very handsome fellow and
> who in his kilt and tartan, leaping, hooting and romping,
> opposite to this London divinity, offered a vivid reminder of
> ancient Caledonian barbarism and of the roughness which
> lurks in all British amusements and only wants a pretext to
> explode.[23]

Despite the element of 'playful' dressing up in this erotically
energized version of nineteenth-century 'Balmorality', what is

of fundamental relevance to our problem is not simply that
James was reminded of 'ancient Caledonian barbarism', but
that he perceived an imminent, explosive and related rough-
ness in Lord Huntly's frolics. Violence lay just beneath the
skin of this civilization. It had, with particular regard to his
treatment of the Highlanders, been Scott's *conscious* intention
as a writer to illustrate the historical discontinuity of the
atavistic from the commercial, civil life of his age. Stevenson,
at the other end of the nineteenth century, took a much more
consciously apprehensive view of this dark, shadowy stranger.
What *Dr. Jekyll and Mr. Hyde* and his Pacific stories illustrate
is the contemporary presence of the bestial. In *Kidnapped* and
Catriona, however, he, to a considerable degree, followed
Scott's prescription. Because of this he employed conventional
literary responses to the Highlander and his society, which, in
fact, appeared before Scott who had considerably and profit-
ably exaggerated them. As Neil Munro, a later Highland
novelist, remarked of Scott:

> No nice consideration about even an approximate realism
> governed Scott's treatment of Gaelic life and character: he
> looked at them as Professor Reinhardt looks at Sophocles, with
> a single eye to their effect as pageantry, and saw them in a light
> that never was on land or sea. He never reported the speech of
> the native either in Erse or English but with a magnificent
> insouciance, and a grotesque improbity which has unhappily
> become stereotyped in most of his successors, and his Gaelic
> characters are equally remote from actual type. I hesitate to
> cavil about novels which at times have been my own delight,
> but the truth is imperative, that Allan Macaulay is the ill-
> begotten offspring of that gigantic humbug, Macpherson's
> *Ossian*, and Rob Roy, in almost every manifestation, is a
> Borderer without one drop of mountain blood.[24]

The need for Highland life as pageantry did not originate in
Scotland. The first symptoms of what was to prove an epidemic, 'tartan fever' (in Scott's own phrase) appeared in the
middle of the eighteenth century in the dire 'Highland' poetry
of William Collins.[25] With bourgeois Europe infected by the
Rousseauish cult of the 'wild man', albeit a safely proscribed
one, it was inevitable that the physical proximity of the
Highlands—tourism was well developed before the end of the

eighteenth century—ensured their being the focus of such fantasy. Most savages were too geographically remote, and the Irish, though nearer to hand, were felt to be too dirty and still too dangerous. The Highland figures present in such literature, supremely in James 'Ossian' MacPherson, were, in fact, compensatory fantasies for the range of emotions which the sceptical rationalism of the Enlightenment had censored and repressed in the lives of the middle classes, who were the economic beneficiaries of these new, rationally derived organizational and productive methods.[26] Violence, a degree of eroticism, maudlin lament, supernaturalism and, indeed, animism as an antidote to the mechanical sterility of Newtonian mechanics were all, at a safe remove, projected onto Highland life. This pre-Jungian, tartan shadow became conveniently incorporated into the sentimental, narcissistic theatricality of the time. As Hazlitt had indicated, modern science and economics were believed to have led the world into an age of rational and, therefore, eternal peace and stability. In one way or another, however, people restlessly chafe against even the fantasy of a wholly stable, tranquil world. They tend to respond with alternative, contradictory fantasies. Scott's enormous sales and celebrity were essentially based on his ability to share and to fabricate such day-dreams. Hazlitt, the only major English romantic writer to enthuse over the historical dimension of Scott's work, put this appeal very well:

> Protestants and Papists do not now burn one another at the stake: but we subscribe to new editions of Fox's Book of Martyrs; and the secret of the success of the Scotch Novels is much the same—they carry us back to the feuds, the heart-burnings, the havoc, the dismay, the wrongs and the revenge of a barbarous age and people—to the rooted prejudices and deadly animosities of sects and parties in politics and religion, and of contending chiefs and clans in war and intrigue. We feel the full force of the spirit of hatred with all of them in turn. As we read, we throw aside the trammels of civilisation, the flimsy veil of humanity. 'Off, you lendings!' The wild beast resumes its sway within us, we feel like hunting-animals, and as the hound starts in his sleep and rushes on the chase in fancy, the heart rouses itself in its native lair, and utters a wild cry of joy, at being restored once more to freedom and lawless, unrestrained impulses.[27]

While it was perhaps more a benevolent prescription than an achieved fact, the social and architectural doctrines of the Enlightenment *philosophes* were designed to create an urban, civil life of checks and balances to protect society against the insurrectionary tendencies of the untrammelled individual will. Amity was to be achieved by a constant process of self-regulation and self-correction through sociable intercourse with one's peers. Rather discouragingly, even among the initial *philosophes* actual relationships were marked by spleen, rancour and ambition.[28] Middle class taste was ironically marked by a fervid appetite for Romantic exoticism. Scottish writers figured prominently in this genre. As Leslie Fiedler has remarked:

> Romantic exoticism seeks to escape the tedium and alienation of bourgeois life by flight in four directions, Back, Out, In and Down: backward in time like Sir Walter Scott; outward in space like Robert Louis Stevenson; inward toward the murky depths of the unconscious like Rimbaud; or down the social scale like Sue and, after him, the so-called 'Naturalists.' All forms of Romantic exoticism are kinds of vicarious tourism—the downward variety vicarious slumming.[29]

'Vicarious tourism' may, of course be seen as a useful safety valve. It was Hazlitt himself who, however, ominously remarked that 'we may depend on it that what men delight to read in books, they will put in practice in reality.'[30] The history of the nineteenth century, in terms of the sociology of bourgeois taste, can be seen as pleasurable, militaristic fantasies darkening towards 1914 into a real appetite for berserking blood and carnage. As Martin Green has pointed out, there was growing desire among the commercial middle class to evolve into a pseudo-aristocratic, military caste.[31] Scott and Stevenson themselves were desirous of the lives of men of action. Both broke with the constricting role of Edinburgh lawyer. As James tellingly remarked of Stevenson in the light of his Pacific adventures: 'Everything was right for the discipline of Alan Fairford, but that the youth *was*, after all, a phoenix.'[32] Scott, denied such opportunity, delighted in playing soldiers during the threat of French invasion. As Henry Cockburn noted:

> Walter Scott's zeal in the cause was very curious. He was the soul of the Edinburgh troop of Midlothian Yeomanry Cavalry. It was

147

not a duty with him, or a necessity, or a pastime, but an absolute passion, indulgence in which gratified his feudal taste for war, and his jovial sociableness. He drilled, and drank, and made songs with a hearty conscientiousness which inspired or shamed everybody within the attraction. I do not know if it is usual, but his troop used to practice, individually, with the sabre at a turnip, which was stuck on the top of a staff, to represent a Frenchman, in front of the line. Every other trooper, when he set forward in his turn, was far less concerned about the success of his aim at the turnip, than about how he was to tumble. But Walter pricked forward gallantly, saying to himself, 'Cut them down, the villains, cut them down!' and made his blow, which from his lameness was often an awkward one, cordially, muttering curses all the while at the detested enemy.[33]

Delightedly exposed as a boy to the questionable Jacobite stories of Stewart of Invernahyle, it was inevitable that Scott, even more than many Scotsmen of his age, would turn to the not too distant Highland insurrection as a day-dream context for his military aspirations. In 1806, responding to the pro-Celtic promptings of the Durham historian, Robert Surtees he wrote:

You flatter me very much by pointing out my attention to the feuds of 1715 and 45:—the truth is, that the subject has often & deeply interested me from my earliest youth. . . . I became a valiant Jacobite at the age of ten years old; and, even since reason & reading came to my assistance, I have never quite got rid of the impression which the gallantry of Prince Charles made on my imagination.[34]

The child may be father of the man in ways less happy than Wordsworth thought. Much of the best-selling work of Scottish middle-class writers has depended on the enormous popular appeal of licentious states of immaturity. Disowning the responsibility of nationhood, we have been among the most lost of boys. By 1813 Scott's Jacobite ardour was not in this respect diminished. Writing to Margaret Clephane, he confessed that:

As for my loyalty to the Stuarts fear nothing that can attaint it. I never used the word Pretender which is a most unseemly word in my life unless when (God help me) I was obliged to take the oaths of Abjuration and Supremacy at elections and so forth and even then I always did it with a qualm of conscience. Seriously I am very glad I did not live in 1745 for though as a lawyer I could not have pleaded Charles's right and as a clergyman I could not have prayed for him yet as a soldier I would I am sure against the convictions of my better reason have fought for him even to the bottom of the gallows.[35]

While this letter may have been partly caused by the desire to cut a dash in the eyes of a young Highland lass, a similar sensibility struggled not always unsuccessfully with common-sense in Scott. Not only was part of the enormous antique bric-à-brac of Abbotsford Highland in origin, but so was at least one servant, Scott's piper. Hence the scene reported by Lockhart in 1818:

> After the Highlander had played some dozen of his tunes, he was summoned, according to the ancient custom, to receive the thanks of the company. He entered *more militari*, without taking off his bonnet, and received a huge tass of acquavitae from the hand of his master, after which he withdrew again—the most perfect solemnity all the while being displayed in his weather-beaten, but handsome and warlike Celtic lineaments. The inspiration of the generous fluid prompted one strain merrier than the rest, behind the door of the Hall, and then the piper was silent—his lungs, I dare say, consenting much more than his will, for he has all the appearance of being a fine enthusiast in the delights and dignity of his calling. So much for Roderick of Skye, for such I think is his style.[36]

Again the image is decorative and theatrical. Perhaps cultures do die not with a bang but a deflating whimper. On the other hand, Highland regiments did and do form the cutting edge of the British army; the *more militari* was by no means wholly symbolic. A more questionable symbolism was evoked in Lockhart's devious mind by this Highland presence in a neo-Gothic, Border mansion:

> It is true, that it was in the Lowlands—and that there are other streams upon which the shadow of the tartans might fall with more of the propriety of mere antiquarianism, than on the Tweed. But the Scotch are right in not now-a-days splitting too much the symbols of their nationality; as they have ceased to be an independent people, they do wisely in striving to be as much as possible a united people. But here, above all, whatever was

truly Scottish could not fail to be truly appropriate in the presence of the great genius to whom whatever is Scottish in thought, in feeling, or in recollection, owes so large a share of its prolonged, or reanimated, or ennobled existence.[37]

It is a desperate nationalism that would ask even the purest and greatest genius to carry such a communal burden. Art expresses but cannot create nationhood. If it attempts to do so we get a false aesthetic simulating real society. As Tom Nairn has cogently pointed out this was, unlike other regenerating European cultures, the fate of the Romantic Movement in Scotland.

Elsewhere, the revelation of the romantic past and the soul of the people informed some real future—in the Scottish limbo, they were the nation's reality. Romanticism provided—as the Enlightenment could not, for all its brilliance—a surrogate identity.[38]

Even granting the possibility that genuine unity can exist in a nation without independence, unity founded on such sentimentality is, at best, self-deceiving and, at worst, politically corrupting. Scottish identity has largely been since the eighteenth century a thing of synthetic symbols initially fabricated by not unrewarded literary intellectuals. *Blackwood's Magazine* centred on John Wilson ('Christopher North') and Lockhart, with its debased German Romantic formulae of nationhood, set the tone for the rest of the nineteenth century. *Blackwood's* allegedly integrative symbolism of *one* Scotland was a concoction well suited to the interests of an increasingly anglicized Scottish establishment. In a country undergoing stressful urban and industrial change, the Kailyard with its soporific pastoralism was a central feature of this policy.[39] No less pervasive and harmful was the 'Celtic' dimension.

The first symptoms of what was to prove an epidemic of writing about and popular enthusiasm for the Highlands appeared in the middle of the eighteenth century. The reasons for this involve a highly complex interaction of local and international political, cultural and literary forces. In Scottish terms, it is certainly arguable that the final collapse of a distinctive Highland society brought about by the failure of the '45 Rebellion rendered the Highlander safe to be assimilated into the imagination of the Lowland Scot. Genocidal impulses could be discarded and apparently benevolent literary ones adopted. Also, in the wake of the Union, Scotland was simultaneously (often absurdly) trying both to anglicize herself and to find historical roots which were, at the very least, different from those of England. As MacDiarmid pertinently remarked, this was 'an exaggerated sentimental nationalism which was obviously a form of compensation for a lack of realistic nationalism'.[40] Because of the very obscurity of Highland history (Gaelic literature was orally transmitted and there was a consequent absence of documentary evidence) and because the popular tide of feeling of the time was so set on the prehistoric and the 'primitive', it was inevitable that the literati should largely seek to locate such sentimental nationalism north of the Highland line. Also the kilts, claymores etc., could be adopted as a distinctive (if wholly superficial) symbolism of the 'real' Scotland; it was to such an 'authentic' nation and capital that the kilted Borderer, Scott, welcomed the gross, pink tartan-swathed German George IV in the early nineteenth century.

While Scott did not initiate 'Highland Scotland', he was undoubtedly, by public acclaim, its greatest proponent. At the simplest level, as we have seen, his fantasy life led him to identify with the Highland warrior. Beneath this there was even an edge of competition, the Highlander for the modern, 'civilized' Lowlander being a pervasive threat to his masculinity. The currency of the Jacobite theme in the consciousness of Scott and his Scotland is, however, more complex than this. At face value, this sympathetic preoccupation with the revolt of a Celtic, Catholic minority by many Lowland Scots is most odd. During the uprisings most Scots had felt as hostile to and more frightened of the Highlanders than the English. In terms, however, of these peculiar legends and semi-mythic personalities endemic to Scottish history, the '45 has become a climactic and tragic *national* event. Scots in general feel free to adopt the accents George Campbell Hay has deemed appropriate to the participating Highlanders:

The rest of it is in our memory. That vow was kept with weary steps and bloody wounds. They set great Goliath rocking, and

151

one against three they fell at last. They closed their spell on this world with honour . . . one spell, one spell only do we get on earth to show the temper of the metal in us, to test the edge of our courage, to win fame for our country or shame.[41]

This national 'myth', crudely assimilated from Highland experience, in which they see their pristine honour being overwhelmed by English main force, is not only extraordinarily self-indulgent but is arguably the product of bad faith. Scotsmen often stress the gallantry of the '45 precisely to the degree they wish to obscure from themselves the shoddy, mercenary self-betrayal of the Union in 1707. To think well of themselves they, at the least, symbolically don the kilt.

The Highlander, then, became in Scottish art, not a true symbol with an inherent power to generate complex meaning, but a sort of vacuum into which all sorts of eccentric, contradictory and politically dubious impulses could be projected. The '45 most conveniently flattered our masculinity and also bespoke inevitable defeat. It was used as a false analogy of the loss of Scottish nationhood. While one would not wholly agree with MacDiarmid's deliberately provocative analysis of this defeatist element in Scott, it seems much nearer the truth than the 'patriotic garrulage' which is still the predominant response to his name and work in Scotland.

> Scott's novels are the great source of the paralysing ideology of defeatism in Scotland, the spread of which is responsible at once for the acceptance of the Union and the low standard of nineteenth-century Scots literature except in the hands of men like the Gaelic poet, William Livingston (1803–70), who were consciously anti-English—a defeatism as profitable financially to its exponents (Scott, Stevenson, Tweedsmuir, &c.) as it is welcome to English interests. 'The cause is lost for ever', the 'end of an auld sang', and that sort of stuff is an actual distortion of history—and that is what Scott did: cf. *The Heart of Midlothian*, in which Scott described the Porteous Riots as if they were temporary accidental disturbances instead of events of an international significance that accompanied a national anger at the Union and led to the Rebellion of eight years after, when the Prince, seeing that the ground was ripe in Scotland, and England at war, came over. That 'the cause was lost for ever' was exactly what Scott's own circle spent their energies in proving, and what

all these new Scott books are endeavouring to ensure in the face of the new Scottish literary and political movement and all the objective facts of Scotland's condition to-day.[42]

Even worse than this abuse of the '45 as corrupt national symbol is the fact that what Scott's fiction actually shows is the radical discontinuity between violent Highland life and moderate, modern Scotland. Scott in the sense of meaningful, organic growth—Highland Scotland merging into a wider national context—is merely sentimentally conservative. The superficial tone and the manipulated, 'private' conclusions of Scott's work point towards placid integration. As Edwin Muir has remarked: the Scott novel 'is content to enunciate moral platitudes, and it does this all the more confidently because such platitudes are certain to be agreeable to the reader.'[43] Modern criticism has generally been a willing participant in such a vision of platitudinous progress. Since Lukács, Scott has been increasingly praised for his moderate, progressive historical good sense, and, as a corollary, his Highland writing has been seen as also embodying these virtues. Scott's conscious intention, deeply influenced as he was by the thought of the Scottish Enlightenment, was to demonstrate the transition from feudal to commercial civilization and the incorporation of Scotland into Britain. Consequently he saw the Highlanders as perfectly suited to a central role in such a moral fable. As he wrote of Rob Roy's personality:

> It is this strong contrast betwixt the civilized and cultivated mode of life on the one side of the Highland line, and the wild and lawless adventures . . . on the opposite side of that ideal boundary, which creates the interest attached to his name.[44]

Here, manifestly, are the twin poles of Scott's dialectic. As Coleridge, an otherwise dissenting voice, remarked, Scott's fiction embodied transition from an age of heroism to one of prudence. Yet if we look at the actual facts of Scottish history and both Scott's life and fictions as they relate to these facts, deeply disquieting contradictions emerge. For an advocate of prudence and moderation, Scott, as we have seen, had deeply martial, if not downright violent, impulses. These feelings existed not simply in the realm of private fantasy but in his sense of politics. At the time of Bonnymuir he imagined

153

himself, mounted and sabre equipped, riding down the pathetically few radicals. Even more tellingly, he envisaged a Highland host come to bring order to the dissident south. Nor in his fiction does he do anything like justice to the fact that the genocidal brutality of the '45 was perpetrated by the 'civilized' Hanoverian side, whereas the Highland troops had behaved with extraordinary restraint throughout. Obsessed with violence, both repelled and attracted by it, Scott projected this obsession onto the Highlanders of his fiction. Thus, rather than having a realistic dialectic between Highland and Lowland values, Scott—*Rob Roy* is the classic instance—embodies his Lowland characters in terms of the comic novel limply derived from Fielding and his Highlanders in terms of Gothic fiction. The result is both bad art and worse history whereby generic fictional forms are imposed in order to justify a highly questionable political vision.

While some of this obsession with violence had obviously private roots in Scott's personality, much of it can be understood in terms of his political beliefs. The great fictional exemplar of the Whig interpretation of history, Scott wanted to verify the theories of Hume and Smith, which had predicated that a new economic order entailed a new harmonious psychological and social order. That is to say, that a commercial and 'improving' society is inherently more stable and less violent than a more traditional one. Thus, while the bloody nature of the Highlanders had to be exaggerated, the actual fact of the enormous and accelerated changes in Scottish urban and rural life had to be disguised. This was especially true of the level of violence and suffering inherent in such a change. Scott, accordingly, seized upon a simplistic and overly optimistic vision of historical development, which he embodied in the controlled environment of historical novels where they could be seen safely cleansed of the grim sort of realities with which a contemporary like Stendhal dealt. When he does talk of Highland social problems, it is not with Burns's acute sense of what was happening but from a safe, generalizing, melioristic distance:

> It is always with unwillingness that the Highlander quits his
> deserts, and at this early period it was like tearing a pine from its

rock, to plant him elsewhere. Yet even then the mountain glens were over-peopled, although thinned occasionally by famine or by the sword, and many of their inhabitants strayed down to Glasgow—there formed settlements—there sought and found employment, although different, indeed, from that of their native hills. This supply of a hardy and useful population was of consequence to the prosperity of the place, furnished the means of carrying on the few manufactures which the town already boasted, and laid the foundation of its future prosperity.[45]

What Scott was doing in his *fiction*, particularly his Highland fiction, was, in fact, writing soothing 'progressive' fables in order to allay intense levels of social and political anxiety which he shared with his vast bourgeois audience. Coleridge, more profound than Hazlitt, realized that beneath the superficial excitation of Scott's art lay a soporific dimension which, for his contemporary audience, was the real attraction of his work:

> His age is an age of *anxiety* from the crown to the hovel, from the cradle to the coffin; all is an anxious straining to maintain life or *appearances*—to *rise*, as the only condition of not falling.
> ... The great felicity of Sir Walter Scott is that his own intellect supplies the place of all intellect and all character in his heroes and heroines, and *representing* the intellect of his readers, supersedes all motives for its exertion, by never appearing alien, whether as above or below.[46]

On the other hand what is recorded in Scott's journals, letters, political pamphlets and speeches is a near overwhelming sense of belonging to an 'age of anxiety'. As Thomas Crawford has pertinently remarked:

> Scott's difficulties as an artist were due not so much to any defect of life in the Scottish people—this was an age of industrial expansion and political and social ferment—as to his Toryism, his pathological fear of radical weavers and contemporary mobs, combined with a refusal to put art first, and a disastrous compromise with the market.[47]

What Crawford does not go on to ask himself is how these creatively crippling politics, placed at the service of his middle-class public, expressed themselves, albeit covertly and in costume, in the fiction. The Lawrentian notion of incongruence between teller and tale is perhaps an exception rather than a rule. Scott's historical fiction is preoccupied with civil discontent and civil war. So, indeed, was his *own* age. Radical unrest threatened both at home and abroad. Thus it is in the Highland novels not Jacobitism but Jacobinism which is the real historical and political problem. Unlike Coleridge, a genuine conservative, Scott consoled his audience by suggesting that the cause and nature of revolution and popular unrest had not to do with governmental malpractices and abuses or the excesses of capitalist economics in the countryside and new proto-industrial towns. Scott relates almost all insurrectionary tendencies to an earlier state of human evolution represented by the 'atavistic' Highlanders in his fiction. Like the earlier thinkers of the Scottish Enlightenment, particularly Hume, Scott sought an antidote to a dark Scottish past in a notion of middle-class inspired progressive social evolution. The 'evolution' of his fiction travels in a contrary direction. In his first novel, *Waverley*, the wilful fanatical ferocity of Scottish history seems at the novel's end safely, aesthetically, confined. The virulent Fergus now exists as a nostalgic portrait. A sense of ancestral threat, however, increases throughout his work. In *Redgauntlet* the past is a threat of chaos to come again. Scottish history, antiques apart, was, in fact, a nightmare constantly preventing Scott from getting a good night's sleep.

The critical movement initiated by Duncan Forbes in seeing the social philosophy of Scott as centrally derived from that of the Scottish Enlightenment is, of course, undeniable.[48] The question not often asked by political philosophers is what shall be the relationship of a *novelist* to a series of political and social theories, particularly those of half a century of lived experience later. Fiction is not theory; it is about what theoretical ideas reveal and create when they are embodied in the actual business of living. This is the true 'novel of ideas'. One can and, indeed, should certainly understand the Scottish Enlightenment as an extraordinarily successful intellectual response to a series of dire religious, social, economic and political problems. Arguably even more than Adam Smith, David Hume's thought stands at the epicentre of this movement. In Hume's work we can perceive a brilliant attempt to lay the bloody Scottish ghosts. In a nation less thrawn, the brilliance of his sceptical epistemology must have destroyed forever a native instinct for fanatical self-righteousness and God-given conviction. Hume himself was in fact haunted by fanaticism's ability to resurrect itself and to return, trailing murderous civil discord in its wake. Consequently, as psychologist and social and political philosopher, he was preoccupied with envisaging a more secure society. This led him to adhere to a general historical theory which saw man evolving away from his primitive, rapacious past by means of metamorphosing economic forms. This historical theory was also a class theory, in that the key role in this forward movement was designated to an expanding middle class, who, out of a new kind of commercial order, would create a foundation of wealth from which would in turn emerge general prosperity, an increase in civil liberty since the new middle class would burst the restrictive feudal bonds pertaining between master and man and create a higher level of culture. As a psychologist Hume seemed to believe that new forms of manners, decorous if not genteel, would be adequate safeguard against the atavistic passions of Scottish history, so that social form and content would go together and middle-class man would exist as amiably one with another as he himself, *le bon David*, managed to do with his friends. Whatever his fears, he certainly articulated a belief that Scotsmen and civilization were compatible phenomena and that, as Scott later suggested, Scots would learn 'what adds dignity to man, and qualifies him to support and adorn an elevated situation in society'.[49] Equally, if their own social group provided for the middle class a means of self-regulation and instruction, he placed faith in their moderation and common-sense to maintain, in a viable and healthy state, the bonds between themselves, the aristocrats and the common people. His radical epistemology apart, Hume is, in most other respects, a highly characteristic Augustan figure, and his thought, like that of the age, seeks an equipoise of tolerance and moderation—precisely the kind of balance that we see reflected in the harmonious structure of Fielding's socially integrative comic fictions. All proponents of Scott as a major writer assume that his latterday endorsement of eighteenth-century values bespeaks a robust and healthy sanity, as opposed to the hypersensitive, perhaps neurotic, response of Romanticism to social problems and pressures. My own feeling is that it much more bespeaks a rather dull and insensitive intelligence and a capacity to fall back, at times aggressively and near hysterically, on certain unexamined historical and political assumptions. This capacity for maintaining inadequate and redundant explanations of what was happening in contemporary history was integral to his literary talent for clinging to inadequate and redundant forms. Scott's central myth has little to do with the revivification or even romance of history, but is centrally concerned with middle-class man, almost like a new Adam, emerging, after some tentative, nostalgic dalliance, from the slough of 'primitive' history. Unfortunately, he was not only derivative but almost half a century too late. We need only look across the Channel to Stendhal to see a far more complex and subtle fiction emerging to deal with a new, ambiguous and frightening world. A world, too, which far from being in harmonious balance is impregnated with avarice, especially bourgeois avarice, and prevented only by fear from tearing itself apart. In Stendhal, balance has given way to stagnation achieved at the terrible expense of willed boredom.

There is no reason to assume or believe that the Scottish middle class was significantly different from other European varieties. Indeed, given that their artistic sense was often a sentimental glaze over a coarse Calvinism (with its assumptions of material, propertied success as significant of spiritual superiority) and that this sentimentality was derived from an already degenerate English source, one cannot see early nineteenth-century Edinburgh as an altogether reassuring phenomenon. Scott's prudent, decorous father-figures, to whom the fanciful, erring sons always return, are eighteenth-century English gentlemen as filtered through the works of Henry MacKenzie. Bailie Nicol Jarvie, that paragon of entrepreneurial virtues of an allegedly more Scottish (Glasgow) strain, has always seemed to me an incipient, comfortable creature of the Kailyard. Are these the accents of a true slave-plantation owner?

> I am a carefu' man, as is weel ken'd, and industrious, as the hale town can testify; and I can win my crowns, and keep my crowns, wi' anybody in the Saut-Market, or it may be the Gallowgate. And I'm a prudent man, as the deacon was before me.[50]

The moderate, prudent, business-like gentleman is one of the key Augustan-derived literary stereotypes which has been consistently confused with a discriminating, specific realism in Scott's work.

Graham MacMaster in his recent book on Scott, *Scott and Society*, provides welcome evidence of the degree to which Scott's fiction darkened in direct proportion to his brooding sense of what was for him a disintegrating society.[51] Further, MacMaster sees five marked phases in Scott's work where, by formal means, we can trace this pattern of change. I do not think that a study of the three Jacobite novels substantiates this concept of radical formal change. There is a darkening of tone due to growing anxiety; the treatment of Gothic sensibility is, in particular, not a subject of playful irony by the time Scott wrote *Redgauntlet*. I would argue, however, that the relatively simple literary conventions which Scott acquired and adapted at the very beginning of his fictional career remained with him till the end. It is a matter of degree and not principle with which we are involved. We are also concerned with the abuse of literary form at the behest of a historicist vision.

In 1898 the American biographer and critic, John Jay Chapman wrote:

> He lived and wrote in the past. That this Scotchman should appear at the end of what has been a very great period of English literature, and summarize the whole of it in his two hours traffic on the stage, gives him a strange place in the history of that literature. . . . He is the mistletoe of English literature whose roots are not in the soil but in the tree.[52]

Chapman was, in fact, discussing Stevenson and not Scott. However, the criticism is not irrelevant to the older writer. Lukács praised Scott for evolving Augustan fiction into a newer, higher realism. Coleridge, inherently more responsive to the development of English prose, thought the reverse. Ironically, Coleridge considered Scott's work to be replete with plagiarism from earlier English and German sources and, like Edwin Muir, saw his fiction as a marked deterioration from the earlier potency of the English novel. In a letter to Thomas Allsop he wrote of Scott with a degree of charitable qualification not always present when he turned to this theme:

Add, that tho' I cannot pretend to have found in any of these Novels a character that even approaches in Genius, in truth of conception or boldness & freshness of execution, to Parson Adams, Blifil, Strap, Lieutenant Bowling, Mr. Shandy, Uncle Toby, & Trim, Lovelace; and tho' Scott's *female* characters will not, even the very best, bear a comparison with Miss Byron, Emily, Clementina in Sir C. Grandison; nor the comic ones with Tabitha Bramble, or with Betty (in Mrs. Bennett's Beggar-girl)—and tho' by the use of the Scotch Dialect, by Ossianic Mock-Highland Motley Heroic, & by extracts from the printed Sermons, Memoirs, &c of the Fanatic Preachers, there is a good deal of *false Effect* & Stage trick; still the number of characters *so good* produced by one man & in so rapid a succession, must ever remain an illustrious phaenomenon in Literature, after all the subtractions for those borrowed from English & German Sources, or compounded by blending two or three of the Old Drama into one—ex. gr. the Caleb in the Bride of Lammermuir.—Scott's great merit, and at the same [time] his *felicity*, and the true solution of the long-sustained *interest* that Novel after novel excited, lie in the nature of the subject— not merely, or even chiefly, because the struggle between the Stuarts & the Presbyterians & Sectaries is still in lively memory, & the passions of the adherency to the former if not the adherency itself, extant in our own Fathers' or Grandfathers' times; nor yet (tho' this is of great weight) because of the language, manners, &c introduced are sufficiently different from our own for *poignancy* & yet sufficiently near & similar for sympathy; nor yet because, for the same reason, the Author speaking, reflecting & describing in his own person remains still (to adopt a painter's phrase) in sufficient *keeping* with his subject matter, while his characters can both talk and feel interestingly to *us* as men without recourse to *antiquarian* Interest, & nevertheless without moral anachronism (—in all which points the Ivanhoe is so wofully the contrary—for what Englishman cares for Saxon or Norman, both brutal Invaders, more than for Chinese & Cochin-chinese?)—yet great as all these causes are, the essential wisdom and happiness of the Subject consists in this: that the contest between the Loyalists & their opponents can never be *obsolete*, for it is the contest between the two great moving Principles of social Humanity— religious adherence to the Past and the Ancient, the Desire & the admiration of Permanence, on the one hand; and the Passion for increase of Knowledge, for Truth as the offspring of

Reason, in short, the mighty Instincts of *Progression* and *Free-agency*, on the other. In all subjects of deep and lasting Interest you will detect a struggle between two opposites, two polar Forces, both of which are alike necessary to our human Well-being, & necessary each to the continued existence of the other—Well therefore may we contemplate with intense feelings those whirlwinds which are, for free-agents, the appointed means & only possible condition of that *equi-librium*, in which our moral Being subsists: while the disturbance of the same constitutes our sense of Life. Thus in the ancient Tragedy the lofty Struggle between irresistible Fate & unconquerable Free Will, which founds its equilibrium in the Providence & the Future Retribution of Christianity. If instead of a contest between Saxons & Normans, or the Fantees & Ashantees, a mere contest of Indifferents! of minim Surges in a boiling Fish-kettle! Walter Scott had taken the struggle between the Men of Arts & the Men of arms in the time of Becket, & made us feel how much to claim our well-wishing there was in the cause & character of the Priestly & Papal Party no less than in those of Henry & his Knights, he would have opened a new mine— instead of translating into Leadenhall Street Minerva Library Sentences a cento of the most common incidents of the stately, self-congruous Romances of D'Urfe, Scuderi &c—N.B. I have not read the Monastery; but I suspect that the Thought or Element of the Faery Work is from the German. I perceive from that passage in the Old Mortality where Morton is discovered by old Alice [Alison] in consequence of calling his Dog, Elphin, that W.S. has been reading Tiek's Phantasus (a collection of Faery or Witch Tales) from which both the incident & name is [are] borrowed.[53]

While he does not wholly follow out the logic of his argument, Coleridge points to the essential critical problem and paradox in Scott's work. How can such a formally and linguistically derivative writer ('Ossianic Mock-Highland Motley Heroic' is particularly fine and apt) have introduced a new dimension of meaning into the novel? In part, Coleridge does not answer this question because of the quantity of Scott's achievement. More important, however, is the fact that Coleridge in this exceptional instance projects on Scott's historical writing his own characteristically near Hegelian dualistic notion of new life emerging out of a creative interaction between past and present: 'a struggle between two opposites, two polar Forces, both of which are alike necessary to our human Well-being, & necessary each to the continued existence of the other.' Coleridge here makes a distinction between those Scott novels which, with partial success, embody this dialectic and those, like *Ivanhoe*, where the dialectic is less than trivial. However, if we actually consider the aesthetic form that Scott gives to his 'polar Forces', we will see that he is not only not interested in doing justice to the past, particularly 'the Stuarts & the Presbyterians & Sectaries', but he, consciously or otherwise, adopts a language and conventions which deliberately disengage past from present.

Thus, though he did not explicitly formulate the question himself, Coleridge's trenchant criticism of Scott leads us to the apparent paradox of why it should be that a new historical content in fiction, indeed a historical content that some prestigious and sophisticated modern theorists believe to embody complex models of historical process and evolution, should introduce itself in the hand-me-down garments of eighteenth-century fiction. Or, put another way, it is arguably more than odd that a genuinely new sense of history, that is to say a new sense of time and causality, did not lead to radical innovations in language, form and the presentation and psychological understanding of character. Coleridge certainly did not think that any such radical innovations were present in Scott. It is perhaps even more extraordinary that, with the exception of this ambivalent letter, he at no time thought that Scott had any penetrative understanding of the processes of history.[54] Thus, to follow Coleridge's close *literary* analysis of Scott and to extend the premises of his judgements, rather than talking hazily about Scott in terms of his work as exemplifying some general theory of social evolution (Lukács) or to pursue that hoary old Scottish chestnut where Sir Walter synthesizes our inner psychological disturbances (head v. heart) and our outer social conflicts, is to be presented with a puzzle as to whether, in fact, it is possible for aesthetic conventions, which were largely redundant by the time Scott came to use them, to be compatible with a radical new content. Is this fictional vehicle, perhaps, like the first motor car, in that it appears to be made to be drawn by horses but is really powered by an internal combustion engine? Did he really manage to pour new wine into old bottles? Or was it old wine artificially aerated: that is to say, that rather than embodying a new dynamic sense into fiction, Scott merely disguised an older static order with historical accretions? My contention is that this is precisely what he did do, and that form and content are wholly compatible in Scott, because they are *both* debilitated versions of the form and content of Augustan fiction. Further, that one major reason why he attracted such a large middle-class audience was due to the fact that their reading of Scott reassured their deep, albeit often unconscious, historical anxieties, that the form of eighteenth-century fiction and all the social, moral and psychological values implicit in such a form provided an adequate explanation of historical process. Scott, rather than pitching them into time and change and involving them with the tormenting questions of their moral participation in history, demonstrated to them agreeable, distanced and safe historical solutions derived from the social and moral equations of the eighteenth century. Indeed, solutions which were capable of arresting history at a point of maximum enjoyment, security and advantage to the middle-class reader of the early nineteenth century. What, in fact, I am suggesting is that Scott's novels are essentially anti-historical: they take the partial solutions of an earlier age, solutions which were authentic to that age, and promulgate them as final solutions, whereas history of its very nature is incompatible with such stasis in that each historical solution, even a progressive one, is by definition also the postulation of a different type and series of problems. There was, perhaps, more of the ideologist in Scott than the creative artist.

The aesthetically reactionary element in Scott's work is nowhere more apparent than in his employment of a redundant eighteenth-century character typology. We have already seen this with reference to his genteel, paternal types. It is also apparent in his young heroes and, more alarmingly, his 'anti-heroes'. Scott's pattern is formulaic and character accordingly becomes stereotype. Infected by the sentimental aesthetics of the picturesque, an aesthetic which stipulated that the charm of an object was dependent on its being observed at a proper *distance*, the young hero is brought into proximity with a past culture and a 'heroic' representative of that culture. Though not participating in violence, which would incriminate him, the scales fall from his eyes and the true nature of his sentimental yearning is revealed to him. Scott's profound common-sense, wisdom even, at such a juncture has been the object of frequent critical acclaim. The hero realizes that his identification with the Highland 'anti-hero' has been wrongheaded. Something akin to a devil histrionically appears from under the deceiving mask. Thus Fergus MacIvor: 'The veins of his forehead swelled when he was in such agitation; his nostril became dilated; his cheek and eye inflamed; and his look that of a demoniac.' Or:

> A petty chief of three or four hundred men!—his pride might suffice for the Cham of Tartary—the Grand Seignior—the Great Mogul! I am well free of him. Were Flora an angel, she would bring with her a second Lucifer of ambition and wrath for a brother-in-law.[55]

Fergus MacIvor is the archetype of the fallen Jacobite angels who threaten the incipiently established Hanoverian bourgeois paradise on earth. Scott was not alone in seeing the Highlanders in a sub-Miltonic context. Burns, from an antipathetic political viewpoint, writes of the 'unfortunate Jacobite Clans who, as John Milton tells us, [had] their unhappy Culloden in Heaven'.[56] Debased mythology does not tend, however, to create adequate fictional character or realistic social observation. Fergus is no Highland chief but a pseudo-mythical figure essentially derived from the eighteenth century's fear of an insurrectionary anti-hero. His type and his origins can be clearly discerned in one of Scott's favourite poems, Johnson's *The Vanity of Human Wishes*. Fergus and Charles XII of Sweden are of the same literary blood royal. Thus locating him as a type with recurrent, demonic desire for power, Scott conveniently locates the cause and nature of all civil revolt. Essentially Fergus is far more a scapegoat than a villain. The complex evil and social guilt of Scott's age, particularly that of his own class and audience, can be conveniently discovered in him. Inevitably, Highland society became similarly incriminated. Scott has Fergus say that Scotland will finally hide its guilt over what has been done to the Highlanders by 'levelling them with a nation of cannibals'. By the time he writes *Rob Roy*, however, he himself is commenting with anthropological crudity on alleged parallels with the American Indians. Both, in fact, are septs of the ur-Hollywood tribe.

> The victim was held flat by some, while others, binding a large heavy stone in a plaid, tied it round his neck, and others again eagerly stripped him of some part of his dress. Half naked, and thus manacled, they hurled him into the lake, there about twelve feet deep, with a loud halloo of vindictive triumph,— above which, however, his last death-shriek, the yell of mortal agony, was distinctly heard.[57]

Thus, too, the voice of old Scotland is that of Mrs. McGregor's absurd, vengeful keening while that of the new is allegedly embodied in the canny tones of the kenspeckle, commercial Bailie.

Scott's general presumption was that the enlightened values consequent upon *laissez-faire* economics removed violence and, indeed, wilfulness from society. While there is a degree of ambiguity concerning this fundamental cultural shift in *Waverley*, he did not, even in that first novel, seriously attempt to test his own almost Burkean premise of old, ferocious impulses finding new forms:

> The wrath of our ancestors, for example, was coloured *gules*; it broke forth in acts of open and sanguinary violence against the objects of its fury. Our malignant feelings which must seek gratification through more indirect channels and undermine the obstacles which they cannot openly bear down must be said to be tinctured *sable*. But the deep running impulse is the same in both cases; and the proud peer who can now only ruin his neighbour according to law, by protracted suits, is the genuine descendant of the baron who wrapped the castle of his competitor in flames, and knocked him on the head as he endeavoured to escape from the conflagration.[58]

Monomania is shown in *Waverley* as a Jacobite preserve: 'Every person of consequence had some separate object, with a fury that Waverley considered as altogether disproportioned to its importance.'[59] The development of his Jacobite fiction shows Scott's own diminishing sense of proportion under the pressure of his self-created debts and a deteriorating national political situation. Murderous revenge in *Rob Roy* becomes a kind of dehumanizing, self-destroying, Gothic force in *Redgauntlet*. Rather than showing national evolution, *Redgauntlet* is a melodramatic clash of opposites. The two young heroes are impotent in the face of the brute force of the past. Alan is ill and Darsie emasculated by being forced to wear feminine dress. A wholly unlikely Hanoverian Campbell *deus ex machina* saves all. Dark horsemen, nocturnal storms, horseshoe marks, intimations of demonism—even of anti-Christ: never has what James termed Scott's 'Gothic upholstery' been more stuffed. 'Wandering Willie's Tale' belongs far more to the Minerva Press than to the realm of the authentic Scottish supernatural. Attempts to make this novel belong to the romance genre, as in Hawthorne's truly sinister histories, are profoundly wide of the mark. The Gothic novel was widely read at the start of the nineteenth century because of its titillating sensationalism. It also had a social and political function, which Scott, particularly in this novel, was employing. As Leslie Fiedler has remarked:

> The classic Gothic Novel was radical in its politics, but radical in an oddly retrospective way; which is to say, its authors attacked the inherited evils of the past as represented especially by the Inquisition and the remnants of the feudal aristocracy. The writers of popular Gothic, on the other hand, fought against the new masters, not the old, the hidden rather than open exploiters: factory owners, capitalists, merchants as well as the pimps and thugs who serve them, and the lawyers and clergy who provide them cover and camouflage.[60]

One of the many unsatisfactory paradoxes of *Redgauntlet* is that minatory Jacobitism should be seen in conclusion as so impotent that it can be safely allowed to take itself off into final exile. One explanation is that the book's Gothic tantrums concerning Jacobitism are artificial. The frequently remarked 'cardboard' element in Scott derives from an aesthetic corrupted by a false historical sense. Scott's enemy, chosen at the behest of his socially aspiring and insecure middle class, had by the early nineteenth century no real substance. Novelists like Stendhal or Dickens, a proponent of the 'popular' Gothic, were fighting the real battles against corrupt power. Scott was almost wholly on the side of the victors: 'Have his patrician birth and aristocratic fortunes given him any right to censure those who dispose of the fruits of their industry, according to their own pleasure.'[61] The book is suffused with sententious social wisdom of this kind. As a social thinker, Scott plays Polonius to Coleridge's Hamlet. At the level of plot this involves discerning the true quality of the either known or discovered father and the accession to the so convenient inheritance. Darsie, the romantically inclined (he and Alan constitute a dualism which to some degree influenced Stevenson as did the sequence with Alan and Nany Ewart), is suitably checked by Alan:

> And yet you impeach my father's courage! I tell you he has courage enough to do what is right, and to spurn what is wrong—courage enough to defend a righteous cause with hand and purse, and to take the part of the poor man against his oppressor, without fear of the consequences himself. This is civil courage, Darsie; and it is of little consequence to most men in this age and country, whether they ever possess military courage or no.[62]

Yet, as we have seen, Scott was personally restless with civil courage and yearned for military action. This, in part, explains his own frequently voiced disgust with the silliness and impotence of his own heroes. They, amidst the bustle of arms and the shock of opposing cultures, lead a near somnambulistic existence. As Hazlitt contemporaneously remarked:

> They are for the most part very equivocal and undecided personages, who receive their governing impulse from accident, or are puppets in the hands of their mistresses, such as Waverley, Ivanhoe, Frank Osbaldistone, Henry Morton, &c. I do not say that any of these are absolutely insipid, but they have in themselves no leading or master traits, and they are worked out of very listless and inert materials into a degree of force and prominence solely by the genius of the author. Instead of acting, they are acted upon, and keep in the back-ground and in a neutral posture, till they are absolutely forced to come forward, and it is then with a very amiable reservation of modest scruples.[63]

Hazlitt's odd notion that Scott somehow gives back with one hand what he has taken away from his heroes with the other can be better understood if we see that Scott's historicism had placed these characters in an impossible position. History in Scott is an emasculating force. Darsie, repeatedly warned by Redgauntlet of the inevitable power and force which the resurrected past has over him, symbolizes this by having to go disguised as a woman when in its power. But the new determinism, while benevolent to its adherents, equally denies individual freedom. Scott supposed that, regrettably, the new world denied man a capacity for vigorous, even violent action. Stevenson with similar regrets and yearnings for action tried to fashion an aesthetic of heroic adventure. 'I am,' he wrote ironically to James, 'an Epick Writer with a "k" to it, but without the necessary genius.'[64] His heroes are frequently more paralysed, though more interestingly so, than Scott's. Neither perceived character as being free within the context of history. Their inert (because determined) wills are merely disguised by the stirring times in which they are placed.

Scott presents us not with such freedom but with a rigid dualism. We either regress to a condition of limitless, capricious craving or assume a supposedly settled sense of secure social place. Such a dualism, of course, does not permit of any genuinely complex psychological or cultural interaction between characters. Having seen the folly of his early ways, the Scott hero opts for a Pomfret-like fantasy of unproblematic life. Worse, the implication is that this private solution represents the resolution of the national dilemma. The nation's past becomes sentimental nostalgia; its future becomes prosperous ease caused by the Union and its resultant burgeoning trade. Scott largely dehistoricized Scottish consciousness without, of course, altering the actuality of Scotland's fraught past and what was to prove its equally fraught future. This uneasy, torpid sleep was broken in the early part of this century by the major writers of the Scottish Renaissance. Writing about Edwin Muir's *Scott and Scotland*, the great Highland novelist Neil Gunn penetrated beyond the conscious rationalizations:

> . . . Scott himself, in a moment of moving self-realisation, cried out against the historical material he dealt in, calling it 'stuffing my head with the most nonsensical trash'. Scott was so great a genius that what he dealt with must have some reality to the

mind of living men. It is not that the history was untrue or was inadequate subject matter for his genius; it was that it no longer enriched or influenced a living national tradition; it had not even the potency of pure legend; it was story-telling or romance set in a void; it was seen backwards as in the round of some time spyglass and had interpretative bearing neither upon a present nor a future. Only some such intuition from Scott's 'secret world' could have drawn from him in his later years these bitter words.[65]

Romance set in a void became the essential characteristic of the nineteenth-century Scottish novel. If Scott's fiction represented an authentic engagement with historical reality, as his proponents suggest, no one has yet satisfactorily explained the absence of the realist novel in Scotland in the nineteenth century when, throughout Europe, it was at the height of its power. Ironically, Scott's historicism dehistoricized Scottish reality. The past became archaic 'romance' and the future a 'fable' of featureless progress. As Cairns Craig, discussing the concluding image of *Waverley* as time as a smooth river, has suggested:

> The image of the amnesiac drift of progress offers vividly Scott's underlying sense that the entry into the modern world is an entry into a storyless environment. Narration and history are divorced for Scott: contemporary history is a silent drift, unparticularised by name or deed; narrative can only connect with a disconnected past. If history is narration then the present is post-history; it inhabits a new realm in which there is progress without narrative. At the very moment, therefore, at which history becomes in Europe a living force, the reality in which people live, act and die, Scott divorces the Scottish present from history.[66]

'Highland' Scotland, however, remained a remarkably good literary export throughout the nineteenth century. Stevenson could neither have been ignorant of nor influenced by the work of best-selling novelists like James Grant and William Black who, respectively, dealt with the martial and, more tricky in a Victorian context, the feminine, erotic elements among the 'Celts'.[67] Indeed, Stevenson brings these elements together in these two novels. As Walter Keir has remarked concerning the malign influence on our fiction of the fantasy of Scottish history initiated by Scott:

He overshadowed the naturalistic novel, so much more sympathetic to the Scottish character, and so much better equipped to deal with the real situation in Scotland, and he did so at the moment of its first promising emergence. He established instead the historical novel as the dominant form. And he handed down to others, less ably equipped than himself, a suspect attitude to Scotland and a suspect literary formula—a suspect literary formula because it tends to shapelessness, and because it emphasises description and narrative at the expense of dramatisation. ('Description and narrative form and essence of the novel,' Scott writes in his life of Fielding).

As for the suspect attitude to Scotland, it was limited, it was largely concerned with what was already dead, and it was 'romantic'. And of course the acceptance of such an attitude was all the more tempting because of the actual conditions in Scotland, because it was becoming increasingly difficult to see Scotland clearly, and establish a genuine identity out of so many confused fragments. Stevenson provides an interesting example of what I mean. Brought up in Scotland whose grey present seemed to contradict this 'romantic' past, he was thwarted by its Calvinism and respectability and its dull materialistic monotony. 'Oh, my sighings after romance,' he writes, 'and O, the weary age that will not produce it.' 'Is there not some escape?' he adds—and of course, there was an escape ready made, an escape to the hills and the heather, to *Kidnapped* and *The Master of Ballantrae*, and to the vicious doctrine that 'stories may be nourished with the realities of life, but their true mark is to satisfy the reader's nameless longings, and to obey the ideal laws of the day-dream.' And this is the side of Stevenson most widely imitated, and, significantly, it was imitated even by Kailyard writers. And this too indicates the line which moves with decreasing conviction from Scott, through Stevenson himself, and then on to Neil Munro and Buchan, and whose final literary importance can not unjustly be estimated by that very destination.[68]

In the main, Stevenson's own comments about *Kidnapped* do little to contradict Keir's acerbic comments. In fact they often corroborate them. The novel's 'Dedication' to Charles Baxter contains the following:

This is no furniture for the scholar's library, but a book for the winter evening school-room when the tasks are over and the hour for bed draws near; and honest Alan, who was a grim old fire-eater in his day, has in this new avatar no more desperate purpose than to steal some young gentleman's attention from his Ovid, carry him awhile into the Highlands and the last century, and pack him to bed with some engaging images to mingle with his dreams.[69]

At best, Highland history has lost even its power to create subconscious anxiety which is still discernible in Scott and had become mere entertainment. This kind of historical writing is simply escapism from the present. We need not, of course, take Stevenson's statement at face value. Mark Twain, not irrelevantly as we shall see, made a similar protestation of *Huckleberry Finn*'s disrelation to serious matters of life and morality. Subsequent to its publication, Stevenson, however, wrote to the critic T. Watts-Dunton in a manner which shows us an awareness that the book had a more complex, uncomfortable life than that of mere adolescent fantasy:

> What you say about the two parts in *Kidnapped* was felt by no one more painfully than by myself. I began it partly as a lark, partly as a pot-boiler; and suddenly it moved, David and Alan stepped out from the canvas, and I found I was in another world. But there was the cursed beginning, and a cursed end must be appended; and our old friend Byles the butcher was plainly audible tapping at the back of the door. So it had to go into the world, one part (as it does seem to me) alive, one part merely galvanised: no work, only an essay. For a man of tentative method, and weak health, and a scarcity of private means and not too much of that frugality which is the artist's proper virtue, the days of sinecures and patrons look very golden: the days of professional literature very hard. Yet I do not so far deceive myself as to think I should change my character by changing my epoch; the sum of virtue in our books is in a relation of equality to the sum of virtues in ourselves; and my *Kidnapped* was doomed, while still in the womb and while I was yet in the cradle, to be the thing it is.[70]

This is an extraordinary compendium of both Stevenson's literary vices and the critical problems he engenders. The vices are only slightly mitigated by his own guilty awareness of them. His Calvinist-inspired surrender to commercial need, his public and 'fate', deny freedom to art. He, the most sensitive of stylists, is capable of crudely changing genre within

171

both his short stories and novels. Acutely aware of distinct types of fiction, he can still disconcertingly and self-destructively change type, a change usually made in the direction of an escape into the 'safe' form of the adventure story and away from the moral and metaphysical difficulties which he has initiated. Thus *Kidnapped* begins as an adventure story, lark and pot-boiler, and develops into a novel of character only for 'a cursed end [to] be appended'. In part, however, *Kidnapped* does transcend the category of boy's adventure story. While not uninfluenced by his friendship with Stevenson, Henry James, who generally abhorred the puerile masculinity he found so dominant in the late nineteenth-century English novel, agreed with Stevenson about the ending and also about the quality of the major part in between.

> There would have been a kind of perverse humility in his keeping up the fiction that a production so literary as *Kidnapped* is addressed to immature minds; and though it was originally given to the world, I believe, in a 'boy's paper,' the story embraces every occasion that it meets to satisfy the higher criticism. It has two weak spots, which need simply to be mentioned. The cruel and miserly uncle, in the first chapters, is rather in the tone of superseded tradition, and the tricks he plays upon his ingenuous nephew are a little like those of country conjurors; in these pages we feel that Mr. Stevenson is thinking too much of what a 'boy's paper' is expected to contain. Then the history stops without ending, as it were; but I think I may add that this accident speaks for itself. Mr. Stevenson has often to lay down his pen for reasons that have nothing to do with the failure of inspiration, and the last page of David Balfour's adventures is an honourable plea for indulgence.[71]

Having compared *Kidnapped* as comparable to *Henry Esmond* as a 'fictive autobiography in archaic form', James went on to describe the novel's success as arising from its fusion of Scottish 'racial' history and individual psychology.

> The life, the humour, the colour of the central portions of *Kidnapped* have a singular pictorial virtue; these passages read like a series of inspired footnotes on some historic page. The charm of the most romantic episode in the world—though perhaps it would be hard to say why it is the most romantic, when it was intermingled with so much stupidity—is over the

whole business, and the forlorn hope of the Stuarts is revived for us without evoking satiety.[72]

Whether 'inspired footnotes' can quite add up to a major historical novel is doubtful. Also, although he himself initiates the question regarding the actual 'romance' of the '45, can we be confident that James fully considers the book's relation to the historical reality so described. For James, however, such a questionable historical foundation does nothing to detract from 'five-sixths' of the novel's success. Action and character are congruent with 'the charm of the most romantic episode in the world':

> There could be no better instance of the author's talent for seeing the actual in the marvellous, and reducing the extravagant to plausible detail, than the description of Alan Breck's defence in the cabin of the ship, and the really magnificent chapters of 'The Flight in the Heather'. Mr. Stevenson has, in a high degree (and doubtless for good reasons of his own), what may be called the imagination of physical states, and this has enabled him to arrive at a wonderfully exact notation of the miseries of his panting Lowland hero, dragged for days and nights over hill and dale, through bog and thicket, without meat or drink or rest, at the tail of an Homeric Highlander.[73]

There is no doubt that Stevenson's near constant state of invalidism in the British climate gave him an acute sense of what it was to be ill and, occasionally, the extraordinary blessing of feeling really well. There was in him, albeit usually repressed, a Keatsian gusto in his appetite for experience. Such physical states are, of course, of the essence of the adventure story. Most of John Buchan is to be found in Stevenson. James, however, felt that Stevenson had not only created a Dumas-like romance but had added to it 'a fineness of grain with which Dumas never had anything to do'. He had added psychological perception to harsh, physical veracity:

> The great superiority of the book resides, to my mind, however, in the fact that it puts two characters on their feet in an admirably upright way. I have paid my tribute to Alan Breck, and I can only repeat that he is a masterpiece. It is interesting to observe that, though the man is extravagant, the author's touch exaggerates nothing; it is, throughout, of the most genial,

ironical kind, full of penetration, but with none of the grossness of moralising satire. The figure is a genuine study, and nothing can be more charming than the way Mr. Stevenson both sees through it and admires it.[74]

Though he develops somewhat, there is, it should be remarked, a considerable degree of transparency in the character of Alan Breck as we first find him. 'His eyes', we are told, 'were unusually light and had a kind of dancing madness in them that was both engaging and alarming.' More disconcertingly, this manic bundle of violent Highland energy is so described after the siege of the round house:

> Thereupon he turned to the four enemies, passed his sword clean through each of them, and tumbled them out of doors one after the other. As he did so, he kept humming and singing and whistling to himself, like a man trying to recall an air; only what *he* was trying, was to make one. All the while, the flush was in his face, and his eyes were as bright as a five-year-old child's with a new toy.[75]

This is far more like a boy's fantasy of violence than violence itself. Given that Alan is also in the throes of composing a Gaelic ode to his own prowess it is, indeed, a Highland comic-cut. If anything, however, James was even more impressed by David Balfour:

> Shall I say that he sees through David Balfour? This would be, perhaps, to underestimate the density of that medium. Beautiful, at any rate, is the expression which this unfortunate though circumspect youth gives to those qualities which combine to exite our respect and our objurgations in the Scottish character. Such a scene as the episode of the quarrel of the two men on the mountain-side is a real stroke of genius, and has the very logic of rhythm of life—a quarrel which we feel to be inevitable, though it is about nothing, or almost nothing, and which springs from exasperated nerves and the simple shock of temperaments. The author's vision of it has a profundity which goes deeper, I think, than *Dr. Jekyll*.[76]

There is certainly a sense of nuances of their relationship more subtle than anything in Scott. The Scott stereotypes of daring Jacobite and stolid Whig, however, remain intact.

In our own more knowing, if perhaps less wise age, another

American commentator, Leslie A. Fiedler, with his tremulous sensitivity to the homo-erotic, has provided a more explicit commentary on the story's 'exasperated nerves and the simple shock of temperaments'. In so doing he places *Kidnapped* in the context of Stevenson's other work:

> *Kidnapped*, like *Treasure Island*, was written for a boys' magazine, and in both all important relationships are between males. In *Kidnapped*, however, the relation of the Boy and the Scoundrel, treated as a flirtation in the earlier book, becomes almost a full-fledged love affair, a pre-sexual romance; the antagonists fall into lover's quarrels and make up, swear to part forever, and remain together. The Rogue this time is Alan Breck Stewart, a rebel, a deserter, perhaps a murderer, certainly vain beyond forgiveness and without a shred of Christian morality. The narrator and foil in this book (certainly, technically, the most economical—perhaps, in that respect, the best of Stevenson) are one: David Balfour is Jim Hawkins and Captain Smollett fused into one single person. David must measure the Scoundrel against himself, and the more unwillingly come to love that which he must disapprove. Here good and evil are more subtly defined, more ambiguous: pious Presbyterian and irreverent Catholic, solid defender of the status quo and fantastic dreamer of the Restoration—in short, Highlander and Lowlander, Scotland divided against itself. It is the Lowlander that Stevenson *was* who looks longingly and disapprovingly at the alien dash, the Highland fecklessness of Alan through the eyes of David (was not Stevenson's own mother a Balfour?); but it is the Highlander he *dreamed* himself (all his life he tried vainly to prove his father's family were descended from the banned Clan MacGregor) that looks back. The sombre good man and the glittering rascal are both two and one; they war within Stevenson's single country and in his single soul.[77]

Intent on fitting *Kidnapped* into the pattern of the dark metaphysic he has partly located and partly contrived in Stevenson—a world where the 'death of evil requires the death of good'—Fiedler, while he may be right about the latent homosexual attraction between the two men, surely mistakes the novel's tone. While he had fantasies of Highland ancestry, the point here is that in the comic form of the novel—it is not like *The Master of Ballantrae* an aborted attempt at tragedy—and in its acceptance of Alan by David we have a respite, albeit a sentimental one, from the 'damned old business of the war in the members'. It is nonsense within the context of the book to describe Alan as 'vain beyond forgiveness and without a shred of Christian morality'. The book was, in fact, a holiday from Stevenson's obsession with the dark, other self. Alan as psychological antidote to this is, however, less than a fully-realized character nor, specifically, a Highland soldier of fortune.

It is difficult, however, to know to what degree the temporary assuagement of Stevenson's divided state is to be meant as symbolic of a wider healing process in Scotland itself. *Catriona* more clearly, indeed literally, indicates a marriage of the two Scotlands. Writing to J. M. Barrie in 1892, just after he had commenced work on *Catriona*, Stevenson wrote:

> I have not yet got to Alan, so I do not know if he is still alive, but David seems to have a kick or two in his shanks. I was pleased to see how the Anglo-Saxon theory fell into the trap: I gave my Lowlander a Gaelic name, and even commented on the fact in the text; yet almost all critics recognised in Alan and David a Saxon and a Celt. I know not about England; in Scotland at least, where Gaelic was spoken in Fife little over the century ago, and in Galloway not much earlier, I deny that there exists such a thing as pure Saxon, and I think it more questionable if there be such a thing as a pure Celt.[78]

If such a racial fusion had taken place, it entails that Stevenson in *Kidnapped* and *Catriona* is not wrestling with a real problem in Scottish society but merely, even playfully, illustrating a successfully passed phase in Scotland's evolution. Even regarding *The Master of Ballantrae*, James is referred to as merely having 'a trick of Celtic boastfulness' which implies that race is not essential to his demonic nature. Stevenson is, in fact, confused and confusing on this subject. He tended, with a considerable lack of conviction, to summon up Highland stereotypes to bolster that shaky sense of identity which has been the Scotsman's birthright since the Union. As a very young man visiting Germany he responded thus to hostile questions about Scotland:

> . . . and thence, as I find is always the case, to the most ghastly romancing about the Scottish scenery and manners, the

Highland dress and everything national and local I could lay my hands upon. . . . There is one thing that burthens me a good deal in my patriotic garrulage, and that is the black ignorance in which I grope about everything. . . . I am generally glad enough to fall back again upon Burns, toddy, and the Highlands.[79]

In a later essay, 'The Foreigner at Home', Stevenson returned to the problem of Scottish identity as a genuine fusion of Highland and Lowland elements.

A century and a half ago the Highlander wore a different costume, spoke a different language, worshipped in another church, held different morals, and obeyed a different social constitution from his fellow-countrymen either of the south or north. Even the English, it is recorded, did not loathe the Highlander and the Highland costume as they were loathed by the remainder of the Scots. Yet the Highlander felt himself a Scot. He would willingly raid into the Scottish lowlands; but his courage failed him at the border, and he regarded England as a perilous, unhomely land. When the Black Watch, after years of foreign service, returned to Scotland, veterans leaped out and kissed the earth at Port Patrick. They had been in Ireland, stationed among men of their own race and language, where they were well liked and treated with affection; but it was the soil of Galloway that they kissed at the extreme end of the hostile lowlands, among a people who did not understand their speech, and who had hated, harried, and hanged them since the dawn of history. Last, and perhaps most curious, the sons of chieftains were often educated on the continent of Europe. They went abroad speaking Gaelic; they returned speaking, not English, but the broad dialect of Scotland. Now, what idea had they in their minds when they thus, in thought, identified themselves with their ancestral enemies? What was the sense in which they were Scottish and not English, or Scottish and not Irish? Can a bare name be thus influential on the minds and affections of men, and a political aggregation blind them to the nature of facts? The story of the Austrian Empire would seem to answer, No; the far more galling business of Ireland clenches the negative from nearer home. Is it common education, common morals, a common language or a common faith, that join men into nations? There were practically none of these in the case we are considering.

The fact remains: in spite of the difference of blood and

Stevenson

language, the Lowlander feels himself the sentimental country-
man of the Highlander. When they meet abroad they fall upon
each other's necks in spirit; even at home there is a kind of
clannish intimacy in their talk. But from his compatriot in the
south the Lowlander stands consciously apart. He has had a
different training; he obeys different laws; he makes his will in
other terms, is otherwise divorced and married; his eyes are not
at home in an English landscape or with English houses; his ear
continues to remark the English speech; and even though his
tongue acquire the Southern knack, he will still have a strong
Scots accent of mind.[80]

This, written only two years after he was preparing to write a
critical, factual history of Scotland, is far from convincing. The
conjunction of Lowlander with Highland men and women in
Kidnapped and *Catriona* becomes merely the explication of a
sentimental thesis and not a genuine confrontation between
different cultural values. Further, by treating a theme that
according to his definition was redundant, Stevenson was able
to avoid not only the radical social problems of Highland
crofters and fishermen but, by entering into Scotland, evade
the real issues in nineteenth-century Scotland.[81] The question
of national identity (especially with regard to active participation in British Imperialism), the new industrial city, 'evangeli-
cal' capitalism and rural decline were the substance of that
history. Stevenson, partly under the guise of various anti-
realist aesthetic theories of varying degrees of inconsistency,
did not respond to them. He surrendered to that commercially
rewarding body of sentimental fantasy, a weird kind of literary
'mythology', perpetrated both by Scottish intellectuals and a
wider public, which has been the compensatory matter of
Scottish history since at least the onset of the Industrial
Revolution. We cannot think of a novelist of worth in any
nineteenth-century nation other than Scotland describing his
national history in such self-deceiving terms:

Nor must we omit the sense of the nature of his country and his
country's history gradually growing in the child's mind from
story and from observation. A Scottish child hears much of
shipwreck, outlying iron skerries, pitiless breakers, and great
sealights; much of heathery mountains, wild clans, and hunted
Covenanters. Breaths come to him in song of the distant

178

Cheviots and the ring of foraying hoofs. He glories in his hard-fisted forefathers, of the iron girdle and the handful of oatmeal, who rode so swiftly and lived so sparely on their raids. Poverty, ill-luck, enterprise, and constant resolution are the fibres of the legend of his country's history. The heroes and kings of Scotland have been tragically fated; the most marking incidents in Scottish history—Flodden, Darien, or the Forty-five—were still either failures or defeats; and the fall of Wallace and the repeated reverses of the Bruce combine with the very smallness of the country to teach rather a moral than a material criterion for life. Britain is altogether small, the mere taproot of her extended empire; Scotland, again, which alone the Scottish boy adopts in his imagination, is but a little part of that, and avowedly cold, sterile and unpopulous. The heart of young Scotland will be always touched more nearly by paucity of number and Spartan poverty of life.[82]

Given the brilliance of Stevenson's powers as a social realist revealed in that marvellous book about the reality of emigration, *The Amateur Emigrant*, this was a tragedy for the Scottish novel. The full extent of the tragedy can be gauged by comparison with a novel which Stevenson not only had in mind when he wrote *Kidnapped* but which he 'adapted' to suit his own ends. What John Jay Chapman called his 'perfectly phenomenal talent for imitation' has rarely revealed more harshly the degree to which that process led, at best, to parody and, at worst, to degenerate work. In a letter written the year before *Kidnapped*'s appearance we find the following:

> Have you read *Huckleberry Finn?* It contains many excellent things; above all, the whole story of a healthy boy's dealings with his conscience, incredibly well done.[83]

Stevenson's critical appraisal is not, however, equalled by his creative response to Twain. The parallels between the two books have not, of course, gone unremarked. As Edwin M. Eigner has noted:

> Yet the similarities between *Kidnapped* and *The Adventures of Huckleberry Finn* are far too numerous to be passed over. Here are just a few of the points which the two books have in common: Both concern newly rich orphans whose lives and fortunes are threatened by greedy men. In each case, the boy's closest living relative kidnaps and attempts to murder him. And

in both books, the boy escapes from his imprisonment under circumstances which lead others to presume him dead. He next spends a few lonely days isolated on a near-shore island and then begins a long journey in the company of an older man of a different, supposedly more primitive race, a man who is a fugitive from justice and a suspected murderer. *Kidnapped*, like *Huckleberry Finn*, is the picaresque story of a boy's wanderings through the heart of his native country. Both works are part adventure story, part travel book, part social satire, and part serious psychological romance.[84]

This is indisputable and mainly unexceptionable. Great novels have emerged partly from a thematic veneration of their predecessors. Eigner's sense of a qualitative parity between *Huckleberry Finn* and *Kidnapped* is, however, much more questionable:

> The most important similarity between Mark Twain's romance and Stevenson's is that both books depend for suspense and significance on the same thematic question: Can the boy transcend his conscience and bring himself to accept his despised companion? Huck, who has been brought up a white man in a slave state, finds himself helping the escape of a Negro. Similarly, David has been brought up a good and loyal Whig in the tense period following the 1745 rebellion. Alan Breck Stewart whose escape David assists and finances is a proscribed rebel. The problem as Stevenson states it has, of course, fewer social overtones than it has in Mark Twain's treatment, but perhaps Stevenson brings out the psychological aspects more clearly.[85]

In great fiction there cannot exist a division between 'psychological aspects' and what Eigner revealingly terms 'social overtones'. They are indivisibly part of what the imagination reveals to us. Hence, critical defenders of Stevenson perpetually get caught in this dilemma. Thus Jenni Calder in her recent introduction to *Kidnapped*:

> What he had was a profound sense of the relationship between society and *character*, rather than between society and history. To get his history right, therefore, was less important to Stevenson than getting his psychology right, in terms of social influences and personality. He used the past to provide him with an authentic environment for his psychological insight.

> . . . Cluny roots Alan firmly in the circumstances which have produced him and which have made his activities necessary. Thus Cluny is part of Stevenson's use of history to provide an authentic ambience for psychological realism.[86]

Such special pleading is based on the evasion of what is fundamentally wrong with Stevenson. It also contradicts James's notion of the relationship between past and present. Character in Stevenson's 'Highland' novels is based on false history. Such art is 'playful' rather than truthful. In comparison to Twain, Stevenson lost not only 'social overtones' but the power of creative dissent to social and political corruption. When, for example, Stevenson creates a figure like the blind preacher on Mull, this is a derivative shadow of the sinister confidence men and religious hysterics who throng the banks of Twain's Mississippi. It is undeniable that nineteenth-century Scotland and the American South are not the same places. Neither the intensity of the Negro question nor the barbaric vulgarity of small town America were present in Scotland. Yet there were and, indeed, are elements of Southern history comparable to Scotland. Twain not only loathed Scott's novels but held him largely responsible for engendering a state of pseudo-chivalric mind in the South which led to the Civil War. While this is probably going too far in terms of the inevitable symbiosis of politics and bad art, the American South and Scotland have tended to dwell in archaic, militaristic nostalgia as an antidote to their stronger, conquering neighbours. Their 'past' undermines their future. Also, Twain's theme of a grasping materialism hidden by gross sentimentality is true of both cultures. 'Soul-butter and hogwash' has been a common currency of human exchange in both regions.

Twain described *Huckleberry Finn* as 'a book of mine where a sound heart and a deformed conscience come into collision and conscience suffers defeat.' David Balfour suffers little of Huck's agony of conscience. He has no comparable inner life. In part this stems from Stevenson's manipulation of form. Twain remarked that 'a boy's life is not all comedy, much of the tragic enters into it.' While Twain himself surrendered the last parts of his book to low comedy, Stevenson's form is comic throughout. We know that David will end as a small but safe laird. It is Scott's form with dashes of Twain's realism which engenders

Kidnapped's mutant nature. Revealingly, elements of *Redgauntlet* are used in order to avoid harsh confrontation with a corrupt world. Like Alan Fairford, David is ill in *Kidnapped* and not fully, critically conscious of the ambience of Cluny's world. Like Darsie Latimer, he is held prisoner so he cannot actively involve himself in the legal corruption. As in the Scott novel, the plot is deliberately structured so that at crucial moments the hero's capacity for judgement and action is suspended. While David, self-preservingly and 'honourably', is involved in violence, this has none of the traumatic quality of Huck's experience when he sees his friend Buck or the pathetic, clownish Boggs gunned down. There is blood in Stevenson's scuppers, but this is only realistic detail in service of a fantasy initiation for (Lowland) youth. Alan Breck is more the small, bad boy than a figure comparable to Twain's 'aristocrats' with their contemptuous, murderous habits. Twain fashioned an innocent eye which reveals his world in terms of both extraordinary humour and terror. Stevenson does not similarly expose adolescence to the world but, as James said, involves it in the safety of a game:

> . . . he speaks as a contemporary absorbed in his own game. That game is almost always a vision of dangers and triumphs; and if emotion, with him, infallibly resolves itself into memory, so memory is an evocation of throbs and thrills and suspense. He has given the world the romance of boyhood, as others have produced that of peerage, the police and the medical profession.[87]

Despite getting married at the end of *Catriona*, David is not really either socially or sexually marked by experience. As in *Kidnapped*, the Highlanders are adumbrated as both loyal and yet trapped by their 'tailforemost', 'traditional' values. Yet, astonishingly, Highland disbelief in the Lowland legal process shown in *Kidnapped* is not examined in terms of the collapse of law caused by political pressure in the second novel. This lack of genuine moral seriousness is exposed by Jenni Calder in attempting to defend *Catriona*:

> *Catriona* is, appropriately, an acutely political book. David's dash to Inverary at first appears to be noble, romantic re-entry into the territory of Highland adventure, but soon emerges for what it really represents: the confirmation of his position in the

Lowland professional scene. His vigour and application, his good sense and canniness become harnessed to the cause of Whig moderation, a moderation that sacrifices truth in the cause of control. He has helped to save Alan Breck, the romantic Jacobite, but he understands that the episode is, on the terms that he has to accept and like his attempted rescue of James Stewart, really an aberration.[88]

Actually, it is the capacity of the Scott-inspired 'best-seller' to have things both ways. In a mature culture the sacrifice of 'truth to the cause of control' might be seen as a theme of tragic seriousness. Indeed, in *Weir of Hermiston* Stevenson at least tackled the problem. *Catriona* is, however, finally and pervasively sentimental. Hence such defences of it:

> Yet the strengths of the earlier part of the novel are the results of Stevenson's psychological perception of history and ironic grasp of character at their very best. He builds his people out of the same material as he builds his city.[89]

Nonetheless, this should not make us countenance hardness of heart in men bent on political execution:

> Prestongrange and Simon Fraser, for instance, both real people: Stevenson handles their personalities and the intricacies of their devious politics with fine control, exemplified almost entirely through their speech. It is out of their own mouths that they reveal who and what they are, and their refined, astute and robustly Scottish sense of what they are doing.[90]

There seems no end to such sentimental evasion in Scottish self-awareness. It pollutes both our creative writing and our criticism. At his best Stevenson struggled with it and infrequently broke free.[91] His Highland novels are sadly not of that order. Out of his own mouth, discussing Walter Scott, he revealed what they and the Scott-inspired tradition they represent really are:

> It seems to me that the explanation is to be found in the very quality of his surprising merits. As his books are play to the reader, so they were play to him. He conjured up the romantic with delight, but he had hardly patience to describe it. He was a great day-dreamer, a seer of fit and beautiful and humorous visions, but hardly a great artist; hardly, in the manful sense, an

artist at all. He pleased himself, and so he pleases us. Of the pleasures of his art he tasted fully; but of its toils and vigils and distresses never man knew less. A great romantic—an idle child.[92]

NOTES

1. *Letters to his Family and Friends*, ed Colvin, 2 vols. (London, 1900), I, p. 194. Henceforth *Letters*.
2. *Letters*, I, p. 193.
3. *Letters*, II, p. 157.
4. This letter to Colvin is in Vol. IV, Tusitala Edition of Letters (London, 1924), p. 113.
5. Ibid., p. 114.
6. *Henry James and Robert Louis Stevenson*, ed. Janet Adam Smith (London, 1948), p. 255. Henceforth *James and Stevenson*.
7. *Letters*, I, p. 316. Stevenson's most extended commentary on Scott's carelessness in matters of dramatic form and style is to be found in 'A Gossip on Romance', Vol. XXIX, Tusitala Edition (London, 1924), pp. 129–31.
8. *Letters*, I, p. 211.
9. Ibid., p. 74.
10. Ibid., p. 301.
11. See Archer's criticisms of Stevenson in *Robert Louis Stevenson: The Critical Heritage* (London, 1981). Archer, a Scotsman, was the foremost drama critic of his day. He was known and his work admired by both Stevenson and James. With John Jay Chapman, he is Stevenson's most trenchant and best nineteenth-century critic.
12. *Letters*, I, p. 270.
13. *James and Stevenson*, pp. 56–7.
14. Ibid., p. 57.
15. Ibid., pp. 89–91.
16. *Hawthorne* (London, 1967), p. 55.
17. 'On Henry James', *The Question of Henry James*, ed. Dupee (New York, 1973), p. 116.
18. See Hawthorne, *The English Notebooks*, ed. Stewart (New York, 1972), for accounts of his travels in Scotland in 1856–57.
19. *James and Stevenson*, p. 141.
20. Ibid., pp. 254–55.
21. Ibid., pp. 139–40.
22. *The Selected Letters of Henry James*, ed. Edel (New York, 1960), p. 53.
23. Ibid., pp. 51–2.
24. *Robert Louis Stevenson: His Work and His Personality* (London, 1924), p. 147.

25. 'An Ode on the Popular Superstitions of the Highlands of Scotland, considered as the subject of Poetry' is a dire source of clichés.
26. See Part Four of Hazard's *The European Mind 1680–1715* (London, 1964).
27. 'On the Pleasure of Hating', *Collected Works*, ed. Weller and Glover (London, 1903), VII, p. 129.
28. See Hazard, *The European Mind* and *The Wild Man Within*, ed. Dudley and Novak (Pittsburgh, 1972).
29. 'In Quest of George Lippard' in *Cross the Border—Close the Gap* (New York, 1972), p. 102.
30. 'Coriolanus', *Collected Works*, Vol. I, p. 216.
31. In *Dreams of Adventure, Deeds of Empire* (London, 1980), Green attempts to define the adventure novel as a major fictional form. What he actually achieves is to reveal the extraordinary level of violence prevailing in British life both in terms of fantasy and imperial practice in the late nineteenth century. See my review of Green's book 'Literary Empires and Scotch Imperials', *Scottish Literary Journal*, Supplement No. 15, Winter 1981, pp. 91–100.
32. *James and Stevenson*, p. 256.
33. *Memorials of his Own Time* (Edinburgh, 1945), pp. 118–19.
34. *The Letters of Sir Walter Scott*, 12 vols. (London, 1932–37), I, pp. 342–43.
35. *Letters*, Vol. III, p. 302.
36. *Peter's Letters to his Kinsfolk*, ed. Ruddick (Edinburgh, 1977), p. 132.
37. Ibid., pp. 131–32.
38. 'The Three Dreams of Scottish Nationalism' in *Memoirs of a Modern Scotland*, ed. Miller (London, 1970), p. 39.
39. See my essay, 'The Literati and the Tradition', in *Order in Space and Society*, ed. Markus (Edinburgh, 1982).
40. *Albyn* (London, 1927), p. 17.
41. This is quoted by Michael Chapman in his interesting book, *The Gaelic Vision in Scottish Culture* (London, 1978).
42. *Lucky Poet* (London, 1972), p. 202.
43. 'Scott and Tradition', in *Edwin Muir: Uncollected Scottish Criticism*, ed. Noble (London and New York, 1982), p. 209.
44. *Rob Roy* (London, 1894), p. 12.
45. Ibid., p. 154.
46. *Coleridge's Miscellaneous Criticism*, ed. Raysor (London, 1937), p. 335.
47. *Walter Scott* (Edinburgh, 1982), p. 18.
48. 'The Rationalism of Sir Walter Scott', *The Cambridge Journal*, Vol. VII, No. 1, pp. 20–35.
49. *Waverley*, ed. Hook (London, 1972), p. 49.
50. *Rob Roy*, p. 182.
51. *Scott and Society* (London, 1982).
52. *Stevenson: The Critical Heritage*, p. 492.
53. *Collected Letters*, ed. Griggs (London, 1972), Vol. V, No. 1229, pp. 34–5.
54. For an explicit denial of the relevance of Scott's novels to history see *On the Constitution of Church and State*, ed. Barrell (London, 1972), p. 83.
55. *Waverley*, pp. 372, 394.
56. See my essay 'Blake, Burns and Romantic Revolt' in *The Art of Robert*

Burns, ed. Jack and Noble (London and New York, 1982), pp. 211–12.
57. *Rob Roy*, p. 268.
58. *Waverley*, p. 36.
59. Ibid., p. 354.
60. *Cross the Border—Close the Gap*, p. 101.
61. *Redgauntlet* (London, 1936), p. 58.
62. Ibid., p. 52.
63. 'Why the Heroes of Romance are Insipid', *Collected Works*, Vol. XII, pp. 65–6.
64. *James and Stevenson*, p. 218.
65. Review of *Scott and Scotland*, *The Scots Magazine*, Vol. XXVI (October, 1936), p. 73.
66. 'The Body in the Kitbag: History and the Scottish Novel', *Cencrastus*, No. 1, Autumn 1979, p. 19.
67. For a masterly analysis of the nature of Black's commercial success see 'Best Sellers of Yesterday: VI William Black', *Edwin Muir: Uncollected Scottish Criticism*, pp. 222–27.
68. 'Scottish History and Scottish Fiction', *Saltire Review*, Vol. 1, No. 1, April 1954, pp. 31–2.
69. *Kidnapped* (Edinburgh, 1980), p. xxiii.
70. *Letters*, II, pp. 41–2.
71. *James and Stevenson*, pp. 157–58.
72. Ibid., p. 158.
73. Ibid., pp. 158–59.
74. Ibid., p. 159.
75. *Kidnapped*, p. 62.
76. *James and Stevenson*, p. 159.
77. 'R. L. S. Revisited', *No! in Thunder* (New York, 1967), pp. 81–2.
78. *Letters*, Vol. II, p. 248.
79. Ibid., I, p. 35.
80. *Memories and Portraits*, Tusitala Edition, Vol. XXIX (London, 1924), pp. 10–11.
81. As a boy of sixteen he had seen such discontent first-hand in Wick. 'An *émeute* of disappointed fishers was feared, and two ships of war are in the bay to render assistance to the municipal authorities. This is the idea; and to all intents and purposes, said ideas are passed. Still there is a good deal of disturbance, many drunk men, and a double supply of police' (*Letters*, Vol. I, pp. 17–18).
82. 'The Foreigner at Home', pp. 9–10.
83. *Letters*, Vol. I, p. 351.
84. *Robert Louis Stevenson and the Romantic Tradition* (Princeton, 1966), pp. 79–80.
85. Ibid., pp. 80–1.
86. *Kidnapped*, pp. xii, xiv.
87. *James and Stevenson*, pp. 132–33.
88. *Catriona* (Edinburgh, 1980), p. xvi.
89. Ibid., pp. xii–xiv.
90. Ibid., p. xiv.

91. See 'Robert Louis Stevenson', *Edwin Muir: Uncollected Scottish Criticism*, for a remarkable account of Stevenson's struggle against Scotland's anti-creative environment.
92. 'A Gossip on Romance', p. 131.

7

Robert Louis Stevenson: Forms of Evasion

by PETER GILMOUR

The setting of 'Benito Cereno' is not secondary to it, but essential, for the isolated ship-load of negroes becomes a burden which Don Aranda bears until the end—and which is born by white men still today. The ship becalmed off the silent coast is a dramatic device used by Melville to concentrate the potentially murderous relationship that exists between colonial whites and dispossessed blacks. To use such a device is to present the antagonism as it has become, in all its terrible richness, not as it might be expediently resolved one way or the other. The cultures of the two races must be present, of course, if only indirectly, if this is to be achieved. The ways in which the dominant whites have created potential oppressors in the subservient race must be implicit in the narrative; it must be possible to imagine both the societies whose ways these are and the societies resolved to subvert the imperial will. If this is not in the narrative, the story may belong to the adventure-story genre; the causes of the conflict and the nature of its resolution may be more or less gratuitous. And if in this genre the white ends the conflict by befriending the black, or by persuading him into happy dependence, then the genre must be seen as presupposing the very imperialism which writers like Melville question.

'You are saved,' cried Captain Delano, more and more astonished and pained. 'You are saved; what has cast such a shadow upon you?'
'The Negro.'[1]

The famous words with which Kurz dies in Conrad's 'Heart of Darkness' ('The horror! The horror!') also reflect backwards into the story; they too presuppose a relationship between the character and the natives in which each side has lastingly affected the other. And Marlowe, narrating, the recipient of these last words, is himself breathed upon by the culture in which Kurz has gone mad. The heart of darkness is experienced by the one and apprehended as a possibility by the other. But it would be to miss Conrad's point to say that the evil is imported into the jungle by the white man, there rioting and spending itself; or that the jungle seduces the white man, previously decent but vulnerable, into evil. The point in Melville's great story as in Conrad's is that evil in such situations is the expression of a relationship. It is not simply the attribute of the white tribe or the black (though a case could fairly be made for seeing the imperialists as the prime movers in this particular dance of death), but a condition generated by the meetings of the two over centuries—a condition which both now in different ways and from different points of view know and sustain. It is a view which disputes that any primitive culture can be seen as merely passive, as simply acted upon, as without effective will. If it is passive, it has become so, and the writer's task is to consider how this has happened. To point to this passivity as a charming feature of primitive societies is questionable, betraying as it usually does the dominant culture's wish to remain dominant. (Some celebrations of the primitive are imperialist by implication. A landscape, for example, can be praised in print or paint because it is thought to induce mildness in the natives.) And there is the further claim, developed in Melville into a challenge, that this disorder between black and white is part of our heritage. Neither side can think or act as if things had been otherwise; the shadow which Don Aranda speaks of is over us still and the possibility of our acting so as to deepen it is eternally present.

*   *   *

189

'The Beach of Falesá' and *The Ebb-Tide*, the South Sea Island stories of Robert Louis Stevenson, have often been praised, and it is my intention in this essay to consider whether they stand comparison with Melville and Conrad, and, if not, whether this is necessarily a reflection on them.

'The Beach of Falesá' begins with Wiltshire, a trader, coming to Falesá. He has heard that Case, the most powerful man on the island, has a 'gallows bad reputation', but to begin with he is impressed by him. Like many of Stevenson's villains, Case is educated and of good family. His only redeeming quality, it turns out, is his kindness to his wife. He arranges for Wiltshire to pick a wife from the native women, writes the marriage certificate himself and then, with Wiltshire married to Uma, disappears. Wiltshire opens his store but, attracting no customers, concludes that he has been tabooed. Even the pastor, 'a big buck Kanaka', recoils from him. Rather to his surprise, Wiltshire now discovers that he is in love with Uma. Even when she tells him that she is the cause of the ban, Case having spread unpleasant rumours about her, he cannot leave her.

> . . . It's strange how it hits a man when he's in love; for there's no use mincing things; Kanaka and all, I was in love with her, or just as good. I tried to take her hand, but she would have none of that. 'Uma,' I said, 'there's no sense in carrying on like that. I want you to stop here, I want my little wifie, I tell you true.'
>
> 'No tell me true,' she sobbed.
>
> 'All right,' says I, 'I'll wait till you're through with this.' And I sat right down beside her on the floor, and set to smooth her hair with my hand. At first she wriggled away when I touched her; then she seemed to notice me no more; then her sobs grew gradually less, and presently stopped; and the next thing I knew, she raised her face to mine.
>
> 'You tell me true? You like me stop?' she asked.
>
> 'Uma,' I said, 'I would rather have you than all the copra in the South Seas,' which was a very big expression, and the strangest thing was that I meant it.[2]

It suits Case, therefore, to have Wiltshire marry Uma. But it must also be said that it suits Stevenson, for it allows him to avoid taking Wiltshire seriously as a trader, as a man for whom profit is an important goal, if not the important goal. He is too infatuated with his native bride to care much about trading. Further, it allows Stevenson to pay no attention to Wiltshire as a white man with racist tendencies. In love with Uma, he isn't troubled by the fact that she is black; his racism is suspended. Thus seen, Wiltshire's relationship with Uma is a sentimental device which allows Stevenson to avoid the challenge of representing Wiltshire as a trader, and as a trader with racist views at that.

Tarleton, a missionary, then reveals that Case was responsible for the deaths or banishment of the previous traders, and confirms Uma's view of his present treatment of Wiltshire. Case, we discover, has the native population at his mercy: even Namu, a pastor, is under his spell. Much of the drama in the second part of the story comes from Wiltshire's discovery of how Case has come to dominate the island. By hanging harps in the trees, so that they whine in the wind, by a careful placing of idols and scarecrows and luminous faces, Case has put himself in a position to exploit the superstitions of the natives. He has convinced them that, intimate with the devil (either controlling him by prayer—Namu's belief—or, horrifyingly, his familiar, doing his will), his command of the island is not to be disputed. Understanding how Case controls Falesá, Wiltshire sees how he can be unmasked. The stage is thus set for the dénouement. But the question now has to be faced whether it is the dénouement of a sophisticated adventure story, or of something more serious. At this point in the narrative there appears the following passage, revealing not just in itself, but by being placed here, just before the dénouement. It is possible that it betrays the terms on which we are to take not just the dénouement, but the whole story; that it betrays its level, the genre to which, in spite of early appearances, it finally belongs. Case may not quite be a 'bad guy'; but it is possible that he is closer to that type than he is to Kurz.

> . . . It's easy to find out what Kanakas think. Just go back to yourself anyway round from ten to fifteen years old, and there's an average Kanaka. There are some pious, just as there are pious boys; and most of them, like boys again, are middling honest and yet think it rather larks to steal, and are easy scared, and rather like to be so. I remember a boy I was at school with

at home who played the Case business. He didn't know anything, that boy; he couldn't do anything; he had no luminous
paint and no Tyrolean harps; he just boldly said he was a
sorcerer, and frightened us out of our boots, and we loved it.
And then it came in my mind how the master had once flogged
that boy, and the surprise we were all in to see the sorcerer
catch it and hum like anybody else. Thinks I to myself: 'I must
find some way of fixing it so for Master Case.' And the next
moment I had my idea.[3]

So Wiltshire thinks of the Kanakas as children, with the sense
of adventure and threat that children have. But is it only he
who thinks of them this way, who represents their responses in
terms of the behaviour of white school-children? And is it only
the Kanakas who have this childish view of Case?

Against the charge that Stevenson too considers the natives
to be like children it can be argued that the narrator is
Wiltshire, not Stevenson. But there is nothing in the South Sea
Island stories to counter the view that, for Stevenson, the
natives were simple, passive, incapable of effective resistance.
The vices in Falesá are imported ones; they are white vices. If
there is a Falesán vice, it is the inability to manage intelligent
opposition. It is easy for Case; his passion as a trader can
express itself unopposed. It may be, though, that this notion of
the natives as childlike and impressionable is another evasion.
If the climax of the story is to be a fight between two white
men, the natives must be represented as interested spectators,
dreading the one outcome, praying for the other, but themselves too unintelligent, too mild, to play a decisive part in
what happens to their island. Everything in the narrative must
be subordinated to the struggle between the decent white man
and the bad white man. Put contentiously, Stevenson's appetite
for adventure stories, in which a boy-scout worthiness triumphs
over shabbiness, led him to misrepresent the natives, to
sentimentalize them, to dodge the challenge of staring them
full in the face. (The appetite may have been rooted, in fact, in
his inability to respond to such challenges.) Certainly it is not
Melville's view of the relationship between traders and natives
in this part of the world.

But although the horrible apprehension had been dispelled, I
had discovered enough to fill me, in my present state of mind,

with the most bitter reflections. It was plain that I had seen the last relic of some unfortunate wretch, who must have been massacred on the beach by the savages, in one of those perilous trading adventures which I have before described.[4]

There is no hint of this in 'The Beach of Falesá' or *The Ebb-Tide*. Evil is apparently peculiar to the whites. But it has to be considered whether even white evil is adequately portrayed.

Case reminds Wiltshire of a boy who pretended to be a sorcerer. True, he says that this is how the Kanakas regard Case, but there is the suspicion that for Wiltshire too Case's career as tyrant-trader can be described in terms of this boyish episode. The episode is concluded when the boy is caned, and shows pain. His malignity is only apparent; it can be banished by authority; there is nothing to fear. Wiltshire, recalling the episode, says: 'I must find some way of fixing it so for Master Case.' The very language invites us to look forward to the dénouement with a certain levity. (Did Billy Budd and Claggart square up to each other thus?) Case has come closer and closer to the bad-guy stereotype. It may not be possible to expose his menace as only apparent (though he does seem to have been characterized more in terms of his practical ingenuity—the harps, the luminous faces—than of the malign will which presumably lies behind it; the reader has to supply the latter, but he gets little help from Stevenson), but the suggestion is that he can be dispatched as effectively and conclusively as the schoolboy sorcerer was exposed.

And this indeed is what happens. Wiltshire stalks Case, creates an explosion in the forest; has a fight with Case; Case is killed. Wiltshire's injuries are not serious, nor are Uma's, who has appeared at the last moment to help Wiltshire. Wiltshire is then the only trader in Falesá, and does well; no other trader arrives to challenge his decency. Nothing of Case survives; all evil has died with him. This shouldn't surprise us, for Case, as we have seen, has been an inadequate incarnation of the malign. There is no heritage of evil in Falesá for his career to complicate. He is not seen as a casualty of the confused meetings between blacks and whites over the centuries, and so he throws no shadow forwards, into the future.

This is very far from Conrad and Melville. The horror of

which Kurz speaks, the evil which, at the last, is at the heart of him, is also outside him and so survives his death. It is not diminished by it. It remains a possibility, for the natives and for Marlowe, because it is as old as the antagonism between the races. And, for Melville, the emphasis at the end of 'Benito Cereno' is on the future too. Don Aranda speaks not only of the present but of what is to come. And the worst is to come. He realizes, as the characters in Stevenson do not, that he is part of a dire historical process. In part an investigation of what is working to generate the worst, 'Benito Cereno' is finally prophetic.

But Wiltshire's defeat of Case is not quite the end of 'The Beach of Falesá'. There is a disturbing last paragraph, in which Wiltshire's racism is allowed to surface.

> My public house? Not a bit of it, nor ever likely. I'm stuck here, I fancy. I don't like to leave the kids, you see; and—there's no use talking—they're better here than what they would be in a white man's country, though Ben took the eldest up to Auckland, where he's being schooled with the best. But what bothers me is the girls. They're only half-castes, of course; I know that as well as you do, and there's nobody thinks less of half-castes than I do; but they're mine, and about all I've got. I can't reconcile my mind to their taking up with Kanakas, and I'd like to know where I'm to find the whites?[5]

It is as though, at the very end, Stevenson is trying to transcend the genre by which he has cautiously allowed himself to be bounded. As though he is trying to suggest that the story has addressed itself to the racial issues inherent in it. But since Wiltshire's infatuation with Uma—which has subdued his racism, his sense of being importantly different from the Kanakas—has run parallel with his contest with Case, there has been no occasion to do so in the story. The infatuation has served Stevenson well. It has allowed him to remain within the adventure-story genre. It has allowed him to proceed as if race were not an issue. But isn't it plausible, it might be argued, that now that Wiltshire has got over his infatuation with Uma he should notice her blackness, be troubled by the status of half-castes? It is a measure of Stevenson's narrative ingenuity that it is plausible. But it can still be suggested that the device of the infatuation has allowed Stevenson to avoid certain imaginative challenges. Wiltshire is never given his head as a trader or as a racist—not to mention as a racist-trader. The story is limited, therefore, because the characterization is limited. And the characterization is limited because the narrator has been placed in circumstances which allow Stevenson to present him as more morally simple than he is. The last paragraph, though it can be defended as consistent, makes us aware of this.

At the start of *The Ebb-Tide* Herrick, one of the main characters, reads Virgil and writes the opening bars of Beethoven's Fifth Symphony on the walls of a hut. He is degraded, and by reading 'O three and four times fortunate, you whose lot it was to die beneath the lofty walls of Troy before the faces of your fathers' and listening to 'destiny knocking at the door' he draws attention to the unheroic nature of his past and to his lack of a future. Captain Davis then arrives with a plan which, if Herrick can overcome his scruples, will give him a future. After a brief struggle with himself, he accepts the plan. But the future which it gives him is no more heroic than his past: the terms of his acceptance insure a continuation of self-disgust. The options in his world are all humiliating ones; but the only alternative is imprisonment and death. He moves from being a derelict among derelicts to a thief among thieves. But because his two fellow thieves lose themselves in drink Herrick also knows, on the schooner *Farallone*, a peculiar strength.

> . . . He who had proved his incapacity in so many fields, being now falsely placed amid duties which he did not understand, without help, and it might be said without countenance, had hitherto surpassed expectation; and even the shameful misconduct and shocking disclosures of that night seemed but to nerve and strengthen him. He had sold his honour; he vowed it should not be in vain; 'it shall be no fault of mine if this miscarry,' he repeated. And in his heart he wondered at himself. Living rage no doubt supported him; no doubt also, the sense of the last cast, of the ships burned, of all doors closed but one, which is so strong a tonic to the merely weak, and so deadly a depressant to the merely cowardly.[6]

So Stevenson is committed to the difficult task of tracing the course of one whose education discloses the possibility of heroism and freedom but who finds himself in a situation where neither seems to be possible. To the Kanaka crew, Herrick is good compared to the past and present captains. They aren't in a position to see either that the terms of his contract have placed goodness beyond him or that his education is tormenting him with a sense of what he has lost. But what is lost can sometimes be recovered. The possibility of moral restitution has to be taken seriously. If it is plausible that Herrick has despaired of it, is it acceptable for Stevenson to write as if, beyond a certain point (which Herrick seems to have passed), there is no such thing? Are we to take the replacement of the beach by the schooner and of the schooner by Attwater's island as a sign that, while the forms of Herrick's imprisonment may vary, the fact of it will not? Have his failures been so many and so serious that his sense of being damned, of being an outcast from grace, is inevitable? How adequate is Stevenson's attempt to develop his dilemma? Is it built into the conclusion of the story, or, an embarrassment, allowed to drop away? Has Stevenson once more (though more directly than in 'The Beach of Falesá') touched on issues which he cannot finally face?

A combination of a 'paltry degree' and the failure of his father's business obliges Herrick to take jobs which boredom prevents him from doing well. He becomes known for his incompetence, not for his 'talent' and 'taste', both apparently considerable. Then, too poor now to support his family (his original motive), he signs on board a ship, his self-respect utterly gone. It is not just that the details of this stage of Herrick's life are skimped (why, if his aim is to be of support to his family, does he leave England for New York?). More seriously, there is some disparity between what happens to him, most unpleasant though it is, and how he comes to feel about himself. The case is not adequately made for his moral and spiritual bankruptcy. If he is to convince us as a man who feels himself to be damned, more than misfortune will have to be shown. But he comes over as a victim rather than as a sinner, and it is only sinners who can feel damnation. A deep feeling of incompetence, of unfitness for worldly matters, has been confused by Stevenson with a sense of damnation. So between

Herrick as we first meet him and Stevenson's account of how he got there there is an unsatisfactory gulf.

> . . . Drenched with rains, broiling by day, shivering by night, a disused and ruinous prison for a bedroom, his diet begged or pilfered out of rubbish heaps, his associates two creatures equally outcast with himself, he had drained for months the cup of penitence.[7]

The story takes Herrick up to the point where, after he has chosen not to commit suicide, he gives himself up to Attwater, asking him if there is anything that can be done with him.

> Attwater slowly put his gun under his arm, then his hands in his pockets.
> 'What brings you here?' he repeated.
> 'I don't know,' said Herrick; and then, with a cry: 'Can you do anything with me?'
> 'Are you armed?' said Attwater. 'I ask for the form's sake.'
> 'Armed? No!' said Herrick. 'O yes, I am, too!'
> And he flung upon the beach a dripping pistol.
> 'You are wet,' said Attwater.
> 'Yes, I am wet,' said Herrick. 'Can you do anything with me?'
> Attwater read his face attentively.
> 'It would depend a good deal upon what you are,' said he.
> 'What I am? A coward!' said Herrick.
> 'There is very little to be done with that,' said Attwater. 'And yet the description hardly strikes me as exhaustive.'
> 'O, what does it matter?' cried Herrick. 'Here I am. I am broken crockery; I am a burst drum; the whole of my life is gone to water; I have nothing left that I believe in, except my living horror of myself. Why do I come to you? I don't know; you are cold, cruel, hateful; and I hate you, or I think I hate you. But you are an honest man, an honest gentleman. I put myself, helpless, in your hands. What must I do? If I can't do anything, be merciful and put a bullet through me; it's only a puppy with a broken leg!'[8]

The night before, Herrick has denounced Attwater as a murderer and a hypocrite; now he abases himself before him. These two responses, besides revealing the hysteria and confusion in Herrick, reflect the two sides of Attwater: Attwater the aristocratic trader and Attwater the missionary. He moves from the one to the other so easily that it is as if they are fed from the same source—monomaniac certainty. The submission he demands is not to God but to himself, as God's appointed. It could be claimed that Stevenson's decision not to pay any further attention to Herrick—but to devote the last two chapters to Huish and Davis—is his way of showing that Herrick knows that Attwater is not the kind of religious figure he needs. He needs a true priest, not a megalomaniac impostor, and so there can be no further development for him. But a feeling of disappointment remains. At just the point when it looks as if Herrick may be moving from despair to faith, or at least from despair to a recognition that there may be something beyond it, Stevenson deserts him. The state of mind of men in Herrick's position is complex, it must be admitted, as Kierkegaard has shown.

> This despair is now well in advance. If the former was the despair of weakness, this is despair over his weakness, although it still remains as to its nature under the category 'despair of weakness' as distinguished from defiance in the next section. So there is only a relative difference. This difference consists in the fact that the forgoing form has the consciousness of weakness as its final consciousness, whereas in this case consciousness does not come to a stop here but potentiates itself to a new consciousness, a consciousness of its weakness. The despairer understands that it is weakness to take the earthly so much to heart, that it is weakness to despair. But then, instead of veering sharply away from despair to faith, humbling himself before God for his weakness, he is more deeply absorbed in despair and despairs over his weakness. Therewith the whole point of view is inverted, he becomes now more clearly conscious of his despair, recognizing that he is in despair about the eternal, he despairs over himself that he could be weak enough to ascribe to the earthly such great importance, which now becomes his despairing expression for the fact that he has lost the eternal and himself.[9]

But Stevenson does not approach this order of understanding. He has followed Herrick's confusions further than he did the contradictions in Wiltshire; he has been truer to him. But, though on a higher plane, a similar signing off occurs. Herrick is abandoned because he stands on the brink of a different condition, a condition Stevenson seems unable to accommodate. The story has been about Herrick at the end of his tether, but what lies at the end of his tether—other than suicide, which he has refused—defeats Stevenson. His narratives are more about men locked in particular conditions than about the experience of change from one condition to another. (Davis cannot really be considered an exception to this. Although he changes, from alert and sober seaman to drunkard and finally to convert, we are not shown him changing. The process of change is left out. It is a case rather of Stevenson changing the labels; and this he does so abruptly that Davis comes over as a succession of types rather than as a character.) And if change out of a low condition presupposes freedom—the individual aware of possibilities for himself and resolved to realize them—then his fiction can be charged with paying only lip service to freedom. What it means to be or to feel free, expressed in the move from a lower condition to a higher, never becomes part of Stevenson's world. The portrait of Herrick as a man knowing one form of humiliation after another, exchanging one prison for another, has been vivid, but nothing is made of his wish to change, to seek restitution, transcendence even. Perhaps Stevenson believed that such a wish betrays delusion, but, if so, it can only be said that this is not shown either. It is not just that the switch from Herrick's point of view has not been prepared for: more seriously, it occurs just when the reader expects most of this particular characterization; when he expects to see what it means for Herrick to grow, to advance in understanding—or to fail to grow.

So it is not possible to know what is happening to Herrick at the end. Does he keep his own counsel and, if so, what is that counsel? Is his state of mind the same as it was before he decided not to commit suicide, or has it changed? When, in the last exchange with Davis, he describes Davis as 'Attwater's pet penitent', is he merely being sarcastic, or is he questioning the point (and indeed the possibility) of penitence altogether? Does he resist Attwater's counsel? What exactly is the nature of that counsel? Is Attwater a conscious or an unconscious hypocrite, aware that he is using his Christianity to ensure submission, or taken in by it, persuaded that he is nonetheless a Christian for being a tyrant?

It is because the characterizations of Herrick and Attwater are not taken beyond a certain point that we never learn the answers to these questions. We don't even learn in what sort of terms answers might be framed; the investigation has not gone far enough. We look for illumination in the text but all we find is the vitriol-throwing episode on the beach and the 'conversion' of Davis. The picturesque and the spectacular combine to distract us from issues which, almost as though by accident, the story has raised. Herrick hovers, unexplored. The symbol of the figure-head—which seemed to point to the possibility of some kind of change for him—is unredeemed. The passage is little more than a gesture in the direction of symbolism; we do not learn enough about Herrick to know for what religious longings exactly this is an image.

> . . . Herrick looked up at her, where she towered above him head and shoulders, with singular feelings of curiosity and romance, and suffered his mind to travel to and fro in her life-history. So long she had been the blind conductress of a ship among the waves; so long she had stood here idle in the violent sun, that yet did not avail to blister her; and was even this the end of so many adventures? he wondered, or was more behind? And he could have found it in his heart to regret that she was not a goddess, nor yet he a pagan, that he might have bowed down before her in that hour of difficulty.[10]

The issue of race has not been ignored, as it is in 'The Beach of Falesá', but because the native population has conveniently been reduced by smallpox to four, it does not figure. Virtually depopulated, the island can be presented as having no culture. (Its culture, in fact, is Attwater's; it is a white island.) Any racial problems are of the past. Attwater distinguishes between the sullen and the obsequious in the old population, but he does not really develop the distinction. The natives are not seen as children, this time, passive and without powers of resistance, but the vision is still well short of Conrad and Melville with their appreciation that evil is as intrinsic to invaded as to invader. Indeed, the view of native cultures which seems to emerge in these stories is oddly close to the colonial presumption that natives are inferior, without effective power, significantly stirred only through contact with the white man. There is a sense in which the Negro—by whose shadow Don Aranda knows he will be haunted until death—haunts these two stories also. But, cast from beyond the bounds of the narrative, the shadow this time is a sardonic one.

So, at the end of *The Ebb-Tide*, because of this weight of unanswered but not unanswerable questions, the impression once more is of evasion. Once more Stevenson stands exposed before 'mysteries abysmal'. Once more he lacks the resource so praised by Henry James.

> What it all came back to was, no doubt, something like this wisdom—that if you haven't for fiction, the root of the matter in you, haven't the sense of life and the penetrating imagination, you are a fool in the very presence of the revealed and assured; but that if you are so armed you are not really helpless, not without your resource, even before mysteries abysmal.[11]

NOTES

1. Herman Melville, *Billy Budd, Sailor and Other Stories* (London: Penguin, 1967), p. 306.
2. Robert Louis Stevenson, 'The Beach of Falesá' (London: Penguin, 1979), pp. 126–27.
3. Ibid., p. 153.
4. Melville, *Typee* (London: Penguin, 1972), p. 309.
5. 'The Beach of Falesá', p. 153.
6. Stevenson, *The Ebb-Tide* (London: Penguin, 1979), p. 220.
7. Ibid., p. 176.
8. Ibid., p. 279.
9. Søren Kierkegaard, *The Sickness Unto Death* (Princeton: Princeton University Press, 1941), p. 195.
10. Stevenson, *The Ebb-Tide*, p. 249.
11. Henry James, *The Princess Casamissima* (London: Penguin, 1977), pp. 22–3.

8

Author and Narrator in *Weir of Hermiston*

by K. G. SIMPSON

> From all its chapters, from all its pages, from all its sentences, the well-written novel echoes and re-echoes its one creative and controlling thought; to this must every incident and character contribute; the style must have been pitched in unison with this; and if there is anywhere a word that looks another way, the book would be stronger, clearer, and (I had almost said) fuller without it.[1]

This is one of several important statements on the practice of fiction made by Stevenson in the course of his debate with Henry James. It is characteristic of the concern with technical and stylistic expertise which so engaged Stevenson.

In *Weir of Hermiston* the 'one creative and controlling thought' is the concept of judgement. Judgement, and the cognate concerns of duty, conscience, and authority, are thematically central to the father-son conflict. While it is recognized that Archie is the principal exemplar of these themes, the point of this essay is to argue that Stevenson attempts to distance himself from his narrator; and in deliberately raising the question of the reliability of his narrator, he offers yet another instance of the limitations of individual human judgement.

Stevenson's concern with judgement in *Weir* may be considered in three respects: in relation to the writer's own personality and values; in relation to Stevenson as a representative

of identifiably Scottish values; and in the context of the movement in the practice of fiction away from authoritative statement on the part of the author-narrator (as in George Eliot,
Thackeray, and Trollope) towards the twentieth-century
novel's reflection, in its form, of the breakdown of absolute
values, and the concomitant decline in the status and conviction of the narrator (the process sometimes referred to as
'Exit author/narrator').

According to Edwin Muir, 'had it been finished *Weir of
Hermiston* would have been something unique in fiction, a
modern saga, a novel combining two elements which are almost
always disjoined: a modern sensibility and a heroic spirit'.[2] The
point at issue is the degree of success achieved in uniting
modern sensibility and heroic spirit. This leads one to a
consideration which repays effort in much greater measure
than hypothesis about the conclusion of *Weir* ever could: on the
evidence available, what is the relationship between values and
technique in *Weir* and, in particular, what consonance is there
between the nature of the material and the technique of
narration? Does *Weir* exemplify its author's contention that in
prose 'idea and stylistic pattern proceed hand in hand'?[3] Does
Weir substantiate James's claim that with Stevenson 'the form,
the envelope, is there . . . headforemost, *as* the idea'?[4]

Any attempt at an answer to this must first take account of
the weight placed by Stevenson, in his theoretical writing, on
narrative technique. 'A Humble Remonstrance' offers the
fullest and clearest statement of Stevenson's views on this. In
response to James's claims in 'The Art of Fiction', Stevenson
wrote:

> What then is the object, what the method, of an art, and what the
> source of its power? The whole secret is that no art does 'compete
> with life'. Man's one method, whether he reasons or creates, is to
> half-shut his eyes against the dazzle and confusion of reality.[5]

Stevenson proceeds to the following pronouncement, which
has the utmost significance for his fiction:

> So far as [literature] imitates at all, it imitates not life but
> speech: not the facts of human destiny, but the emphasis and
> the suppressions with which the human actor tells of them. The
> real art that dealt with life directly was that of the first men who

told their stories round the savage camp-fire. Our art is occupied, and bound to be occupied, not so much in making stories true as in making them typical; not so much in capturing the lineaments of each fact, as in marshalling all of them towards a common end. . . . The novel, which is a work of art, exists, not by its resemblances to life, which are forced and material, as a shoe must still consist of leather, but by its immeasurable difference from life, which is designed and significant, and is both the method and the meaning of the work.

Several aspects of this are noteworthy: the timely warning against excessive reliance on James's 'illusion of reality'; the primitivist nostalgia, that hankering after an earlier age when life and art were one, which has affected many modern writers but which may be related in Scotland to the post-Union insecurity, precisely the crisis of values and subsequent nostalgia out of which Macpherson's Ossian poems were born; the emphasis on 'marshalling [facts] towards a common end', which, in *Weir*, is the author's concern with destiny and judgement (compare Stevenson's definition of the novel as 'not a transcript of life, to be judged by its exactitude, but a simplification of some side or point of life, to stand or fall by its significant simplicity',[6] about which there is more than a tinge of a characteristically Scottish reductionism); the recognition of the interinvolvement of 'method' and 'meaning'; and, above all, the importance of narrative voice as the basis of the version of 'human destiny'.

On another occasion Stevenson described the process whereby the writer selects and shapes the material of his fiction as 'the sentiment assimilating the facts of natural congruity'.[7] For Stevenson, the artist 'must suppress much and omit more'.[8] His annoyance with the readiness of the public to regard fiction as 'slice of life' is reflected in his protest to James: 'They think that striking situations, or good dialogue, are got by studying life; they will not rise to understand that they are prepared by deliberate artifice and set off by painful suppressions.'[9] For Stevenson this capacity for modulation and subordination is one of the particular strengths of fiction: one of the advantages of continuous narration over drama is that the writer 'can now subordinate one thing to another in importance, and introduce all manner of very subtle detail, to a degree that was before impossible'.[10]

Hugo is praised by Stevenson for setting before himself 'the task of realizing, in the language of romance, much of the involution of our complicated lives', and, in contrast with the 'unity, the unwavering creative purpose' of some of Hawthorne's romances, Hugo achieves 'unity out of multitude'; and 'it is the wonderful power of subordination and synthesis thus displayed that gives us the measure of his talent.' Stevenson distinguishes between Hugo's romances and 'the novel with a purpose', in that 'the moral significance, with Hugo, is of the essence of the romance; it is the organizing principle.'[11]

One side of Stevenson was striving for precisely this, but he was never to achieve it entirely satisfactorily. The imaginative expression of such moral purpose was perhaps incompatible with the Calvinist emphasis on predetermination. Underlying this judgement on Hugo is a compound of feelings: Hugo 'learned to subordinate his story to an idea, to make his art speak'. The aim of the artist is, for Stevenson, configuration; the writer is the source of a pattern, an alternative to the pattern of life which is the provision of Fate. 'The motive and end of any art whatever is to make a pattern', wrote Stevenson. Hence,

> That style is therefore the most perfect, not, as fools say, which is the most natural, for the most natural is the disjointed babble of the chronicler; but which attains the highest degree of elegant and pregnant implication unobtrusively; or, if obtrusively, then with the greatest gain to sense and vigour.[12]

Assessment of the degree of implication accomplished by Stevenson in *Weir* involves examination of the narrative technique employed in the novel. It is essential to consider not only the attitude of the narrator to his subject but also the attitude of the novelist to his narrator. Why did Stevenson choose the particular narrative mode employed in *Weir*, and why did he choose this particular narrator? How reliable is the narrator of *Weir*? Can it be that he is the object of authorial irony?

In *Weir* Stevenson uses first-person narration, as he did in many of his books. Percy Lubbock, noting that Stevenson may not have seen how logically his preference for first-person narration followed from the subjects that most attracted him, observed that Stevenson never had any occasion to use the first-person for enhancement of plain narrative as his subjects were 'strongly romantic, vividly dramatic'.[13] Hence the value of the use of Mackellar in *The Master of Ballantrae*: the fantasy of much of the material is contained within the form of Mackellar's doggedly realist account.

In *Weir* the narrator is similarly personalized by his style (though it is not that of Mackellar), but he is not identified specifically. This fact has given rise to some divergence of opinion as to the identity of the narrator. For instance, Leslie Fiedler goes so far as to comment on the deleterious effects of the choice of third-person narration, adding,

> Stevenson's instinctive bent was for first-person narrative; and when . . . he attempts to speak from outside *about* his fiction, his style betrays him to self-pity (we *know* Archie is really the author, and the third-person singular affects us like a transparent hoax), sentimentality and the sort of 'fine' writing he had avoided since *Prince Otto*.[14]

The answer to this must be that though Stevenson has not identified his narrator he has personalized him quite distinctly, and that instances of 'fine' writing have to be attributed to him and not to Stevenson. Thus such passages are further exemplification of human limitation, and in particular limitation of judgement; and as such they are entirely consonant with the central thematic concern of the book.

In *Weir* the narrator is soon present in the first chapter as a source of opinion and judgement. He states that 'chance cast [Jean Rutherford] in the path of Adam Weir'; volunteers the view that 'it seems profane to call [the acquaintance] a courtship'; and recounts that 'on the very eve of their engagement, it was related that one had drawn near to the tender couple, and had overheard the lady cry out, with the tones of one who talked for the sake of talking, "Keep me, Mr. Weir, and what became of him?" and the profound accents of the suitor reply, "Haangit, mem, haangit" ' (195).[15] Fairly rapidly the narratorial omniscience is personalized, though not identified, with the narrator appearing thus in his own voice: 'The heresy about foolish women is always punished, I have said, and Lord Hermiston began to pay the penalty at once' (196). Such comment inevitably leads the reader to ponder the identity of the narrative voice; and the tension between apparent omniscience and personalization creates problems for Stevenson the further the narrative advances.

Stevenson's recognition of the importance of narrative voice leads to the elevation of the narrator of *Weir* to the status of sophisticated and conscious artist. The skill with which the material of the narrative is structured betokens a refined intelligence, and this might be held to strengthen the case for identifying the narrator with the author. Juxtaposition is used to considerable effect: witness the juxtaposing of the exchange between Hermiston and Kirstie on the death of his wife, and the ensuing account by the narrator entitled 'Father and Son' (204); the report of the conversation between Archie and Dr. Gregory and the effect thereof on Archie's feelings for his father reveals a fine sense of ironic ordering (215); Archie's impassioned plea (with which Chapter Four ends) is deliberately juxtaposed with the reductive account of Hermiston parish which follows it (227); Archie's restraint and 'Roman sense of duty' are contrasted with the ensuing depiction of the restraint which life has imposed upon Kirstie's innately passionate nature (230–31); and, perhaps most tellingly, Chapter Six ends with Christina's romantic dreams while Chapter Seven, 'Enter Mephistopheles', begins with the arrival which is to prove their undoing. All of this suggests a fairly high level of conscious artistry. So, too, do the manifest ability to render character by means of distinctive style, and the capacity to use language in a way that reveals awareness of the symbolic or mythical dimension of the events of the novel. For instance, the exchange between Archie and Frank after Archie's denunciation of the hanging of Duncan Jopp occasions the following comment:

> And the one young man carried his tortured spirit forth of the city and all the day long, by one road and another, in an endless pilgrimage of misery; while the other hastened smilingly to spread the news of Weir's access of insanity, and to drum up for that night a full attendance at the Speculative, where further eccentric developments might certainly be looked for. (212)

The narrator is aware of the action on one level as *peregrinatio* threatened by Satanic temptation, while at the same time, with characteristic Scottish reductionism, he presents the devil-figure as basely and pettily human.

Frequently, too, the tone and the demeanour of the narrator are such as to encourage identification of narrator with author. Early in the first chapter the narrator offers himself as a source of authoritative comment, not just on the behaviour of the characters but on the extent to which it is typical of various classes or categories of human beings. He wishes to appear as someone who knows the ways of the world and the responses of men and women. At the same time he knows the Weirs and those with whom they come in contact. Of Archie's refusal, after the conversation with Glenalmond, to express further his feelings for his father, the narrator comments:

> With the infinitely delicate sense of youth, Archie avoided the subject from that hour. It was perhaps a pity. Had he but talked—talked freely—let himself gush out in words (the way youth loves to do and should), there might have been no tale to write upon the Weirs of Hermiston. But the shadow of a threat of ridicule sufficed; in the slight tartness of these words he read a prohibition; and it is likely that Glenalmond meant it so. (207)

The narrator is sufficiently confident to account for Archie's solitariness as follows: '. . . something that was in part the delicacy of his mother, in part the austerity of his father, held him aloof from all'; and to direct thus the reader's response to Hermiston: 'Sympathy is not due to these steadfast iron natures. If he failed to gain his son's friendship, or even his son's toleration, on he went up the great, bare stair-case of his duty, uncheered and undepressed.' And consideration of Archie's situation leads him to this generalization: 'Parsimony of pain, glut of pleasure, these are the two alternating ends of youth; and Archie was of the parsimonious.' The narrator never loses this readiness to relate the particular behaviour of his subjects to general human patterns. Of the final encounter between Archie and Christine the narrator observes that 'the schoolmaster that there is in all men, to the despair of all girls and most women, was now completely in possession of Archie' (283).

In such comment it is difficult not to hear the voice of Stevenson himself, and the same may be said of those passages where the narrator widens the range of his authority, discoursing on the distinctive attitude of the Scot to the past (233), or observing: 'not even the most acute political heads are guided through the steps of life with unerring directness. That would require a gift of prophecy which has been denied to man' (264–65). Noteworthy too is the narrator's readiness to formulate or interpret the response or behaviour of his characters. Of Hermiston's atmosphere of industry the narrator remarks that 'it was still present, unobserved like the ticking of a clock, an arid ideal, a tasteless stimulant in the boy's life' (206). In the following description of the attempts at converse between Archie and his father the choice of analogy is, quite deliberately, not to Archie's advantage:

> The father, with a grand simplicity, either spoke of what interested himself, or maintained an unaffected silence. The son turned in his head for some topic that should be quite safe, that would spare him fresh evidences either of my lord's inherent grossness or of the innocence of his inhumanity; treading gingerly the ways of intercourse, like a lady gathering up her skirts in a by-path. (209)

This fondness for analogy persists throughout *Weir*. Early in the final chapter comes this account of Christina's appearing before Archie: 'His first sight of her was thus excruciatingly sad, like a glimpse of a world from which all light, comfort, and society were on the point of vanishing' (283).

It is significant that, in his essay on Burns, Stevenson noted the importance of style to Burns, and claimed that 'it was by his style, and not by his matter, that he affected Wordsworth and the world.'[16] Almost immediately, however, he recognized another major quality in the poet, exclaiming 'What a gust of sympathy there is in him sometimes.' Precisely this combination of qualities is exemplified in Stevenson himself. James was to see the union of the sympathetic and the ironical in Stevenson as an essentially Scottish characteristic, finding in the Scottish background 'a certain process of detachment, of extreme secularization', and claiming: 'Mr. Stevenson is . . . a Scotchman of the world. None other . . . could have drawn with such a mixture of sympathetic and ironical observation the character of the canny young Lowlander, David Balfour.' James wrote of Stevenson's 'talent for seeing the familiar in the heroic, and reducing the extravagant to plausible detail', and the character, Alan Breck, he found 'a genuine study, and nothing can be more charming than the way Mr. Stevenson both sees through and admires it'. Parts of *The Silverado Squatters* James referred to as 'this half-humorous, half-tragical recital'.[17]

Such ambivalence of attitude, such 'compassionate irony' (the term is Furnas's),[18] is frequently the response of the narrator of *Weir*. This is exemplified in the account of the marriage of Jean Rutherford and Hermiston, and in that of the relationship between mother and son in such comments as 'The sight of the little man at her skirt intoxicated her with the sense of power, and froze her with the consciousness of her responsibility' (198). The union of sympathy and irony informs the description of the trial of Duncan Jopp. Here a meticulous realism of presentation is accompanied, without strain, by a compassion that is reminiscent of Dickens. But, in a way that Dickens was not always able to do, Stevenson has his narrator relate thus the particular to general human traits:

> There was pinned about his throat a piece of dingy flannel; and this it was perhaps that turned the scale in Archie's mind between disgust and pity. The creature stood in a vanishing point; yet a little while, and he was still a man, and had eyes and apprehension; yet a little longer, and with a last sordid piece of pageantry, he would cease to be. And here, in the meantime, with a trait of human nature that caught at the beholder's breath, he was tending a sore throat. (209)

It is essential to note here that the compassionate irony encompasses the account of Archie's response to the trial.

In Chapter Six, 'A Leaf from Christina's Psalm-Book', the same applies: common to the description of the Hermiston congregation and Archie's response to it is the same compassionate irony. This is precisely the attitude that is evinced towards the whole episode of the romantic involvement of Archie and Christina. Here is the description of Christina's awaiting Archie near the Weaver's Stone on the Sunday evening:

By the time the sun was down and all the easterly braes lay plunged in clear shadow, she was aware of another figure coming up the path at a most unequal rate of approach, now half running, now pausing and seeming to hesitate. She watched him at first with a total suspension of thought. She held her thought as a person holds his breathing. Then she consented to recognise him. 'He'll no be coming here, he canna be; it's no possible.' And there began to grow upon her a subdued choking response. (259)

It is not only Christina's attitude that is in flux here: the narrator's own attitude is a composite one, as the fluctuation between amusement and sympathy indicates. The treatment of the romance between Archie and Christina is not Kailyard. Stevenson's narrator does not suppress the 'sugar bool' incident: he *chooses* to present it (when he could have omitted it) because it enables him to demonstrate his amused sympathy. And, to a large extent, *Weir* is about the narrator's attitude to his subject.

For all the apparent omniscience of the narrator, for all his readiness to pronounce with what seems to be authority, Stevenson is able to demonstrate that his narrator is far from being infallible; indeed he represents further exemplification of the central thematic concern of *Weir*—the limitation of human judgement. Despite the appearance of conviction, the word, 'perhaps', recurs with remarkable frequency in the narrative, as, for instance, in this comment on Archie and his father: 'there were not, perhaps, in Christendom two men more radically strangers' (208). A characteristic of the narrator is to embark upon an authoritative judgement, only to have to retreat into tentativeness. Of Archie's disinclination to socialize in the country the narrator writes: 'The habit of solitude tends to perpetuate itself, and an austerity of which he was quite unconscious, and a pride which seemed arrogance, and perhaps was chiefly shyness, discouraged and offended his new companions' (229). The narrator has, too, a tendency to beg the crucial question (Archie, who had just defied—was it God or Satan?—would not listen (212)); and he is, at times, made to say things which are simply silly. He remarks, for instance, of Archie's setting fines at the Speculative: 'He little thought, as he did so, how he resembled his father, but his

211

friends remarked upon it, chuckling' (213); to which the reader is entitled to ask if it is likely that he would think such a thing. Similarly, the narrator says of Archie: 'He hated to be inhospitable, but in one thing he was his father's son. He had a strong sense that his house was his own and no man else's' (272). If the narrator has failed to observe the various other points of resemblance between father and son, then his vision is truly blinkered.

It should be noted too that on several occasions the narrator acknowledges his own inadequacy of judgement. In the course of the exchange between father and son his narrator remarks of Archie that 'he had a strong impression, besides, of the essential valour of the old gentleman before him, how conveyed it would be hard to say' (219). The narrator interrupts Kirstie's account of the death of Gilbert Elliott with a joke at both his expense and that of his source, Kirstie, 'whom I but haltingly follow, for she told this tale like one inspired' (236). The most telling admission, and subsequent demonstration of the circumscription of the narrator's judgement occurs in the midst of the account of young Kirstie's romanticizing. The narrator comments:

> Had a doctor of medicine come into that loft, he would have diagnosed a healthy, well-developed, eminently vivacious lass lying on her face in a fit of the sulks; not one who had just contracted, or was just contracting a mortal sickness of the mind which should yet carry her towards death and despair. Had it been a doctor of psychology, he might have been pardoned for divining in the girl a passion of childish vanity, self-love *in excelsis*, and no more. It is to be understood that I have been painting chaos and describing the inarticulate. Every lineament that appears is too precise, almost every word too strong. Take a finger-post in the mountains on a day of rolling mists; I have but copied the names that appear on the pointers, the names of definite and famous cities far distant, and now perhaps basking in sunshine; but Christina remained all these hours, as it were, at the foot of the post itself, not moving and enveloped in mutable and blinding wreaths of haze. (255–56)

Here the narrator is the target of a strong authorial irony. What is meant by 'a mortal sickness of the mind which should yet carry her towards death and despair'? Is the narrator ignorant of subsequent events and the nature of the revised ending? And, after the admission that 'every word is too strong', the narrative lapses into the stylistic excesses to which it is prone. Such 'fine writing' as appears in *Weir* is to be attributed to the narrator and further exemplifies his subjection to the ironic overview of the author. Likewise, sentimental excess in the writing (e.g. the description of Kirstie (281)) should be regarded as the response of the narrator.

Stevenson allows his narrator to reveal—and at times acknowledge—his fallibility. 'I have said she was no hypocrite', he writes of young Kirstie, 'but here I am at fault . . . the steps of love in the young, and especially in girls, are instinctive and unconscious' (259). The account, which follows soon after, of the lovers' tentative approaches to one another ('He was sounding her . . . a thrill of emotion' (261)) is self-consciously weighty and florid. From such obvious excesses Stevenson has taken care to distance himself. The following, also, has to be read as the comment of the narrator, from which the author has distanced himself:

> *Tantaene irae?* Has the reader perceived the reason? Since Frank's coming there were no more hours of gossip over the supper tray! All his blandishments were in vain; he started handicapped on the race for Mrs. Elliott's favour. (267)

When the narrator strikes this note he is being set up quite deliberately by the author. Adopting his authoritative 'public' voice, for instance, the narrator expounds upon the futility of condescension towards the Scots peasantry (269). All unwittingly he is made to sound more than a little patronizing himself.

The narrator both recognizes his own limitation of understanding and draws attention to the limited effectiveness of language in rendering experience when he offers the following account of Frank's discovery of the romance between Archie and young Kirstie:

> Here was Archie's secret, here was the woman, and more than that—though I have need here of every manageable attenuation of language—with the first look, he had already entered himself as a rival. It was a good deal in pique, it was a little in revenge, it was much in genuine admiration: the devil may

decide the proportions! I cannot, and it is very likely that Frank could not. (274)

The manner in which this chapter ends is significant. The triumph of Frank's discovery leads to the comment that 'there was nothing vindictive in his nature; but, if revenge came in his way, it might as well be good, and the thought of Archie's pillow reflections that night was indescribably sweet to him' (276). It is difficult to reconcile the claim that 'there was nothing vindictive in his nature' with the evidence that the narrator has presented or, for that matter, with his entitling Frank's appearance 'Enter Mephistopheles'. How is the judgement of the narrator to be viewed? Is this simply one of his blind spots? Or is he, in the manner adopted intermittently by Fielding's narrator in *Tom Jones*, feigning fallibility? This latter possibility makes *Weir* into an even more complex work of irony, and at the same time it exacerbates the problem of comprehension for the reader: when is the narrator genuinely fallible, and when is he, as participant in Stevenson's ironic *schema*, obliged to simulate fallibility? On the occasion under consideration, after the apparent proof of his fallibility, the narrator—ironically—attempts to reassert his authority by resuming his omniscient Olympian manner as follows:

> Poor cork upon a torrent, he tasted that night the sweets of omnipotence, and brooded like a deity over the strands of that intrigue which was to shatter him before the summer waned. (277)

The effect of such 'fine writing' and flaunting of narratorial authority is counter-productive: it merely re-emphasizes the limitations of the narrator. Thus, one of the most potent ironies in *Weir* is that often when the narrator believes he has accomplished a particular effect, he has in fact achieved something quite different. Generally when he speaks with his authoritative voice the true omniscience is not his but Stevenson's. Not only his attitude to the characters, but also his attitude to himself and his narrative function, is in constant flux. The irony is that the narrator does not share in the author's and readers' awareness of this.

All of this would combine to suggest that *Weir* is a masterpiece of irony; that Stevenson, sublimely detached, leaves his narrator to over-reach and so demonstrate his limitations. This view of the novel is tempting, but there are major objections to it and it requires some qualification. Paradoxically, the difficulties arise principally from precisely that narrative energy and flux already identified, and in particular from Stevenson's use in *Weir* of the technique that has come to be known as Free Indirect Speech.[19] Intermittent rendering of the character's thought-processes by means of F.I.S. permits of identification and evaluation. As Spitzer pointed out, mimicry implies a mimic as well as a person mimicked.[20] With F.I.S., where mimicry is at the heart of the technique, this applies equally; and it should be added that mimicry implies not just the presence of a mimic but the presence of a mimic with an attitude towards his subject. Here once again irony may be critical or sympathetic (or a compound of these constituents in varying proportions), and irony again functions as a means of directing response. Perhaps the least complex instance of this in *Weir* is the occasion when the narrator adopts the voice of genteel society in order to subject it to irony. The response to Frank's tales about Archie is presented thus:

> He had done something disgraceful, my dear. What, was not precisely known, and that good kind young man, Mr. Innes, did his best to make light of it. But there it was. And Mr. Innes was very anxious about him now; he was really uneasy, my dear; he was positively wrecking his own prospects because he dared not leave him alone. (271)

As a passage of ironic writing, that could stand comparison with Jane Austen. The irony is compounded by the fact that the voice of genteel society relays the view of things—a totally inaccurate one—which Frank has been circulating.

Roy Pascal has noted that F.I.S. both evokes a particular character and places him in a context of judgement by the narrator.[21] This is true of each of the principals in *Weir*. In the early stages the use of F.I.S. is concise and economical. Here, for a moment, the narrator enters the mind of Mrs. Weir, both rendering her terms and evoking an attitude of compassionate irony:

215

It was only with the child that she had conceived and managed to pursue a scheme of conduct. Archie was to be a great man and a good; a minister if possible, a saint for certain. (198)

There is comparable access to her mind and her terms in the ensuing account of her philosophy of tenderness and in her defence of Hermiston to Archie. In the case of Hermiston sympathy is rather less a constituent of the attitude evinced, but there is the same concision in the use of F.I.S., as here, for instance:

> There might have been more pleasure in his relations with Archie, so much he may have recognised at moments; but pleasure was a by-product of the singular chemistry of life, which only fools expected. (208)

Where there is more extensive use of F.I.S. it is in the case of Frank that it is most readily identified and consistently understood, possibly because the narrator's attitude to Frank is in the main unequivocal. Here is Frank's version of his enforced departure from Edinburgh society:

> Any port in a storm! He was manfully turning his back on the Parliament House and its gay babble, on port and oysters, the racecourse and the ring; and manfully prepared, until these clouds should have blown by, to share a living grave with Archie Weir at Hermiston. (265)

Such masterly ironic self-revelation is reminiscent of Jane Austen and, in the Scottish tradition, of Burns and Galt; and there is a potential for it in *St. Ives* which Stevenson chose not to exploit. It is sustained through Chapter Seven of *Weir*. The narrator presents thus Frank's reaction to his desertion by Archie:

> Innes groaned under these desertions; it required all his philosophy to sit down to a solitary breakfast with composure, and all his unaffected good-nature to be able to greet Archie with friendliness on the more rare occasions when he came home late for dinner. (266)

And this is his response to the Hermiston household: 'For the others, they were beyond hope and beyond endurance. Never had a young Apollo been cast among such rustic barbarians' (268). The mastery of this mode here is accomplished not because Frank is a shallow fool who lends himself readily to this sort of treatment; rather, it is because the narrator's attitude to Frank does not fluctuate.

With some of the characters, and Archie most conspicuously, the narrator's attitude does fluctuate, and it is here that Stevenson encounters some difficulties. For instance, the account of Archie's reactions during the trial of Duncan Jopp has passages of F.I.S., such as

> He thought of flight, and where was he to flee to? of other lives, but was there any life worth living in this den of savage and jeering animals?. . . . It seemed to him, from the top of his nineteen years' experience, as if he were marked at birth to be the perpetrator of some signal action, to set back fallen Mercy, to overthrow the usurping devil that sat, horned and hoofed, on her throne. . . . He saw the fleering rabble, the flinching wretch produced. He looked on for a while at a certain parody of devotion, which seemed to strip the wretch of his last claim to manhood. (211)

Part of the difficulty in differentiating Archie's thoughts, rendered in F.I.S., from those of the narrator derives from the frequent similarity between their respective styles. This may be at least in part a result of the origin, as Lorck pointed out, of some instances of F.I.S. in the intense imaginative identification of narrator with character.[22]

In the lengthy sixth chapter, 'From Christina's Psalm-Book', there is sustained interplaying of external narration and F.I.S. Here F.I.S. is used to reflect character and to convey narratorial irony, while at the same time it participates in expressing the flux of the narrator's own response. In the account of Archie's reaction to the Hermiston congregation the use of Archie's own terms, the mimicking of his way of seeing, is used to reflect less than entirely favourably on him. In this, for instance, Archie appears as civilized urban man in whom the natural origins are concealed beneath a veneer of patronizing sophistication:

> The rest of the congregation, like so many sheep, oppressed him with a sense of hob-nailed routine, day following day—of physical labour in the open air, oatmeal porridge, peas bannock, the somnolent fireside in the evening, and the night-long nasal

217

slumbers in a box-bed. Yet he knew many of them to be shrewd
and humorous, men of character, notable women, making a
bustle in the world and radiating an influence from their low-
browed doors. He knew besides they were like other men;
below the crust of custom, rapture found a way; he had heard
them beat the timbrel before Bacchus—had heard them shout
and carouse over their whisky-toddy; and not the most Dutch-
bottomed and severe faces among them all, not even the solemn
elders themselves, but were capable of singular gambols at the
voice of love. (246)

Again the use of the individual's (inflated) terms against him
is redolent of Jane Austen.

Especially in the scenes at Hermiston the appearance of
inflated language often indicates the return of the narrative to
Archie's viewpoint, Archie being thus represented as the
urbane or unnatural in an otherwise predominantly natural
world. Here Archie's strong but unfocused romantic mood is
conveyed through its own terms, only to be undermined by
reductive detail:

Vagrant scents of the earth arrested Archie by the way with
moments of ethereal intoxication. The grey, Quakerish dale
was still only awakened in places and patches from the sobriety
of its winter colouring; and he wondered at its beauty; an
essential beauty of the old earth it seemed to him, not resident
in particulars but breathing to him from the whole. He surprised himself by a sudden impulse to write poetry—he did so
sometimes, loose, galloping octosyllabics in the vein of Scott—
and when he had taken his place on a boulder, near some fairy
falls and shaded by a whip of a tree that was already radiant
with new leaves, it still more surprised him that he should find
nothing to write. (246–67)

The echoes of Edward Waverley in the Highlands are more
than accidental. The irony is further compounded by the
narrator's immediate uncertainty: 'His heart *perhaps* beat in
time to some vast indwelling rhythm of the universe.'

Throughout the record of the romance between Archie and
young Kirstie the narrator's attitude is a composite one,
alternating between amused observation and sympathetic
identification. Here fluctuation of narrative perspective, a
feature throughout *Weir*, reaches its most pronounced. The

narrator offers this skilful mimicry of Archie's highly romantic view of things:

> Brightness of azure, clouds of fragrance, a tinkle of falling water and singing birds, rose like exhalations from some deeper, aboriginal memory, that was not his, but belonged to the flesh on his bones. His body remembered; and it seemed to him that his body was in no way gross, but ethereal and perishable like a strain of music; and he felt for it an exquisite tenderness as for a child, an innocent, full of instincts and destined to an early death. And he felt for old Torrance—of the many supplications, of the few days—a pity that was near to tears. (247)

The centre of interest then shifts to young Kirstie, and in the representation of her response F.I.S. is used intermittently (e.g. 'If he spared a glance in her direction, he should know she was a well-behaved young lady who had been to Glasgow. . . . Even then, she was far too well-bred to gratify her curiosity with any impatience' (248)). Equally, the narrator adopts from time to time the persona of the detached and amused observer of the enduring social comedy ('Presently he leaned nonchalantly back; and that deadly instrument, the maiden, was suddenly unmasked in profile' (249)). In the same tone the particular is related to the general ('According to the pretty fashion in which our grandmothers did not hesitate to appear, and our great-aunts went forth armed for the pursuit and capture of our great-uncles, the dress was drawn up so as to mould the contours of both breasts, and in the nook between, a cairngorm brooch maintained it' (250)).

There follows this quite remarkable passage in which narrator's observation and F.I.S. are so fused that it is difficult to differentiate them:

> Archie was attracted by the bright thing like a child. He looked at her again and yet again, and their looks crossed. The lip was lifted from her little teeth. He saw the red blood work vividly under her tawny skin. Her eye, which was great as a stag's, struck and held his gaze. He knew who she must be—Kirstie, she of the harsh diminutive, his housekeeper's niece, the sister of the rustic prophet, Gib—and he found in her the answer to his wishes. (250)

The preposterous nature of these analogies leads one to wonder if they are Archie's or the narrator's. Similarly, in the

219

ensuing comment it is not easy for the reader to ascertain
whether the narrator is distancing himself by means of irony
from young Kirstie's romantic illusions or is, to an extent,
identifying with them ('Christina felt the shock of their
encountering glances, and seemed to rise, clothed in smiles,
into a region of the vague and bright').

From Kirstie's viewpoint the narrative perspective moves
on into this sequence where it fluctuates markedly:

> She took to reading in the metrical psalms, and then remem-
> bered it was sermon-time. Last she put a sugarbool in her
> mouth, and the next moment repented of the step. It was such a
> homely-like thing! Mr. Archie would never be eating sweeties in
> kirk; and, with a palpable effort, she swallowed it whole, and
> her colour flamed high. At this signal of distress Archie awoke
> to a sense of his ill-behaviour. What had he been doing? He had
> been exquisitely rude in church to the niece of his housekeeper;
> he had stared like a lackey and a libertine at a beautiful and
> modest girl. It was possible, it was even likely, he would be
> presented to her after service in the kirk-yard, and then how
> was he to look? And there was no excuse. He had marked the
> tokens of her shame, of her increasing indignation, and he was
> such a fool that he had not understood them. Shame bowed him
> down, and he looked resolutely at Mr. Torrance; who little
> supposed, good worthy man, as he continued to expound
> justification by faith, what was his true business: to play the
> part of derivative to a pair of children at the old game of falling
> in love. (251)

Here the narrative has moved from F.I.S. rendering of
Kirstie's viewpoint, through a comparable rendering of
Archie's, to a characteristic narratorial interpretation of
Torrance's feelings. The section that follows shows a fluctuation between narratorial comment and recurrent F.I.S. such
as 'All would have been right if she had not blushed, a silly
fool! There was nothing to blush at, if she *had* taken a sugar-
bool. Mrs. MacTaggart, the elder's wife in St. Enoch's, took
them often. And if he had looked at her, what was more
natural than that a young gentleman should look at the best-
dressed girl in church' (F.I.S.). 'And at the same time, she
knew far otherwise, she knew there was nothing casual or
ordinary in the look, and valued herself on its memory like a

decoration' (Narrator). 'Well, it was a blessing he had found something else to look at!' (F.I.S.). Thereafter there are passages of F.I.S. ('Here was a piece of nicety for that upland parish, where the matrons marched with their coats kilted in the rain, and the lasses walked barefoot to kirk through the dust of summer, and went bravely down by the burn-side, and sat on stones to make a public toilet before entering!') which are succeeded by narratorial interpretation ('It was perhaps an air wafted from Glasgow; or perhaps it marked a stage of that dizziness of gratified vanity, in which the instinctive act passed unperceived'). The brief return to F.I.S. ('He was looking after!') gives way in turn to the narrator's comment ('She unloaded herself of a prodigious sigh that was all pleasure, and betook herself to a run' (253)).

Throughout this chapter irony informs the flux of the individual vision. When Archie climbs the hill and enters the hollow of the Deil's Hag, he sees before him 'like an answer to his wishes, the little womanly figure in the grey dress and the pink kerchief sitting little, and low, and lost, and acutely solitary, in these desolate surroundings and on the weather-beaten stone of the dead weaver' (259–60). These terms, this way of seeing, are his. The narrative takes account of the flux of his response in that soon his thoughts are shown to have become quite different: 'This was a grown woman he was approaching, endowed with her mysterious potencies and attractions, the treasury of the continued race, and he was neither better nor worse than the average of his sex and age' (260). Within one sentence here F.I.S. has merged into narratorial judgement. While, in all of this, the views of the characters are demonstrably in flux, this is equally true of the view of the narrator.

In *Weir* Stevenson often fails to achieve F.I.S. in its purest form. At times the nature of the language used to reflect the activities of the mind is at odds with the nature of that mind as it is revealed through dialogue. Because of the narrator's readiness to interpret, F.I.S. is rarely sustained for long, and there is often a stylistic fusion between the rendering of the character's thought-processes and the narrator's subsequent commentary. Roy Pascal has noted that 'Lerch maintained that in S.I.L. (*style indirect libre*) passages the narrator disappears from the scene to be replaced by the character, whose self-expression borrows the narratorial form only in order to assume the full authoritativeness of narratorial statements.'[23] The situation in *Weir* is an unusual one: narratorial authority is shown to be suspect, but, paradoxically, the narrator is reluctant to absent himself for long from the process of narration. Here, for instance, the narrator comes close to rendering Archie's response from Archie's own viewpoint, but he is unwilling or unable to suppress his own attitude:

> He hated to seem harsh. But that was Frank's look-out. If Frank had been commonly discreet, he would have been decently courteous. And there was another consideration. The secret he was protecting was not his own merely; it was hers: it belonged to that inexpressible she who was fast taking possession of his soul, and whom he would soon have defended at the cost of burning cities. (273)

The following exemplifies the constant shifting of the narrative perspective:

> He met Archie at dinner without resentment, almost with cordiality. You must take your friends as you find them, he would have said. Archie couldn't help being his father's son, or his grandfather's, the hypothetical weaver's grandson. The son of a hunks, he was still a hunks at heart, incapable of true generosity and consideration; but he had other qualities with which Frank could divert himself in the meanwhile, and to enjoy which it was necessary that Frank should keep his temper. (273)

Of this, the first two sentences are the narrator's; the third would be F.I.S. but for the term, 'hypothetical'; of the last sentence, the first part is F.I.S., and 'but he had other qualities . . . ff.' is the narrator's view.

Such flux of the narrative perspective in *Weir* reflects the complexity of, and indeed the deep divisions within, Stevenson's own values. Stevenson's own restlessness, for instance, finds expression in the constant shifting of narratorial stance. With justification Edwin M. Eigner has noted the extent of the opposition between activism and scepticism in Stevenson himself, suggesting that the problem of *The Great North Road* is that of *Hamlet* in the nineteenth century.[24]

222

In part, the fluctuation of the narrative in *Weir* can be seen as a manifestation of Stevenson's dramatic capacity: through his narrator he becomes, momentarily, the particular character. Thus the narrative of *Weir* fuses static and fluid, fixed points of reference and the flow of the mind, reality and version of reality. Rightly Kurt Wittig noted that 'in his determination to enter into his characters, Stevenson seizes on, and recreates, the sensuous impressions which they receive, together with the images, metaphors and comparisons which the impressions themselves evoke in their minds'; hence, 'as it exists only in the mind, it is not a static picture, but one that changes with the character's prevailing mood.'[25] To this one has to add that in *Weir* the effect is compounded by the fact that the picture changes too with the changing attitude of the narrator.

This practice is very much in line with Stevenson's theoretical writing on the subject of narration. He wrote of Balzac: 'I wish I had his fist—for I have already a better method—the kinetic—whereas he continually allowed himself to be led into the static.'[26] And he drew the following contrast between his theory and practice of fiction and those of James:

> [James] spoke of the finished picture and its worth when done; I, of the brushes, the palette, and the north light. He uttered his views in the tone and for the ear of good society; I, with the emphasis and the technicalities of the obtrusive student.[27]

In various weightings of emphasis, however, there was a characteristic degree of conflict or contradiction. Stevenson could exclaim: 'Vital—that's what I am at; first, wholly vital, with a buoyancy of life. The lyrical, if it may be, and picturesque, always with an epic value of scenes, so that the figures remain in the mind's eye forever.' But this claim has to be set alongside the following: 'Unconscious thought, there is the only method . . . the will is only to be brought in the field for study and again for revision. The essential part of the work is not an act, it is a state.'[28]

Such complexities and contradictions are reflected in *Weir* in the fluctuating attitude of the narrator to his subject, and in the fluctuating relationship between Stevenson and his narrator. And the source is in the personality and values of the author. His letters record the flux of Stevenson's moods and feelings while he was at work on *Weir*. On 27 December 1893 he wrote: 'I am worked out and can no more at all', while the following day found him rejoicing: 'I have got unexpectedly to work again and feel quite dandy.'[29] The rootlessness and restlessness cannot be explained simply in terms of a reaction against a life of ill-health. They originate in the deeper psychological recesses of Stevenson the man and Stevenson the Scot. Muir noted that the expression on photographs of Stevenson is 'continually on the point of changing . . . flying away perhaps to some place so absurdly childish or romantic that even its owner is not quite prepared to countenance it'.[30] Various factors account for this: the expressive energy innate within the older Scottish literary tradition endured but found itself allied uneasily to a rootlessness which the Union fostered; and the need to escape to a fluid world of the imagination is a reaction against the Calvinist legacy. In this context one can appreciate James's comments on Stevenson's 'sort of ironic, desperate gallantry, burning away, with a finer and finer fire', and the 'beautiful golden thread [which] he spins . . . in alternate doubt and elation'.[31]

If Stevenson is something of a paradox, it is not just the case, as G. Gregory Smith suggested, that 'his is the paradox of the Scot'[32]: his is the paradox of the Scot as imaginative writer. Scotland, by virtue of both the cultural disorientation which followed the Union and the effects of the Calvinist influence, failed to experience Romantic idealism (or at least Scottish literature failed to reflect any such experience). From the eighteenth century onwards Scottish writers have known and expressed that alienation and that rootlessness which have emerged in European literatures only after the phenomenon of Romantic individualism's turning inward in the face of the pressures of mass society. It is in this respect that Stevenson is an embryo twentieth-century writer.

In a curious way the deleterious effect of Scottish values on Scottish literature (which Muir noted)[33] anticipates, in a specific cultural context, the general crisis of the novel in recent times, wherein the order, configuration, and authority inseparable from the traditional novel are regarded as suspect, since they are so much at variance with the chaotic flux of life. In this light the following comment of Furnas becomes acutely relevant: 'The more that miniature politics apparently distracted [Stevenson], the less sure he grew that art is the supreme human activity, the better he wrote, the more skilfully he sought such compassionate irony as *Hermiston* shows.'[34] As well as being the exponent of such irony, Stevenson is also, unwittingly, its subject.

If, as is often claimed, there is much of Stevenson in Archie, so there is much of him in the narrator of *Weir*. But as Archie is not Stevenson, so the narrator is not Stevenson. The use of the narrative persona in *Weir* represents Stevenson's attempt at self-confrontation and self-objectification. Was it inevitable that it would be less than entirely successful? It would seem so, in that the personalized narrator that Stevenson creates cannot credibly be omniscient; equally the choice of narrative method serves to restrict the role of the author-substitute to that of fallible observer. In *Weir* Stevenson encounters the difficulties which result from the combination of intermittent F.I.S. with personalized narration. F.I.S. is scarcely appropriate to personalized narration: the capacity to use F.I.S. implies considerable authority, if not omniscience, whereas personalization implies the individual view with all its natural limitations. In *Weir* the shifting of focus, the fluctuation between personal impression and authoritative statement, may occasion doubts as to the degree of control exercised by the author over both the intricate and often-ironic shifts of perspective and the concomitant direction of the reader's response.

The problem is largely explicable in terms of the incompatibility of the Calvinist legacy and art (which finds expression in the father-son conflict). In the writing of *Weir* Stevenson seems at last to have purged himself of his need to objectify himself as a limited being (this in itself is a manifestation of the Calvinist influence, and it is reflected in the almost-obsessive need for self-denunciation). Thus the use of F.I.S. in *Weir* reveals, ambivalently, a potential capacity for empathy and a highly reductive view of human limitation. The example of *Weir* shows that Stevenson could not permit the author-substitute to surrender completely the authorial right to authority.

That Stevenson found it impossible to relinquish narratorial authority and delegate it to his characters is more than accidental in the light of the author's own personality, values, and nationality, and the way in which these find expression in *Weir* in a concern with authority and judgement. Roy Pascal has commented that the 'hidden, omniscient narrator is the aesthetic counterpart of a now discredited providential God'.[35] This illuminates very clearly the central problem of Stevenson: Stevenson longed to discredit such a God but found it impossible so to do. Of his works, *Weir* in particular reflects the resultant tension between the impulse towards technical and narratorial experimentation and the awe of authority with which Calvinism endowed him. If *Weir* is an ironic study of human limitation, exemplified by both characters and narrator, perhaps the final irony is that it also demonstrates the extent to which Stevenson's own judgement succumbed (perhaps had to succumb) to racial and cultural pressures.

NOTES

1. 'A Humble Remonstrance', *Memories and Portraits* (London, 1924), Tusitala Edition, Vol. XXIX, p. 136.
2. 'Robert Louis Stevenson', *Edwin Muir: Uncollected Scottish Criticism*, edited and introduced by Andrew Noble (London and Totowa, N.J., 1982), p. 235.
3. 'On Some Technical Elements of Style in Literature', *The Works of Robert Louis Stevenson* (London, 1912), XVI, p. 247.
4. *Henry James and Robert Louis Stevenson: A Record of Friendship and Criticism*, edited with an introduction by Janet Adam Smith (London, 1948), p. 267.
5. *Memories and Portraits*, p. 135.
6. Ibid., p. 142.
7. Cited G. Gregory Smith, *Scottish Literature: Character and Influence* (London, 1919), p. 18.
8. 'A Note on Realism', *Works*, XVI, p. 238.
9. *The Letters of Robert Louis Stevenson*, edited by Sidney Colvin (New York, 1969), II, pp. 216–17.
10. 'Victor Hugo's Romances', *Familiar Studies of Men and Books* (London, 1924), p. 30.
11. Ibid., pp. 35, 48.
12. 'On Some Technical Elements of Style in Literature', *Works*, XVI, p. 245.
13. Percy Lubbock, *The Craft of Fiction* (London, 1921), p. 218.
14. Leslie Fiedler, 'RLS Revisited', *No! In Thunder* (London, 1963), p. 88. J. C. Furnas, *Voyage to Windward: The Life of Robert Louis Stevenson* (New York, 1951), p. 427, also praises the use of 'third-person narration' in

Heathercat and *Weir*. In contrast, Kurt Wittig, *The Scottish Tradition in Literature* (Edinburgh, 1978), p. 263, notes that 'though the word "I" occurs rarely, it is told in the first-person singular'.

15. References are to the Everyman edition of *The Master of Ballantrae* and *Weir of Hermiston* (London and New York, 1925), with an introduction by M. R. Ridley.
16. *Familiar Studies*, p. 85.
17. *The House of Fiction: Essays on the Novel by Henry James* edited with an introduction by Leon Edel (London, 1957), pp. 125, 137, 130.
18. Op. cit., p. 429.
19. Hereafter referred to as F.I.S. See Roy Pascal, *The Dual Voice* (Manchester, 1977) for an excellent account of the characteristics and the development of the technique.
20. Cited Pascal, p. 18.
21. Ibid., pp. 74–5.
22. Ibid., p. 22.
23. Ibid., p. 22.
24. Edwin M. Eigner, *Robert Louis Stevenson and Romantic Tradition* (Princeton, 1966), pp. 52, 64.
25. Op. cit., p. 259.
26. Cited Janet Adam Smith, p. 267.
27. 'A Humble Remonstrance', *Memories and Portraits*, p. 141.
28. Cited Janet Adam Smith, pp. 41, 42.
29. Cited Furnas, p. 425.
30. Op. cit., p. 236.
31. Cited Janet Adam Smith, pp. 268, 269.
32. Op. cit., p. 288.
33. Op. cit., p. 229.
34. Op. cit., p. 429.
35. Op. cit., p. 139.

Notes on Contributors

KENNETH GRAHAM is Professor of English literature in the University of Sheffield. He is a graduate of Glasgow and Oxford. He was Henry Fellow at Yale (1959–60) and subsequently taught at Aberdeen and Southampton. He was A.C.L.S. Visiting Fellow at the University of Virginia, 1966–67 and Brooks Visiting Lecturer in the University of Queensland in 1982. He is the author of *English Criticism of the Novel, 1865–1900* (Oxford, 1965); *Tales of Edgar Allan Poe* (Oxford, 1967) and *Henry James: The Drama of Fulfilment* (Oxford, 1975). He has written various articles, reviews and broadcast talks on the English and American novel, and is at present engaged in a comparative study of James, Conrad and Forster and a history of criticism and literary theory from 1800 to 1890.

ANDREW JEFFORD studied at the Universities of Reading and East Anglia, where he has done research work on Nabokov and Stevenson. He is particularly interested in Stevenson's later short fictions and in the excellence of his prose.

JAMES WILSON has written two novels published by Hutchinson: *Interrupted Journey* (1958) and *Straw in the Wind* (1960). Editions of these have appeared in five European languages. He has contributed criticism to books on film and drama, has been Director of 'Films of Scotland', a B.B.C. television and radio producer, and a journalist with *The Scotsman*. For television he wrote, directed and produced two films on Stevenson's travels: *The Donkey that Walked into History*, which retraced the journey with Modestine across the Cevennes from Le Monastier to St. Jean du Gard, and *The Silverado Episode*, which dealt with the honeymoon period in California's Napa Valley. This second film also featured the Silverado Museum in St. Helena, and he has written elsewhere about its remarkable collection of first editions, manuscripts and memorabilia.

HONOR MULHOLLAND is a graduate of Strathclyde, Edinburgh and MacMaster Universities. She has completed theses on Robert

Notes on Contributors

Lowell and Wordsworth's *The Prelude* and was assistant editor of *Order in Space and Society: Architectural Form and its Context in the Scottish Enlightenment*, ed. Markus (Edinburgh, 1982). She is currently doing research at Strathclyde on Nathaniel Hawthorne.

CAROL MILLS lives in Elgin. She has taught in several Scottish Universities—most recently at Strathclyde—and is a past member of the council of the Association of Scottish Literary Studies. In addition to Stevenson she has research interests in early Scottish literature. Her publications include 'Henryson and Romance Tradition' in *Bards and Makars*, ed. MacDiarmid and Aitken.

ANDREW NOBLE is a graduate of Aberdeen and Sussex Universities and is Senior Lecturer in English Studies at Strathclyde. He has recently published *Edwin Muir: Uncollected Scottish Criticism* and co-edited with Dr. R. D. S. Jack *The Art of Robert Burns*—both from Vision Press. He has written numerous other articles on Scottish, English, American and Russian literature and is completing a book on Burns and the English Romantics and preparing to write a history of Scottish literature from 1920 to 1945 and to work with the Architecture Department at Strathclyde on Utopian theory.

PETER GILMOUR is a graduate of Strathclyde and Stirling Universities with particular interest in the relationship between philosophy and literature. He is now an arts tutor with the Open University in Scotland. As well as criticism he writes creatively and has had several short stories published.

KENNETH SIMPSON is a Glasgow graduate who now lectures at Strathclyde. He has contributed essays to Vision Press's *Tobias Smollett: Author of the First Distinction* and *The Art of Robert Burns* as well as numerous articles and essays dealing with such writers as Galt and John Home. He is currently engaged in research on the Scottish literary situation in the late eighteenth century.

Index

Index

Index